POST WAR BRATS

Receipt

Received From:

The Sum of: (in words) Ten Pounds

Amount in Figures: £ 10-00

For Rent Books
For

Cash Credit Card
Cheque Money Order

Date 2 Aug 05

Balance Outstanding: £ —

Rec'd By: [signature]

Signature

55785

SCU1520

First edition
published in 2005 by

WOODFIELD PUBLISHING
Bognor Regis, West Sussex, England
www.woodfieldpublishing.com

© The Named Contributors, 2005

All rights reserved.
No part of this publication may be reproduced
or transmitted in any form or by any means,
electronic or mechanical, nor may it be stored
in any information storage and retrieval system,
without prior permission from the publisher.

The right of the Named Contributors
to be identified as Authors of this work
has been asserted in accordance with
the Copyright, Designs and Patents Act 1988

ISBN 1-903953-93-6

Post War Brats at Large

Recollections from the RAF careers and subsequent lives of members of 51st Entry of RAF Aircraft Apprentices

COMPILED AND EDITED BY
BEN MITCHELL

Woodfield

Acknowledgements

To Sqn Ldr Frank Tilsley for the 'Story of Halton' introduction, which first appeared in the March 1945 issue of the RAF Journal.

To ACM Sir Michael Armitage for honouring the Entry by writing the Foreword.

To Robbie Roberts who came up with the title for the book.

To the authors of the stories, without whom there would be no book.

To the benefactors who donated the money in order to publish the book.

To Sam Bugg for the design of the covers in liaison with Woodfield Publishing.

And finally to Ben Mitchell who collected the stories, edited them and put the book together.

Contents

Foreword iv

Preface v

Introduction: The Story of Halton
SQN LDR FRANK TILSLEY (MARCH 1945) vii

1. Arrival at Halton
   FRED HOSKINS 1

2. Lest We Forget or 'Chiefy, Chiefy, Chiefy'
   SLIM POCOCK 7

3. Why Do Bad Things Always Happen in Threes?
   ERIC MOLD 8

4. Navy Days or How Not To Carry a Teapot
   DON ELLIS 13

5. There I Was At 3,000 Feet…
   DAVE WILLIAMS 17

6. From Wales to the Orient
   BEN MITCHELL 19

7. The Victory Parade
   KEN COOK 24

8. The Lighter Side of RAF Bomb Disposal
   BRIAN CREASEY 25

9. No Fault Found
   JACK WETHERELL 30

10. The End of an Era or the Demise of the V-Bomber Force
    SANDY SANDERS (568) – EX-CREW CHIEF – 55 SQN 32

11. We Were There
    ROBBIE ROBERTS 36

12. From the 1947 Diary of 582491 A/A Hoskins F D, Aged 17⅛
    FRED HOSKINS 38

13. Canada, Here I Come
    ERIC MOLD 42

14. The Aden Protectorate Levies
    JUNIOR ROOTS 46

15. Feat(s) of Clay – or How to Dodge the Column for
    24 Years and Still Get a Pension
    W.G. (BILL, MICK, SAM – TAKE YOUR PICK) CLAY (514) 48

16. Much Ado about Nothing – or Come Back Eric Mold,
    All Is For Given
    TODDY HOOD 51
17. Hardships
    GUS THOROGOOD 56
18. Nothing to Do With Me Chief!
    GINGE MUSHENS 57
19. An Honorary Aussie
    JACK SMITH 59
20. Two of Our Aircraft Are Missing
    ROY MANINGTON 62
21. Stand by Yer Boats, 'ere Comes the Air Chief Marshal
    ERIC MOLD 63
22. A Memory of the 51ST, by an Outsider
    AIR CHIEF MARSHAL SIR MICHAEL ARMITAGE KCB CBE (56TH ENTRY) 67
23. Conversion – Piston to Jet
    DAVE WILLIAMS 68
24. Food, Glorious Food
    FRED HOSKINS 73
25. Whoops!
    ERIC MOLD 76
26. We WAAFs Were Not All Angels
    LEE DOWNTON 76
27. Flying Training – Rhodesia Style
    GEOF BRADSHAW 79
28. Trains – or You Can Only Fool Them Some Of The Time!
    JOHN MCLAREN 82
29. My 16 Years as a Navigator
    PETER BLACKMAN 84
30. My 'Basic' Career
    JACK SMITH 107
31. A Middle East Safari by Land, Sea and Air
    JOE WOODFORD 109
32. Travels With A Reluctant 'Pig' Or Never Fear,
    Freddy's Fixed It For Christmas
    TODDY HOOD 112
33. Journey North
    GINGE MUSHENS 116
34. Some Dreams Do Come True
    ERIC MOLD 119
35. I Learnt About Flying from That…
    FRED HOSKINS 119
36. Go (Middle) East Young Man
    ROBBIE ROBERTS 129

37. Flight Commander at Halton
    DAVE WILLIAMS 134
38. The Christmas Mail Pick-Up From Aldabra
    JOHN OAKES 138
39. CB or Not CB? That is the Question
    TOM MCHARRY 140
40. Rags to Riches or A Chequered Career
    JOHN MCLAREN 142
41. My Last Operational Sortie in the RAF
    SANDY SANDERS 147
42. Girl Katie
    ERIC MOLD 149
43. Schoolboy Impressions
    JMR 153
44. The Shepherd
    GEOF BRADSHAW 154
45. It Was Only a Golf Prize
    STAN DOWNTON 159
46. For Whom the Bell Tolls
    GINGE MUSHENS 161
47. Full Circle
    JACK WETHERELL 163
48. An Unofficial Modification
    FRED HOSKINS 166
49. The Ring
    ERIC MOLD 167
50. Trials and Tribulations
    ROBBIE ROBERTS 173
51. 16 Block Drain Clearance: A Confession
    NOBBY CLARKE 176
52. By The Stroke of a Pen (What's in a Name?)
    TAFF DENHAM 178
53. There Was I ... With My Neptune's Cold War Diversion
    DON ELLIS 180
54. The Great Escape (Halton Version)
    GINGE MUSHENS 183
55. The Last Man Left in the Air Force
    (AUTHOR UNKNOWN – SENT IN BY JACK WETHERELL) 187

Foreword

I well recall the 51st Entry from the days when, as a member of the junior Entry in No.1 Wing, I was housed in Block 15 Room 1 under C/A/A Dorman.

With such a lively bunch of skates, skivers and diverse characters in your Entry that I can recall, it was no great surprise to me that the experiences and achievements of so many members have been found worthy of publication. I shall certainly be buying a copy of the publication, partly out of curiosity to learn how, if at all, some of these outlaws were tamed by the Service, and partly out of genuine admiration for an Entry that I know contributed so much to the high reputation that Halton has always enjoyed.

I wish the book every success.

Air Chief Marshal Sir Michael Armitage KCB CBE (56th Entry)

Preface

On the 21st of August 1945, just 6 days after the end of the second World War, 252 young men aged between 15½ and 17 years arrived by train at Wendover station, where they piled onto the platform with a motley collection of luggage. They were gathered together in a long snake and "marched" to Halton Camp. Here they were registered, medically examined, attested and issued with RAF uniforms – the 51st Entry of RAF Aircraft Apprentices (Trenchard's Brats) had arrived!! 63 members of the Entry left for No. 1 Radio School, RAF Cranwell while the remainder stayed at No.1 School of Technical Training, RAF Halton. Little did those lads realise how much the following three years would shape their future lives. After a Passing Out Parade on the 28th July 1948 the Entry was posted *en masse* to RAF St Athan for "improver training" at No.32 Maintenance Unit. Twelve months later, the Entry dispersed to their first postings – the 51st Entry were now "at large"!!

During the following years some carried on in their trade, others volunteered for aircrew, many were commissioned (two attained Air rank); civvy street beckoned others. Many kept in contact, others met up again at RAF Stations worldwide and at Halton Aircraft Apprentice Association (HAAA) reunions. The first Entry reunion was held in Tring following the Passing Out of the 151st Entry on 20th June 1991 – the 51st Entry Association was formed the following year and annual reunions have since been held at Bromsgrove. On these occasions, stories have been swapped – some amusing, some amazing, others incredible – but all part of the rich history of the 51st Entry. Members have been persuaded to write the stories of their exploits and these are now preserved for posterity in this book, which, hopefully, will be of considerable interest to members of the Entry, their families and friends, and to a wider public who have an interest in the history of aviation and the RAF.

The 51st Entry would not have formed its own Association if it had not been for the efforts of three members of the Entry. For many years the late Roy 'Dinger' Bell was the Entry representative for the HAAA and he, together with a few stalwarts, attended the HAAA triennial reunions for all Entries at RAF Halton. Ken Savage had been liaising with Dinger prior to the first reunion and had been advertising in numerous Service and retirement magazines in an attempt to bring the 51st Entry back together. Following the success of that first reunion, it was decided that the Entry should have its own Association. At the 1992 HAAA triennial,

Dinger commandeered a bomb trolley and used it as a platform to address the 38 members of the Entry who were present that day – as a result, the 51st Entry Association was formed with Dinger as Chairman, Ken as Secretary and David (Ben) Mitchell as Treasurer. With the passing of Dinger in 2001, Don Ellis took over as Chairman.

A newsletter, edited by Ben, is published bi-annually and the Entry has its own website – www.51stentry.co.uk – with Bill Williams as webmaster. Ray Belsham is the archivist with a large collection of photographs and memorabilia, so the 51st Entry is still very active despite their advancing years. Many have fallen by the wayside, but such is the *esprit de corps* that at a recent reunion, the gathering was asked:

"How long should we continue to hold reunions?"

The reply: "Until the last one puts the lights out!"

This book is dedicated to those members who, sadly, will not be attending the reunion on 21st August 2005 to celebrate the 60th anniversary of the 51st Entry of Aircraft Apprentices joining the Royal Air Force.

Introduction: The Story of Halton

Sqn Ldr Frank Tilsley (March 1945)

Halton, the RAF's 'Public School' as it has sometimes been called, is spread over the northern slopes of the lovely Chiltern Hills, a mile or two from the pleasant little village of Wendover. The nearest town of any size is the market town of Aylesbury, into which Apprentices can go at the weekend for a change of scenery, cinema or for shopping expeditions.

The Aircraft Apprentice Scheme was begun immediately after the World War 1 and is 25 years old this year. It was begun because it was clear that after the 1914-1918 war, it would be impossible to recruit the large number of Mechanics needed for the RAF from skilled craftsmen trained in civil firms, and it was therefore necessary for the RAF to train its own Mechanics. This scheme had the added advantage of maintenance personnel being trained in RAF methods. It was decided therefore to enrol boys in a Service apprenticeship scheme, taking them at as early an age as 15, and giving them a 3-year course in technical and educational training, on condition that the boys would sign on for 12 years regular service from the age of 18. It was thought that under Service conditions, boys would get an adequate training comparable to the 5-year apprenticeship in civil life.

To say that this scheme has been a success is to put it mildly. Anybody who has been in the RAF any length of time, must have been struck by the frequency with which outstanding officers and men turn out to have been ex-apprentices. The ex-apprentices – all 18,499 of them – have exerted an influence out of all proportion to their numbers, not only on the technical side, but also in other branches and in the air. A very large proportion of them have gone into flying duties, and they have earned 165 DFC's, in seven cases with a bar, and in two cases with two bars. They have also won 25 DSO's and two DSO's and bar. Altogether, ex-apprentices have collected 865 decorations, including a VC, and 1,773 of them have been Mentioned in Dispatches. 920 of them have already given their lives on active service. But decorations and rolls of honour do not reflect altogether the high quality and widespread nature of the contribution made to the RAF by the ex-apprentices. They have been described, and not inaccurately I think, as the backbone of the modern Air Force. These boys have risen to positions of the greatest responsibility – 4,124 have been commissioned. Several of these have attained the rank of Group Captain, and two have become Air Commodores.

It is among the technical NCO's however, that you get the most impressive sense of their quality. During the winter of 1941/42, I was adjutant to the Chief Technical Officer on a Station in the North of England. It seemed to me that whenever I remarked on the exceptional ability of one of our NCO's, the Squadron Leader would say "Of course he's good, he was a boy at Halton". I became so impressed by this, that I began to mark the personnel cards on my state board with a Red 'A' for those men who had been apprentices, and in time I found that I had marked nine of our dozen best NCO's. One of these NCO's was in the office one day and asked me what the Red 'A' was for. I told him "It was to indicate Apprentice, or rather, an ex-apprentice" He examined the board with great interest then, and at last he said "That's a good idea Sir, but you are one short" and he took down the Squadron Leader's card and marked it with a Red 'A'.

A Tour of Halton

I began my tour of Halton in the 'Wing', which is the part of the Camp where the boys live, as distinct from the School, in which they are given their theoretical education, and the Workshops, where they do their practical work. The Wing consists of a group of two and three storey buildings, situated round the parade ground. The buildings are brick, fairly modern, roughly sensible; as though the architects secretly disapproved of the lovely countryside with its rolling hills and well-wooded slopes and thought it was up to somebody to strike a practical note. They have succeeded in striking a practical note.

Before the war there were four Wings, each accommodating about a thousand boys, and roughly corresponding to the Houses of a school, though of course, much bigger. Each Wing had its own Commanding Officer, and occupied a separate block of buildings with dormitories, mess rooms and so on, and they had a separate life in which rivalry with the other Wings formed a conspicuous and enthusiastic part. There is now only one Wing, and the tradition of rivalry is carried on by the three squadrons into which it is divided.

The various sports play a big part in this rivalry, and in the lives of all apprentices. Even in wartime, with a rather more crowded programme of work, two afternoons a week on Wednesdays and Saturdays are given over to games on the seemingly endless and superb playing pitches which slope down like vast green carpets from the school to the airfield, where the boys get a certain amount of their practical experience and do their modest quota of flying experience. I watched several of these games, both soccer and rugby, on the fine turf in the bleak winter sunshine, and realized how inevitably Halton Camp has come to be called the Public School of the RAF. In fact Halton plays games against most of the large Public Schools which are accessible. Soccer with Eton, Malvern and Charterhouse; rugby with Harrow, Stowe, Beaumont, Bedford and Merchant Taylors; and cricket on a similar scale. Hockey, boxing, swimming and athletics are practised on the same high standard at both the Station level and Inter-squadron. Inter-squadron games all count to a major trophy awarded annually – the Barrington-Kennet Trophy, a magnificent model of an SE.5 aircraft, mounted in silver. Subsidiary silver trophies are apparently numberless. There are two large glass showcases full of silver cups and shields in the library and many more locked away in safes.

The library is very pleasant. Large, roomy, comfortable, with well arranged shelves and a fine collection of books. Fiction included a good selection of the more enterprising modern novels. The common rooms contain billiards tables, table tennis tables, darts boards and so on. There were separate rooms for NCO apprentices – the apprentices have a promotion system not unlike the RAF itself (Leading, Corporal and Sergeant), though NCO apprentices do not receive additional pay. I visited two or three of the dormitories, which were like dormitories in any modern barracks, rather bare and forbidding, but blatantly clean and tidy. At the end of each room was a rack containing rifles. "Each boy is given a rifle immediately he arrives here" I was told. "It is in his personal possession throughout his training. We try to keep the same boys together throughout their whole time here. All the boys in this room, for instance, arrived at the same time and in the same trade, so they all do their workshops and schools periods together too".

I thought them a fine lot of boys and asked how they compared with those of pre-war days. Different officers had different ideas about this, but all agreed that owing to war conditions, and more particularly to evacuation, the educational standard of boys arriving at .the School was not so high as before the war. All the officers who knew Halton in the old days thought that the discipline now, in the early stages of training, was not so good as it used to be. The standard, however, is soon brought up to the desired pitch. "What do you expect" said one officer, as we walked down one of the roads, "When fathers go away in the war, and when so many children were evacuated to strangers?" The apprentices were streaming past us through the biting wind and rain and hail, each boy as straight and well turned out as a Guardsman, and each boy giving us a cracking salute or a smart turn of the head. "No" he said, "Discipline isn't what it was. Take smoking. At one time no apprentice could smoke anywhere at any time. Now they can smoke, under certain conditions, at the age of 18".

I had a look at the Institute (the NAAFI), which is like Institutes everywhere, buzzing with cheerfulness and conversation and the clatter of cups and glasses, and the champing of buns. Buns and tea are the main commodities pushed over the counters of the Institute. The boys eat heartily in the dining rooms, and the food is good. I liked the system in use in the dining rooms. Instead of queuing up in the usual Service manner, the boys go straight to their own tables. The boys of each dormitory have a table, which is called for some reason a mess-deck. The food is then served out to them by mess-stewards – the boys taking this duty in weekly turns.

The School

I thought the School a rather pleasanter building than most of the others, though a school first, last, and all the time-wide corridors, a scholastic quietness, that intimidating smell of cleanliness. If you'd gone in there blindfolded, you could have guessed you were in a school. Each boy spends 10 hours a week in the School, as against 9 hours on physical training, organized games and drill, and 20 hours in the Workshops. At least that is the normal allocation, although times are sometimes altered to fit in with changing conditions. When war broke out, the training of apprentices had to give way rather to the training of men. I was told "The period of training was reduced to 2 years. We recently got it back to 2½ years, and the next intake will be back to the normal 3 years". (The 51st Entry!) The education in the School is closely allied to the practical work in the workshops, but there is also an English and General Studies section aimed at broadening the mind and sharpening the intelligence in a more general way. The School notice board is an education in itself, bringing the up-to-date news of the world into focus in a few minutes, reading by means of newspaper cuttings, maps, pamphlets etc, all neatly displayed and cunningly arranged. I had difficulty in tearing myself away from that board. If you are interested in science, which I am not, then the laboratories would probably be the highlight of your visit to the School. Personally I was most impressed by the school library. Halton seems to go in for libraries in a big way.

The Principal Education Officer, a Wing Commander, told me that negotiations were in progress with the Board of Education and the Institute of Electrical & Mechanical Engineers, for the award to apprentices at the end of their Halton Course, of a National Certificate in Mechanical & Electrical Engineering. This is being arranged for the benefit of the boys when their 12 years service with the RAF is completed, and they return to civil life – or rather, to be exact, when they start out in civil life for the first time. As things are now, they leave the

Service with no recognized diploma to testify to their engineering experience and skill. I asked what happened to old Halton boys when their service with the RAF ended and they looked round for civilian employment. The answer was that very few Halton boys have, in fact, ever gone into civilian employment, for the service of even the earliest intakes ended at a time when the RAF was beginning to expand, and the great majority of them chose to remain. With later intakes, of course, there was no choice anyway because of the war and the National Service Acts.

The Hub of the Scheme

Workshops, of course, are the real hub of the Aircraft Apprentice Scheme. The workshops are first rate and much superior in space, roominess, layout and in many other ways to several industrial workshops I have seen. This goes not only for the new workshops, which were only recently completed, but for the old workshops too. A variety of modern aircraft, including a Horsa glider, are housed quite comfortably in one shed alone.

Boys are entered for one of five basic trades. These are Fitter (Engine), Fitter (Airframe), Fitter (Armourer), Electrician and Instrument Maker. For workshop training, they are divided into small classes of 10 to 15, and each class is given over to one instructor. As far as possible, this instructor remains with his class for the whole of the first year's training, and teaches them the basics of their particular trade. During the next 2 years, the training leans more and more towards the application of their trade to aircraft and to Service requirements. Fitters, for instance, spend the first period of their course in acquiring basic knowledge and skill of hand – in short, they learn how to use the tools of their trade. I was shown practical work done by first year boys, which I should have thought good for highly qualified and experienced tradesmen. There seems to be a pretty keen spirit of competition in the workshops. Class lists, showing marks obtained for the various subjects, are posted on notice boards so that the boys can see how they are progressing. For those who did exceptionally well, there were prizes in the shape of Flight Cadetships at the Royal Air Force College, Cranwell. On successful completion of the 2 year Cadet course, permanent commissions were granted in the General Duties Branch – but these have been suspended during the war. Now, the boys who would have gone to the College, are reported to the Air Ministry with a view to selection for 'duration of hostilities' commissions in the Technical Branch after they have had experience in their trade at Service units.

I liked the way that the boys in the workshops got on with their jobs without too much supervision. You could see them working at their benches, or at the machines, sometimes two or three of them arguing out some point for themselves, or two or three of them turning up their notebooks to reconcile a point of practice with a point of theory. Dotted here and there were little informal classes, clustered beside benches and machines, following a lecture from an instructor. The work here seemed rather more like an industrial workshop than a training school of a fighting Service, though the general tidiness, orderliness and cleanliness, the 'Service virtues' as they have sometimes been called, were very marked.

The Boys of Halton

The boys, who come in within the present age limits of 15½ and 17, are from all walks of life and from all sorts of schools. The only common factor here is that they have to achieve an educational standard which will enable them to get through a competitive examination in which there are four papers – Mathematics, Science, English Composition and a General Paper; the most important of these being the maths paper. Many of the boys are the sons of serving officers and men. They come from all parts of the United Kingdom. Their sense of this is shown in the nickname they chose for the new mascot of their pipe band, which is a goat. They tried to make the name from the initial letters of the four countries England, Wales, Ireland and Scotland, which gave the letters 'E W I S'. Someone then thought of London, the capital, giving them an 'L', and the goat's name – 'Lewis'.

It occurred to me that the trouble about entering boys as young as 15½ for a career as conclusive as this, is the fact that boys of 15½ often change their minds very decidedly a little later on. I asked what happened if boys changed their mind once they were launched on this programme. The answer was that the number of boys who wanted to leave Halton is negligible. On rare occasions boys are removed from training, but only when it is considered pointless to continue further with their training. Sometimes during the first year at Halton, boys are often settling down, but after this period they mostly come to like their life very much. I talked to enough boys to feel sure that this is the case. I expected that the attitude of the third-year boys would be mostly enthusiasm at the prospect of shortly going into the Service proper. But his seemed to be very much tempered by a sense of regret at leaving Halton. It is certainly easy to understand this attitude, particularly with the boys who are keen on games, for Halton, as I have said, offers simply grand opportunities for games. There are, however, facilities for boys with other tastes, in the activities run by the Halton Society, which organises facilities for gliding, model engineering, chess, stamp collecting, nature study, model aircraft, amateur dramatics, and pretty well every other hobby and activity you can think of. Also the Camp is well provided with such amenities as a cinema, swimming baths, gymnasium, a stage (which has recently been built), and so on.

You can appreciate, therefore, that many boys look forward to the great event of the 'passing out' with some reluctance. The Passing Out Parade, of course, is the great bi-annual event at Halton, to which the boys parents flock in such numbers that in Peace time special trains were laid on to cope with them. By this time the examinations are all over, and the boys have been classified, according to the results, as aircraftmen of the rank of AC.2, AC.1 or even LAC. AC.1, however, is the standard aimed at. As one engineering officer put it: "What really counts in the RAF are first-rate AC.1's, and that's what Halton aims to turn out – first-rate AC.1's who are capable, with experience, of working their way up to the higher ranks". Halton has certainly done this and some of us feel that it has perhaps done rather more, on the evidence of its records. Before finishing, mention must be made of Cranwell and Ruislip. Cranwell was where the fitter apprentice scheme first began, and where the first few entries started their careers until the scheme was transferred to Halton. Afterwards, apprentices of the Wireless trades, previously trained at Flowerdown, near Winchester, transferred to Cranwell and there continued their training. Ruislip was the home of the Apprentice Clerk scheme, which continued until the early years of the war.

1. Arrival at Halton

Fred Hoskins

"They don't march anywhere nowadays" was the taxi driver's response to my comment, as he drove me from Wendover Station to RAF Halton, that my last journey along that road had been on foot, thirty years before, with two hundred or so other youngsters. I was on my way to the Princess Mary's Hospital for a medical examination on leaving the RAF, but my mind flew back to that day in August 1945 when I took one of the biggest steps in my life on joining the RAF as an Aircraft Apprentice at the age of fifteen. The memory of that day is still vivid. As we alighted from the train, a sudden roar of engines made us all look up to see a flight of Lockheed Lightning P.38 fighters passing overhead. They were easily identified by their twin booms and twin engines, with a central nacelle for the pilot. Moreover, this was only a few days after the ending of World War II and the fact that the aircraft were still painted with the black and white stripes used for identification from D Day onwards reinforces the recollection.

I had left home in Bournemouth that morning and travelled to Waterloo and then on to Marylebone for the train to Wendover. My father was in Ceylon with the RAF and my mother, worried, I suppose, came with me as far as Marylebone – but no further because that was where all we recruits assembled for the last stage of our journeys by train to Wendover station. I was not keen for her to accompany me at all, but I was not alone in that embarrassing regard. Fortunately, we all seemed to be sympathetic to each other and the bold lads who had travelled alone were kind enough not to make fun of the rest of us – perhaps their mothers had been with them too, but had broken away at an earlier station. The ones who became the butt of jokes were those who had arrived dressed in the uniform of the Air Training Corps. Most of us had also been cadets but, illogically in view of our desire to make our careers in the RAF, made a point of keeping quiet about it.

The Sergeants who met us at Wendover station marched us through the gates of Halton and on to No.1 Wing. They called out our names and divided into us into parties for allocation to rooms in the barrack blocks, each party in the charge of an Aircrew Sergeant, only recently trained and now redundant with the war so recently ended and having no further requirement for replacements. A photograph records that I was one of 18 boys in 'A' Party of the 51st Entry and placed in Room 1 of

Block 16 of No.1 Wing. The NCO in charge of us was a redundant air gunner. Very shortly it was made clear to us that we were not only in 1 Wing but, much more important, in 'C' Squadron and that we were not to forget that it was known as 'Shiny C'. Flight Sergeant Marsh, who conveyed that information to us, and the reason for it, appeared to be from a world far from the one we had known and far from the one from which the pleasant young Sergeant Air Gunner had come.

The barrack rooms contained about 20 beds and these beds were of the MacDonald type. That is to say, they were made of solid iron and assembled from a number of parts held together by iron pegs. Apart from the solidity of the iron, the main feature of the beds was that the bedstead was in two sections supported by six legs, and the foot of the bed slid along into the main section so that during the day the bed was only half its full size. The beds were opened only when it was time to prepare them for sleep. There was no springing, the base of the bed being comprised of iron slats on which were placed three squares of hard mattress known as 'biscuits'. The bed legs were fixed to the base sections by iron pegs, and the bed head was a plate of iron with lugs that slid onto rods that extended from the legs at that end. A bolster, or pillow, was provided, together with two sheets, a pillowcase and five blankets. We found that all these items had to be folded and stacked in a special way on getting up each morning. First the bed was telescoped and then the biscuits were piled on it. Four blankets had to be folded to exactly the same size. With the two sheets folded in between and this sandwich, blanket, sheet, two blankets, sheet and blanket, had to be wrapped in the last blanket so as to make a rectangular block and display the neatly squared front folds of blankets and sheets, looking something like a large striped liquorice allsort. The pillow was placed behind, and on top were placed the pyjamas, also folded neatly and square of course.

This was only the start of the ritual laying out of kit which took place daily, and we quickly learned to make our beds with blankets only partly unfolded so as to save time in folding and stacking in the morning.

My other memory of that first day is that we were taken to the cookhouse and given a very good meal. It has to be remembered that wartime rationing was still in force, and although we had not starved during the war, little luxuries or a bigger helping than usual were things which were greatly appreciated, and we really enjoyed that meal, thinking that the RAF was the place to be if this was what we were going to get to eat. Although I cannot remember the main course, I recall that we had plum pie and custard which was really delicious. At that time, of course, we had yet to sign on. A few days later, after signing on, the food did not seem quite so good!

During the course of the next few days we were marched hither and yon about Halton, being examined medically and given some aptitude tests to determine the trades to which we would be allocated. Several months before being called to Halton, all potential apprentices had to sit qualifying examinations in English, General Knowledge, mathematics and science and, on arriving, boys were allocated to parties according to their examination results. 'A' Party comprised the boys at the head of the list and so we were almost certain to get the trade of our choice. As my father was in the RAF, I was a 'Service Entrant' and given some priority, hence my being in 'A' Party. Aircraft Apprentices were trained to be the elite of the RAF's technical tradesmen. Ours was to be a course lasting three years and at the end of that time we would qualify as 'fitters' in the highest group of trades and much greater than mere mechanics. Apprentices were expected to become NCO's and thus the backbone of the servicing organisation. There were six trades open to us, engines (usually known as 'fitters', somewhat illogically as that was a grade of proficiency that applied to other trades), airframes (known as 'riggers' from the days of bi-planes braced with wire), instruments, electrical, armament and radio/radar. Radar had caught the imagination of many people during the war and was thought to be the trade with a bright future. Those who were in that trade thought themselves, without reason, superior in brainpower to those who wielded hammers and spanners. My choice of trade was radar. Of 18 in 'A' party, six of us were selected for radar training and in due course sent to the Radio School at Cranwell.

As far as I can recall, as soon as we had been passed medically fit for service we were attested. That is to say, an officer explained the meaning of what we were about to do and then, on the Bible, we took an oath of allegiance to King George VI, his heirs and successors, and promised to obey the orders of all those set in authority over us. The age bracket for enlistment as apprentices was 15½ to 17, and so not one of us was of an age to be competent in law to take such an oath, or any oath – but we did not know this at the time. Our parents had been required to sign a document giving consent to our enlistment. The period of enlistment was for twelve years from the age of eighteen, which was a heavy commitment for boys of our age. In my case it represented a period stretching almost as far ahead of me as the length of my life behind me.

Having enlisted, we were kitted out with uniform and all the accoutrements believed necessary in the life of apprentices and airmen in 1945. At the Clothing Store we were confronted with bewildering heaps of kit as well as the uniforms we were so anxious to wear. As to the latter, we were not measured. A middle aged civilian tailor simply looked each one of us over and called out to the storemen the sizes of trousers and tunics he assessed as appropriate to us. In most cases his years of experience were enough to give the right answer, subject to a few minor tailoring alterations. Caps and boots had to be fitted and I am sure we had had our hair cut beforehand. This was just as well, because our heads were almost literally shorn. They were certainly clipped to the skin to a level about one inch above the ears and there was nothing above that level longer than an inch.

Attested and kitted out, we donned our uniforms and started our initiation into the world of Flight Sergeant Marsh. That world was centred on the Henderson Barrack square with the 3-storey barrack blocks on the periphery. In the barrack rooms we swept and polished the brown lino floors, cleaned the wash basins and ablutions, and polished the brass fittings on our webbing equipment, buttons on our uniforms, our cap badges and, of course, the distinguishing badge known as the 'wheel'. Apprentices wore these on the upper left arm, and it was a brass circle about 1½ inch in diameter, surrounding a four bladed propeller with blades at 45 degrees to the vertical. Our pride in this badge is shown by the fact that so many ex-apprentices can still produce the ones they wore in their young days. The other distinguishing mark for apprentices was a coloured cap band, which at Halton denoted the wearer's Wing. The cap bands were red, green or blue. Ours in No.1 Wing were red. At Cranwell we found that the cap bands were chequered. In the barrack rooms we also learned to fold blankets as I have described above and to lay out other items of kit for daily inspection. Another task was to mark all our kit with our service number. A printing set was supplied, with ink, to mark cloth items and a set of metal punches to mark things such as our 'button sticks'. These were flat pieces of thin brass with a long slot into which were slid the buttons for cleaning, and they enabled four buttons to be polished at the same time and kept the polish off the uniforms. I still have my button stick, with, stamped on it, the number 582491, allocated to me on being attested, and my boot brushes, of very high quality, are still serviceable after all these years.

Our kit also included a hairbrush, knife, fork and spoon, mug, mess tins, a linen ration bag intended to contain dry rations, i.e. tea and sugar, and a linen and felt roll with needles, thread and some blue/grey wool for sewing on buttons, darning socks and repairing clothes. This was a called a 'housewife', pronounced 'hussif'. We were given a canvas kitbag and a full set of webbing equipment, which included backpack, sidepack, water bottle, waistbelt, shoulder straps, bayonet frog and the pieces which connected the shoulder straps to the waist belt and had clips for the shoulder straps of the backpack. It was as complicated as it sounds, possibly even more so because the backpack was in two sections, with a multiplicity of straps and buckles to connect the two and to hold a rolled greatcoat or blanket and a steel helmet. The two uniforms issued to us were Service Dress, with brass buttons and belt buckle, usually known as 'Best Blue'. A greatcoat, Service Dress cap (known as a 'bull'), Field Service cap (known as a 'foo') and two pairs of boots completed our external clothing. Working inwards, we had three shirts with six separate collars and two black ties, three pairs of socks, three pairs of underpants and three vests. The general idea was 'one on, one off, and one in the wash'. The uniforms were made of thick and hairy serge, the shirts of a hard wearing cotton and the underwear of a thick material which I believe was called 'union'. The underpants were huge by more modern standards, with legs reaching almost to the knees, and with high waists to match the waists of the trousers. On one boy in our room the pants literally reached from his knees to his armpits! The underpants had buttons down the front and did not have elasticated waists. Instead they were kept up by passing the leather tabs of the braces through loops of tape at the back and sides, and buttoning the tabs to the six brass buttons sewn around the waist of the trousers. Trousers and underpants were thereby united into one nether garment. The trouser buttons on the fly and for the braces were pressed out of thin sheet brass and had four holes for sewing on. Being thin metal they cut through the thread very quickly, so the issue of hussifs proved to be very helpful as they were frequently in use. The same method of holding up the underpants was also used on the thinner aertex type issued later. Those first ones really were heavy and hot, but as most RAF stations were windswept and remote, I feel sure that there were many times when these qualities had been appreciated.

Other items of clothing included shorts, vests and canvas shoes for Physical Training (PT), Wellington boots, a long sleeved pullover and a sleeveless one, a cap comforter, which was a short tubular woollen scarf which could be turned into itself and folded to make a cap, and a groundsheet. The latter was a rectangle of rubberised cloth with a triangle of the same added to one end, together with a collar and a couple of buttons. It was intended for sleeping on in the field and for use as a cape to keep off the rain. For this, it was draped round the shoulders and the collar buttoned round the neck. More buttons closed the front. Being a basic rectangle, the cape did not hang evenly but with uneven points hanging a long way down in some places while leaving the body and legs exposed elsewhere. Usually it succeeded in directing a stream of rainwater onto the knees, and as water gradually permeated the rubber proofing and saturated the cloth it was useless both as a protection against rain and as a groundsheet.

Having been clothed by the RAF, all our civilian clothes were packed and sent home. We were neither permitted to wear civilian clothes, nor to have them in our possession on camp. Later, most boys had one or two items such as a sweater or shirt. Officially we were not even allowed to wear civilian clothes on leave, but I think most of us did.

Outside the barrack block we swept the roads and generally made everything tidy in order to satisfy Flight Sergeant Marsh's high standards. There was little hope of achieving this aim of course, and even less chance of doing so on the barrack square. Despite experience in the Air Training Corps or our schools' cadet corps, our drill was never going to be good enough – at least not as regards those of us who were destined for No.1 Radio School and would be transferred to RAF Cranwell after a few days.

It seemed as though we were never off duty during that brief stay at Halton, but we did have a little spare time, just a half hour or so in the evening. Being hungry youngsters we tended to spend this in the NAAFI canteen. At Halton this was known as 'the tank' and was on the opposite side of the square to our barrack block. Needless to say, we were not permitted to take the shortest distance between two points, which would have taken us across the square, but were required to go around the edge. It was on the way to the tank that we found that outside one of the barrack blocks there was flying the red and white flag of the Polish Air Force, indicating the presence of a squadron of apprentices comprised of boys deported from Poland to the labour camps of the Soviet Union from whence, after a few years, they had travelled via Persia and the Middle East to England. Theirs is a story better told by themselves.

In the tank there was tea to be had at one penny the cup, rock cakes at the same price and still lemonade at twopence a pint or a penny a half. Fizzy drinks would have cost rather more. There were more exotic items at higher prices, such as beans on toast, but we had not been in long enough to earn any pay and had little money from our school days. It was in the tank that apprentices could buy necessary items such as polish for boots and buttons, soap, toothpaste and the like. However, so far as we were concerned, the main purpose of the tank was to provide a supplementary source of food. For us recruits were kept busy polishing and sweeping in the evenings, there was no opportunity for other entertainment other than the tank and perhaps to watch the pipes and drums practising on the square in the evenings. The pipe tune I remember above all others from those days is 'The Green Hills of Tyrol'.

After a few more days, 63 of us in the new Entry of apprentices were assembled to travel to Cranwell to start our training in No.1 Radio School.

2. Lest We Forget or 'Chiefy, Chiefy, Chiefy'

Slim Pocock

None of us in the 51st will ever forget that man! He nailed us to the wall as the Junior Entry, he gave us hell in the second year and he lied through his teeth for us as the Senior Entry. Together with WO 'Boggy' Marsh and their team of tormentors, he moulded us into something which we can all be proud of judging from appearances at our Reunions – you'll know the name – 'Chiefy Thomas'!! (Sometimes known, amongst other names, as 'McLaren's mate'!) I hadn't heard of him for years, but recently browsing through my Service History for some reason or other, he came blazingly to mind. It was like this:-

I had been commissioned as a Navigator on Boxing Day 1951, and after Christmas leave I was posted to RAF Melksham to No.10 School of Recruit Training as a Flight Commander to three intakes of National Service recruits. This was to give me, Pilot Officer Prune, a job for 3 months while awaiting a Conversion Course on the Lincoln bomber – needless to say, in Lincolnshire. A clever move on the Air Ministry's part if you think about it – an ex-brat i/c National Servicemen – in other words, a former poacher now employed as a gamekeeper! I duly arrived at Melksham, and, at 09.00 hrs on the Monday morning, having been issued with my regulation book swagger stick, I turned up at my office by the side of the 'sacred acre'! There I was met by the 'archetype' Rock Ape – sorry – Regiment Warrant Officer. He was Scottish – he was big – he spoke in a broad Scots accent – and he frightened the daylight out of the recruits! He thought he could frighten me, but after 3 years at Halton, he was on a loser! Anyway, he gave me the regulation tour, and after stamping his feet on the wooden floor whilst saluting, and consequently almost demolishing the building in the process, explained that his No.2 was on leave but he would introduce me to him in a day or so upon his return.

True to his word, at 09.00 hrs on the Wednesday, there was the now familiar 'beetle crusher' tattoo on the door, accompanied by an exaggerated salute and the voice said "Sir, this is Flt Sgt T——". You've guessed it! I cut him off in his tracks and said "Don't bother Mr Bloggs – we have met before – and should the Flt Sgt desire a long weekend pass between now and Christmas, he can forget it!". The W.O.'s face was a picture! He caught his breath and was speechless! A situation which was aggravated when 'Chiefy' burst out laughing and uttered one word, or rather two, "You bastard!".

For the next hour or so, the three of us had a very interesting chat over a NATO Standard Orderly Room coffee or two, and would you believe, Chiefy Thomas had been keeping tabs on his 'lads' – he knew exactly where the majority of us were and what we were doing. Quite an effort on his part!

After I left Melksham in the April, I didn't hear of, or see, Chiefy Thomas for years, but I think it was in the 60's when I bumped into him again and he was at the Recruiting Office in Leeds – or possibly it was Hull. He was a bit older, no wiser, but still smart with knife edge creases and shiny boots. See – we obviously taught him something!

A few more of his kind in the right places would be of good value, even more so in today's world of crazy standards.

Slim (582600) (and get off my polished bedspace!)

3.   Why Do Bad Things Always Happen in Threes?

Eric Mold

19th of August 1952 was a splendid day. A huge anti-cyclone had been solidly entrenched over northwest Europe for a week or more, making the 19th one more of those gorgeous lazy, hazy, summer days. I was flying Vampires with 67 Squadron at the time. We'd just moved from RAF Gutersloh to the brand new NATO airfield at RAF Wildenrath, and were in the process of settling into our new quarters. After the Met briefing that morning, Willie Wilson, my Flight Commander, came up to me and said "OK Eric, jump into your kite and nip over to Tangers (RAF Tangmere) and bring back the boss's kite". In those days we were assigned our own planes. Mine was F for Freddie, the boss's was Q for Queenie.

At the time, all of our kites were going through 'Operation Beef'. We were flying them to Tangmere, where a crew of civvy technicians were replacing the old four channel VHF radios with new nine channel sets (Wow! – nine channels, big deal). It was F Freddie's turn to get hers. A few minutes later I was on my way, climbing out from Wildenrath. The countryside of Holland and Belgium unfolding below was soon replaced by the Frisian Islands and the North Sea. The sun reflecting off of the sea seemed to pierce the haze like a flaming steel rapier. Soon, the Channel narrowed down to the Dover Strait, with Kent and the Thames estuary to starboard and Cap Griz Nez to port. I pulled back on the throttle and started to ease down towards my destination.

In those days, flying a peppy little jet like the Vampire, was one of the most wonderful things a chap could do. Uncomplicated, simple, very few gadgets to mess around with to go wrong or to try to figure out. All you needed was a topographical map and good eyesight. In fact you only really needed the map for the detailed stuff. The geographical features of that part of the world are so well defined, that most of us could go practically anywhere without a map.

With only a four channel radio, you couldn't talk to many people even if you wanted to. There weren't many people to talk to anyway. Very little in the way of air traffic control. Just give Sector a call when 'coasting in'. A quick call to Tangmere for a radio bearing or two, for it was still buried in the haze, somewhere up ahead, beneath the nose. The Vampire glided like a bird, almost silently. I have actually gained height at idle power in a Vamp while soaring in a standing wave over one of Germany's famous gliding ridges. The Isle of Wight passed under the nose and soon Tangmere came into view. Careful, don't confuse it with the airfield at Ford – it's been done before. A call to the air traffic control tower "Downwind, three green lights, final". I 'kiss' the tarmac with a typically perfect Mold touch-down and taxied over to the hanger where they were doing the modifications. Queenie was sitting there, so I parked alongside her, shutdown and got out. A civvy greeted me, he was one of the working party that were doing the mods. He told me that Queenie was ready to go, so I dumped my parachute and helmet on her wing and said "I'll just pop down to the Mess for a bit of lunch and be right back". (On a subsequent visit to Tangmere, in the late 80's, I was distressed to find the Station deserted and that lovely old and historic Officers Mess completely vandalized.) After a quick soup and sandwich, I strolled back to my kite. Little did I know that my glorious day was about to come to an abrupt end. I signed the Form 700, did a walk around check, put on my parachute and climbed aboard. Securely strapped in, I started the engine and a few seconds later waved 'chocks away' and then taxied out to the duty runway. I asked for and received take-off clearance, so rolled to the take-off position and opened up the throttle. The Vamp, on hot days like that, especially when fitted with drop tanks, was not what you would call 'quick out of the box'. I was well past the half-way point on the runway before she lifted off. Then it happened! About 10 ft in the air, going like the clappers, rapidly running out of runway – the engine seemed to stop. Wow! Suddenly the world stood still. I slammed her back on the ground, squeezed the brakes as hard as I could and tried, successfully thank God, to miss a dispersal pen which I was heading directly into. I bounced across the grass, through a hedge, down a bank, across a little river and ended up in a field on the far side. Phew! That was a close one! To my astonishment, the engine was still running, so I closed the high pressure cock, turned off the switches and jumped out. Almost immediately the Wing Commander Flying and a couple of other bods came running up, soaking wet after wading across the stream. "Are you OK?" he shouted. I assured him I was and I tried to explain what had happened. By this time a Jeep had arrived in the field where I had ended up and gave us a ride back to Station Headquarters. I was a bit mystified as to what had caused the problem, as I was sure it was nothing that I had done or had omitted to do. The Wing Co didn't know much about Vampires, so could not contribute very much. However, after a few phone calls, I was told that I would have to stick around for a few days because they were going to hold a Court of Inquiry.

I had no way of getting back to Germany anyway, and I was not anxious to face my boss after leaving his plane, which was the Queen of the squadron, in a mass of shreds in some poor farmer's field. Since I had nothing to do but wait, I decided to go home to see my dad who, at this time, knew nothing of this. The next evening I tapped on his door. Surprised to see me he said "What are you doing here?". "Oh, I just had a prang down at Tangmere" I replied rather nonchalantly. "Are you all right?" he asked. I assured him I was and he said, "Well you're bloody lucky, Harry Brooks went out over the North Sea last night and so far they haven't come back". I was shocked. Harry, my brother-in-law of nine weeks, was a navigator on Vampire Mk.10's operating out of RAF Coltishall. In June he had married my 19 year old sister, who was a fighter controller, also based at Coltishall. What's more – there was a honeymoon baby on the way. I had only met Harry once, at my sisters wedding. Nick, his pilot, was there as well, he was the Best Man. Apparently, they were practicing low level intercepts at night. They must have become disorientated and went straight into the sea. No trace of them or their plane was ever found. I spent a few melancholy days moping around my dad's apartment and eventually got a message to report back to Tangers, to give my evidence to the court. I was pleased to learn that they had pretty well determined that I did, indeed, have an engine problem. Having given my evidence, I was free to go. A couple of days later, Curly Winter came over to get me in the Meteor Mk.7. When I got back to the squadron, everyone was very sympathetic, not just about my own prang but also the news, or rather lack of it, of Harry and Nick.

I can hear my boss, Sqn Ldr David Giles, saying it now. "Come on old chap, cheer up, you've had a rough few days so take MLB (our wing leader, Mike LaBas's kite) and do a nice low-level cross country trip". We all liked low-level trips. MLB was the queen of the wing. She was hangared by our squadron and we looked after her. She had all of the latest mods, beautiful paint job, DFC painted tail – she was immaculate. We looked upon it as a special treat to have the chance to take her up. So, trying to shake some of the gloom of the last few days out of my head, I jumped into MLB and headed out to the duty runway. Cleared for take-off, I taxied into position and let her rip. I couldn't believe it, about 10 ft off of the ground – the engine RPM dropped back to idle. This must be some kind of horrible dream. I slammed her back on the ground, jammed on the brakes and this time managed to come to a stop before I ran out of concrete. Phew! I can't believe this. The same problem on two consecutive trips! A bit shaken up, I taxied slowly back to the squadron where Sgt. Russell was waiting to marshal me in. Suddenly the brakes failed completely. No one had thought to tell me that my wheels were on fire! The plane rolled on, but without the differential brakes, I couldn't steer it. I screamed at Sgt. Russell "Get out of the way, I can't stop the bloody thing". Later he thanked me for saving his life. In the meantime, I was heading directly for the hangar wall. Crunch! MLB entered the hanger the hard way, through her own, custom made, hole in the wall. Thank God those German hangers were rather Jerry built (joke – get it?) Suddenly everyone was around me. Gp Capt Johnny E Johnson, our Station Commander (J.E.J. to us), went red faced and screamed "You're grounded, you'll never fly any of my kites again". Mike LeBas, looking forlornly at his newly trashed pretty little plane, didn't say much, but then he never did. The only person that was nice to me was Sgt. Russell. I pleaded "It was the engine, the engine". No one believed that the same thing could happen to the same person on two consecutive trips. Accidents just didn't happen that way. I was pretty upset. J.E.J. added "It had bloody well better be the engine or else you've had it". I was kind of 'sent to Coventry' for the next few days, only putting in appearances when summoned to testify before the Court of Inquiry.

Slowly the word came out. It was another technical fault. In fact we were in for a whole epidemic of them. Apparently a barometric device, which is designed to gradually reduce the engine speed in the climb to prevent overheating the tail pipe, had failed. The result was that it suddenly, regardless of the throttle lever position, bled off the engine RPM to idle – just enough to taxi. I was completely exonerated of any blame for both accidents. I could hold my head up high once more and

POST WAR BRATS AT LARGE ~ 11

start going to the morning Met briefings again. The first morning, J.E.J. jumped up, grabbed me, gave be a big hug and christened me 'Pranger' – a name which stuck for a while. After all, I was probably the most experienced person at pranging Vampires. Anything you want to know about pranging Vampires – ask Pranger.

I only had one other significant event during my Air Force flying career. It was in a Starfighter when I was in the Royal Canadian Air Force. We were coming in to land at Zwiebrucken, the weather was terrible, right on the limits, probably a bit below. We were 'On course, on the glide path'. My wing man was tucked nicely into my starboard side, 'On course, on the glide path'. We were in the landing attitude, just a few knots above touch down speed, 'On course, on the glide path'. Finally, 'Look ahead and land'. Then THUMP! The plane swung violently to the right, and instinctively I applied hard opposite rudder but it was too late. I touched down on the port wheel with what seemed like 45 degrees of left bank, the nose pointing towards the infield. As the kite careened down the runway on its left ear, so to speak, I was worried about my wing man. He was surely going to clobber me and then we'd have a massive bar-b-cue in the middle of the runway. But that didn't happen. After pulling the drag chute and zig zagging across the runway a few times, I finally got the beast under control, coming to rest almost at the end of the concrete, with the plane listing heavily to port. The left gear had collapsed, little wonder after that assault on the touch down point. Still expecting my wing man to crash into me, I cut the engine and scrambled out of the cockpit. He was nowhere to be seen, but then the visibility was only a couple of hundred yards. He had slid off the runway, coming to rest on his belly a few hundred feet further back than I did. My poor old Starfighter looked rather sorry for herself, lying there on her side. Apparently what happened was that when the controller said "Look ahead and land", my wing man did just that. He took his eyes off his leader (me), something you never do when flying in close formation. It caused him to collide with my starboard side, a split second before touch down. Both of us were unharmed and both planes were eventually repaired and flew again. But it was a scary moment.

The funny thing is that when all of these shenanigans were going on, time seemed to slow down very significantly. All seemed serene and there was plenty of time to do things. The aircraft speed too seemed to slow down drastically as well. Why is that?

The following postscript to Eric's story was sent in by Geof Bradshaw:-

When we arrived at RAF St Athan from Halton in 1948, we were told that those who had applied for aircrew training would have to resubmit their applications. I allowed my 'friends' to persuade me to stay on the ground and it wasn't until late 1951 that I thought "B....r my friends" and put in my application. Consequently, by the time I reached the jet conversion stage on Vampire 5's, Eric's problem had been recognised and a cure found. This consisted of a button in the cockpit, which was to be pressed in the event of an unexplained power loss on take-off. The button activated an electro-magnetic hammer, which delivered an admonitory thump to the recalcitrant barostat to remind it of its purpose. I never had to use it and I don't know anyone who did, but I suppose it *could* have worked. After completing my conversion course, I was posted to 60 Sqn who were operating Vampire 9's, which had obviously been 'properly' modified, because I don't remember any mysterious 'buttons' in their cockpits.

Note: A copy of Geof's postscript about the modification to resolve the problem which Eric had experienced twice when taking off in different Vampires, was sent to Eric. He responded by saying that he never knew about the modification, as it was obviously introduced after he had left 67 Sqn, but the modification sounded like the typical type of solution that could have been dreamed up in Room 16-1 at Halton on the back of a Woodbine packet!

4. Navy Days or How Not To Carry a Teapot

Don Ellis

After spending 12 months at St Athan overhauling Merlin 224's for the Berlin Airlift, I was posted to RAF Wyton in company with Jimmy Middleton, Gus Thorogood, Kipper Morton, Neil Hull, Jock Mackie, Taff White and Jock Wardlaw. At Wyton there were four squadrons, totalling 32 Lincolns (those were the days!) and all the fitters and riggers were employed in ASF (Aircraft Servicing Flight) as card-carrying members of a Planned (?) Servicing Team By November 1949 the weather on the fringe of East Anglia was getting decidedly chilly. Our Flight Sergeant, F.S. Sharpe, who claimed he was Sharpe by name and sharp by nature, was generally known round the hangar as 'Teef-an'-Trousers'. He came into our smoke laden crewroom one morning breaktime and sang out "Anybody want to go to Gibraltar?". About half the occupants of this black hole of Calcutta, me included, put our hands up, thinking that Gib must be warmer than Wyton in November. He evidently made a note of our names, while we speculated that one of our aircraft was stuck in Gib for an engine change, but surprisingly we heard no more about it.

Christmas and New Year came and went, and some time during January 1950 I was summoned to the office to be told that my name, together with that of some pen pusher in Tech Records, had been drawn out of the hat for the Gibraltar trip. Even then we weren't told any more than that. In time, we learned that the RN Home Fleet and Training Squadron had offered a number of places on board HM ships, on their Spring Cruise, to officers and airmen of Bomber Command. We were to report to an assembly point at RAF Upwood on some January night very soon.

The call came and from Upwood, a group of us set off by train to London, then from Waterloo to Weymouth, whence we were taken out onto Weymouth Pier on a damp misty day. We could see a number of ships of various sizes at anchor, well off shore, with small boats running to and fro. Eventually we were split into groups and I and my fellow Wytonian found ourselves in a party of six destined for HMS Vengeance. I can't remember much about the other four lads, except that one was the AOC's driver from No.1 Group at Bawtry. After a time, a motorboat came alongside to take us out to our ship, which we were pleased to discover was a Light Fleet Carrier. Once on board we were assigned to a Mess Deck, about as big as our lounge in Chippenham, and already occupied by nine Leading Seamen and a National Service Ordinary Seaman messman. Despite our having increased the complement of the mess by 60%, we were made very welcome and we then discovered that we not only slept there but ate all our meals there too. Perhaps one of the reasons for our popularity was the fact that we all were old enough to draw our tot and we were soon introduced to the mysteries of 'sippers' and 'gulpers'.

Most of the nine Killicks (Leading Seamen) in our Mess were Regulators (Ship's Police), including (inevitably) Stripey, who had three Good Conduct Badges. Several had been up to Petty Officer rank and down again at least once, but that's the Navy for you. I chummed up with another member of the Mess – the ship's crane driver (a very important job when flying was in progress) and he was also the ship's diver, in the days of brass helmets and lead boots. One of the first jobs they had to do after our arrival was to issue us with hammocks and teach us how to sling them, and of course how to lash up and stow. When all the hammocks were slung, they were above the mess table and in fairly close contact with each other. All very friendly! One routine which was new to us was a visit, at 21.00 hrs nightly, by the Officer of the Day, duly togged up in

Mess Kit and preceded by a Royal Marine bugler, presumably to ensure that all the ratings were behaving themselves. We heard our messmates refer to their officers generally as 'pigs', and they really made it sound as though they meant it!

We were told that we had no duties whilst on board and were free to go wherever we wished, provided we asked first. I think we all had a go at steering the ship, but our favourite spot, while they were flying, was up on the island where we had an excellent view of all that was going on. I took full advantage by having my camera and a supply of film, and there was plenty to photograph. Vengeance's complement of aircraft was Fireflies and Sea Fury's, and to see them all ranged up on the after-end of the flight deck, started up and awaiting take-off, was quite a sight – and sound! There were two other carriers, Indomitable and Victorious, equipped, I think, with Sea Hornets and Firebrands, and a Barracuda as the Admiral's 'barge'. Mishaps on landing were commonplace. A Sea Fury burst a tyre on landing and was saved from going over the side by the arrester wire. Another caught its tail wheel instead of its hook, whereupon the wire dragged the whole assembly out and catapulted it along the flight deck. The aircraft was prevented from rolling forward into those ranged at the sharp end, or indeed from going overboard, by a hydraulically raised barrier which automatically rose out of the deck before each landing. It was interesting on this occasion to see that the flight crew were ready for anything and produced a roller-skate sized dolly to put under the tail while the aircraft went forward of the barrier. A common problem was that of an aircraft nosing over after the hook had engaged, with the resultant sparks when the prop blades hit the deck. Down on the hangar deck, there were spare props mounted on every available bit of bulkhead space. One of the most spectacular occurrences that we saw was a Firefly whose hook engaged satisfactorily, but whose starboard wheel hit the deck very hard indeed. The impact caused the underwing pod, containing the radar scanner, to break away and hurtle along the deck like a torpedo until it hit the island. We were asked whether any of us would like a flight, but after having watched a few catapult launches, as well as all the deck landing escapades, we were all brave enough to say "No thank you!".

It wouldn't be fair if I didn't mention the handling crews on the flight deck. To say they were slick would be doing them an injustice. Obviously they had to take cover in various hidey-holes while aircraft were taking off and landing, but the speed with which they reacted to all the emergencies was remarkable, as was the variety of handling equipment available. I mentioned earlier, my friend the crane driver. He was never required to heave a broken aircraft overboard while we were on board, but he was always at his post while flying was in progress. Full of admiration as I was for the ground crew, I wouldn't have swopped my cold hangar at Wyton with any of them!

I can't remember the names of all the ships in our squadron – after all it was back in the days when we still had a Navy. Whenever we were flying, we had an attendant destroyer a few cables astern – just in case. We also had in company the RN's latest battleship, HMS Vanguard, of which more later. During our passage to Gib, other exercises went on as well as the flying, including refuelling one ship from another and transferring people from one ship to another by jackstay. Happily they never asked us if we would like to try that out! After about 10 days, we arrived off Gib and flew off a number of Martinet target tugs which we were delivering. We had a few more days flying within sight of the Rock, then docked and were allowed shore leave. Not only had the Home Fleet and the Training Squadron arrived, but we had been joined in the harbour by the Mediterranean Fleet too, and anyone who has ever set foot on the Rock can imagine Main Street and its environs thronged with getting on for 10,000 matelots (and a few crabfats!) on a fine evening. One shore leave story is worth repeating, and before I relate it, I must point out that the member of our Mess who narrated it knew nothing, in 1950, of political correctness. I am equally sure that he had no intention of offending anybody. He went ashore with the intention of buying a present for his 'party', (Pompey slang for girl friend), and went into an Indian shop to examine the stock. He saw something which took his eye and asked the price. Having been told, he retorted "You robbing Black B*****d!", to which the aforesaid RBB replied "Me no Black B*****d – Me British *Object!*".

While we were alongside in Gib, we were told that Vengeance was remaining in the Med for the time being and that we would be going home in HMS Vanguard. We were fallen in on Vanguard's quarterdeck, and, after being inspected by an Admiral with an unpleasant smell under his nose, were put to work up on the bridge polishing saluting guns. After a couple of hours with the Brasso, we were told that it had all been a big mistake and that, as on Vengeance, we had the run of the ship. After we had sailed, I was given a conducted tour, starting in the magazines and climbing what seemed like 100 ft up an ammunition hoist into one of the 16 inch turrets. Once more I was glad that I had joined the RAF! A tale from Vanguard, which only a couple of years previously had taken the Royal Family to South Africa, was of a sailor during the tour taking his Mess teapot to the galley to 'wet the tea'. He was apprehended by the ship's police, charged and punished for 'carrying a teapot in an unseamanlike manner'. He was holding it by the spout!

On our passage home through the Bay of Biscay, in very rough conditions, we stood by a cargo ship whose cargo had shifted, for about 36 hours. Our 43,000 ton battleship was making pretty heavy weather of it herself, because (we were told) she had no heavy ammunition in her magazines, and whenever we altered course the weather decks (those open to the sea) were cleared of people to minimise the risk of being swept overboard.

All in all, the whole adventure turned out to be a very memorable experience and surprisingly some of what I learned proved to be of value when I was required to take promotion exams after commissioning. One thing which I did learn however, was that life in my chosen uniform was an awful lot better than that of the average matelot.

P.S. When I got back to Wyton, I wrote to my oppo, Jim Hitchcock from the 50th (who had remained with the 51st at St Athan after having spent some time in hospital), and told him about the trip. We arranged that I would visit him at his home in South London on Easter Monday with all my photos, he being very much an aircraft enthusiast (and still is!). A couple of weeks before Easter he wrote to tell me that two girls, his cousins, would also be visiting on Easter Monday and he wondered whether I still wanted to come. I felt that I wasn't going to let a little thing like that upset my plans, so I went, and I fear that Jim and I bored the two girls to distraction with my pictures. However, we took them up to the West End in the afternoon in the hope that we could get into a theatre to see a show (we couldn't), but to cut a long story short, one of those girls was Pam and we married nearly three years later. If I hadn't spent those three weeks with the Navy!

5. There I Was At 3,000 Feet…

Dave Williams

When 'it' happened, three Meteor Nightfighter NF.11's, two wingmen and one in the box, were forming with my aircraft, one of the many 'formations within formations'. There were 640 aircraft in all, making well-rehearsed tracks for RAF Odiham at fairly low altitude and speed.

'My' Squadron, 151(F), stationed at RAF Leuchars in Fife, had detached a number of Meteors to RAF West Malling in Kent, joining-up with other NF Meteors from four other Squadrons. We stayed there for a week or so, rehearsing over and over again our part in what was to be possibly the largest display of military airpower that this country has ever seen. I refer of course to 'The Queen's Review Fly-past of the Royal Air

Force' on July 15, 1953. More than 300 aircraft were statically displayed at the Review Base, RAF Odiham, while more than 600 would fly in formation over the Station. Included in the fly past would be aircraft of the Commonwealth Nations.

The managing of this formidable undertaking fell to Air Vice Marshal The Earl of Bandon, inevitably known as 'The Abandoned Earl'. His remit would be to arrange for a mass of aircraft of many types and differing performances, to be in perfect formation at the arranged time and altitude, overhead the Review Base. There were more than 440 jet types in the formation, which meant that some aircraft were not too far above their stalling speeds while others would be struggling to keep up. The AVM would ensure that the myriad details involved in such a 'do' would cohere to produce an occasion of which both the RAF and the country in general could rightly be proud.

When I recall the Fly Past today, and ponder the organisation required to pull it off, I can hardly believe that it was accomplished so immaculately, as it most certainly was. Imagine if you will, six hundred plus aircraft of differing types flying to a series of rendezvous, forming themselves into small formations, then changing course and other variables to join other small formations to make larger formations and so on, until the whole thing came exactly to perfection overhead a fixed point at precise speed, precise altitude and absolutely precise time. Today, my mind boggles!

I didn't fly over Odiham on that particular day!

I commenced this story with the words "When 'it' happened". Well, what happened, after all the rehearsals and briefings, was that my NF.11 played the fool and frightened at least my small formation and we twitched for a day or two afterwards. I think my allocated speed and altitude for the initial positioning were 300 kts and 3000 ft respectively, but that is of little relevance to what was to occur. My numbers two and three wingmen were inching into position, as was number four, slightly behind and below me, when, to my utter disbelief, my aircraft began, with no input from me, to bank to port and wouldn't respond to aileron. I yelled something on the radio to the others, but they had just about gone by that time. By 'gone', I mean they had left the formation by climbing rapidly out of my maverick Meteor's way, full of self preservation spirit. Thanks be that they were able to pull out as quickly as they did, or there almost certainly would have been a tragic outcome. I made the necessary calls after extracting myself from the crowded sky, one of which was to request a 'contingency' NF.11 to take my place. He had been flying at 10,000 ft, just hoping for something like this to happen I'm sure.

Having got the hell out of the formation, I quickly learned that below a certain speed, the Meteor behaved itself as usual, but a knot above and down went the port wing again. I called London Radar, where they already knew about my 'adventure' and they instructed me to fly very low down a 'valley' (?), and to approach West Malling 'with care'. They must have considered that before broadcasting it I suppose. I was already taking care thank you! I did as instructed after I had checked stalling speed and other bits and pieces, and the aircraft was behaving entirely normally, except above that airspeed. I landed without incident at West Malling, where the Engineering blokes were waiting to have a look at things. Almost immediately, a Sergeant Airframe Fitter discovered the cause of the 'naughty'. We were carrying under-wing fuel tanks, which were replenished by removing a fairing covering the fuel intake – not unlike a car – which presented an aerodynamically satisfactory shape to the airflow and not interfering with flying characteristics. This fairing was secured by four 'Dzeus' clips, two on either side. Only two – on the same side of the fairing – had been secured. At the 'certain speed', the fairing turned through almost 180 degrees, presenting the airflow with a horrible mess and ruining the aerodynamics of that wing, hence the uncontrolled rolling motion. I was grateful that all was well below that 'critical speed'. I hate to think what happened to the man responsible for securing the fairing!

6. From Wales to the Orient

Ben Mitchell

The 51st Entry arrived at RAF St Athan near Barry in South Wales in August 1948, to do their 12 months 'improver training' in order to complete their apprenticeship. I was posted to the Instrument Workshop repairing Mk.14 Bombsights, and after a couple of months was detached along with Jock Wardlaw and two Polish apprentices – Joe Dryjinski and Joe Pazik – to No.3 MU at RAF Milton near Didcot. We found ourselves billeted in a Nissan hut, a stones throw from the railway line to the West Country, and our job was to repair bombsights which were rejected by the civilian AIS Inspectors, who were checking the bombsights prior to delivery to Units from storage. An AC.2's (Aircraftsman 2nd Class) pay in those days was 4/6d a day (22p in 'new' money!), so we didn't go 'out on the town' very often. Spare time was spent stealing coal from a railway siding for the Nissan hut stove and jotting down the names of the Great Western steam locomotives as they passed by. I recall that we had to do guard duty at a storage depot at RAF Kingston Bagpuize. There were two hangars full of surplus equipment, which was auctioned off at periodic intervals. At weekends, the MT drivers from the MU, who were mostly cockneys from the East End of London, always volunteered for weekend duty. Their mates from the East End used to turn up with a lorry and they would load it with equipment from the hangar, which would no doubt appear on the stalls down Petticoat Lane!

It was back to St Athan after the detachment and the day for postings to the 'real Air Force' arrived in August 1949. Along with Chris Brill, Jock Espie and Taff Evans, I headed further West into Wales and landed up at RAF Pembroke Dock. My first servicing task in ASF (Aircraft Servicing Flight) was to do a Man 'C' Minor inspection on a Sunderland. I asked my Instrument Cpl to show me what to do. He said "You are one of those clever b......d's from Halton who know everything, so get on with it". I never forgot him – Cpl Norris – and would loved to have come across him in later years, but I never did. Working on the Sunderlands on the water was often a good scrounge, especially in summer when you could sunbathe on the wing away from the shore where you couldn't be seen. In order to get some electrical power on the aircraft, the leading edge of the wing between the fuselage and the port inner engine dropped down to make a platform and exposed a Jap engine with a yo-yo starter. It was all a bit precarious, but I never heard of anyone falling in the sea. When you wanted to get a dingy from the Marine Craft Section to take you ashore, you flashed them with an Aldis lamp. One job that ASF had was to refurbish a Walrus, and I fitted a complete new pitot-static system pipework from the pitot head to the instrument panel. It took three months for all the trades to complete the task and when it went on air test, it landed in a fairly choppy sea at RAF Calshot and was written off! Jock and I played darts for the Market Tavern, just along from the Station entrance, and a few doors down from the Market Tavern was another pub, the Navy Tavern, run by Tommy Tucker's parents. Also on the sporting front, Jock, Taff and I were in the Tech Wing 7 a-side hockey team that won the Station Knock-out tournament. The following August, I was summoned to the Orderly Room to be told that I was posted to RAF Leuchars (near St Andrews) – a long way to go for a weekend at home on the Isle of Wight!

Upon arrival at Leuchars, I reported to the Orderly Room to be told, "I don't know why you have been posted here. Nobody wants you! We will send you up to ASF, but if you have any other preferences, then let me know". I started working on Lancasters, and then bumped into Jimmy Hutchison, who was on 237 (PR) OCU, and told him that nobody wanted me. He said "Why not come up on 237, we are moving down to RAF Benson (near Oxford) next month". I went along to the Orderly Room and asked what were the chances of being posted to 237? A few phone calls and I found myself with a new job. 237 (PR) OCU was a Photographic Reconnaissance Operational Conversion Unit, operating 8 Spitfire XIX's, 10 Mosquito 34's, 2 Harvards, an Oxford and a Tiger Moth – quite an interesting bunch of aircraft.

When the Squadron arrived at Benson in October 1950, we were billeted in the floor above the King's Flight ground crew, and the 237 hangar was a newly built corrugated one situated just up a slope from the King's Flight hangar, which was one of the standard brick built hangars of the pre-war era, of which there were four on the Station housing photo reconnaissance Spitfire and Mosquito Squadrons, plus 82 Sqn Lincolns. The King's Flight operated four Vikings – the King flew in No.1, the Queen in No.2, the Princess's in No.3 and No.4 was the flying workshop. I recall that one day, they were changing a propeller and it dropped from the crane. Our Squadron bods lined up outside the offices, which overlooked the King's Flight apron, shouting rude remarks and cheering. The next day, a notice went up stating that there was to be no loitering in front of the Squadron offices!

One of the student pilots on a course was Dave Muff – ex-S/A/A (Sgt Apprentice) of the 47th. He had completed his course, flying Spitfires, and took off on a gash trip and ended up flying into a hillside in Kent with fatal consequences. Another ex-S/A/A who was also on the Spitfire course, was Straw Hall of the 50th. I remember that he used to hare around the Station and to work on a Triumph Tiger 100 motorbike.

Our stay at Benson was a short one and the Squadron moved in August 1951 to RAF Bassingbourn in the Cambridgeshire area, which had been occupied by the USAF. When we arrived, the Yanks were gradually pulling out, but not before my National Service oppo and I used to go round their barrack block, purchasing cartons of 200 Camels, Lucky Strikes, Marlboroughs etc for a pound. My oppo, who played semi-pro football for Grantham Town at weekends, sold them to his mates for 30 shillings, so we had a good racket going. On one of the last days before the USAF finally departed from the station, a long 'line astern' formation of Corgi scooters did a circuit of the perimeter track and drove up the ramp into a USAF freighter.

The Squadron were about to replace their ageing Mosquitos with Mk.3(PR) Canberras, so in February 1952, I was sent off to RAF Binbrook, along with members of the other trades, to get some gen on the servicing of the instruments on these new aircraft. Immediately upon my return, I was told to report to the Orderly Room because my overseas posting had come through. On the way to Station Headquarters, all the possibilities were running through my mind – Germany, Malta, Cyprus, Suez Canal Zone, Aden, Ceylon, Singapore, Malaya, Hong Kong. In reply to my first question "Where is it?", the PWR clerk said "Singapore".

I had just two weeks for a spot of leave to say farewell to my parents in the Isle of Wight and then it was off to the PDC (Preliminary Dispatch Centre) at RAF Warton near Lytham, complete with all of my worldly belongings in my kitbag. I had said my farewells to Hutch, not knowing that we were to meet up again on 194 Sqn at RAF Kuala Lumpur in Malaya in 1954. The first days at the PDC were to get kitted out with KD (khaki drill) and the necessary inoculations. For these, we lined up, baring both arms, with one doc or nursing orderly on either side injecting whatever. The syringe held a lot of doses, and they only changed the needle when it began to be difficult to get it into the arm! I was destined to travel on the Empire Orwell, just one week after arriving at Warton, but at the last minute I was taken off the draft for this troopship and was told that I would be allocated another draft in due course. In the meantime it meant doing fatigues during the day and trips into Blackpool in the evening – while the money lasted. Dancing in the Winter Gardens was the favourite haunt. I also remember going to one or two of the Blackpool football matches, in the days when Mannion, Mortensen and Matthews were in the team. It was a further three weeks before I was put on the draft for the Empire Pride, and I headed for Liverpool Docks by train and we sailed on April 1st 1952.

The 'Pride' was an ex-German cargo ship and was very basic. No bunks – just hammocks. No canteens, lounges etc. A hatch opened up on the poop deck at 19.45 hrs each evening for 45 minutes, serving beer and cigarettes. In order to get some beer, you had to take your 'mugs, enamel' to collect it in! We were all allocated to a Mess Deck, with overhead racks for our kitbags. Tables with bench seats for approximately 20 men was our home for the next 28 days. Two men from each table were detailed to be the Mess Orderlies for the day, and their job was to collect the food in large dixies from the galley and serve it to the men on their mess deck table. Hammocks could not be slung until 20.00 hrs and on the first nights, the matelots showed we 'crabfats' how to sling them. At 6 ft 3 in, I was a bit too long for the hammock, with my head and feet resting on the ropes at either end of the hammock. After the first night, I found myself a space on the floor of a gangway, along with many others who did not take to a hammock. Everything on board was 'basic' to say the least. No luxuries such as showers, but the matelots showed us how to 'sluice down' from a wash basin. The 'heads', as the toilet area was called in Naval language, was a vast open area at the bow of the ship. Numerous rows of seats were situated over long troughs. Each seat was partitioned off, but without a door – so you could be squatting opposite a fellow 'user'! At approximately 10.00 hrs every morning, a shout would go out "Clear the heads" and a huge jet of sea water would flush out the whole of the toilet area.

Our journey through the dreaded Bay of Biscay was one of the smoothest ever according to the crew. We anchored at Port Said, but were not allowed to go ashore. Instead we were entertained on board by the Gillie-Gillie man in his fez and could purchase souvenirs from the bum-boats who plied their trade in small dinghies which swarmed around the boat. You shouted out what you wanted, they told you how much and threw a rope up to the deck. You pulled the basket up, put the money in, lowered it to the bum-boat and then hauled the basket up containing the purchase. The journey through the Suez Canal was interesting in that the first part of the canal was very narrow, with the ships sides almost touching the banks. At various places along the canal were British Army bases and the troops lined the canal banks, as we did the ships rails, shouting light hearted banter to each other – "Get your knees brown", "Who's the King of England" etc.

Our first trip ashore was at Aden and then Colombo in Ceylon. I always remember my introduction to the betel nut. The pavements of Colombo were spotted with red stains, and upon asking what they were, I was told that the Tamils chewed the betel nut and then spat out the red juice. I was later to see the same red stains on the streets of Singapore and Kuala Lumpur. Two days out from Singapore we were told where we were being posted to, and my posting was to FETW. I enquired what this meant and where was it, because everybody else seemed to be told a Unit or Station – RAF Changi, RAF Seletar or RAF Tengah. I was told that it was the Far East Transport Wing at Changi.

We finally arrived in Singapore, 28 days after leaving Liverpool. We disembarked and boarded a fleet of buses and arrived at around midday outside the Malcolm Club at Changi. As I stepped off the bus, who should be there to welcome me – my fellow 51st Instrument Basher – Robbie Roberts. (One of these days I must ask him how he got to know that I was arriving on the Empire Pride.) He immediately led me to the Malcolm Club bar, where he introduced me to the local brew – Tiger. Later that evening, I 'came to' on a bed in Block 151 Centre, which was an enormous 'room' with approximately 50 beds. The Blocks were all three stories and the floors were known as 'Bottom', 'Centre' and 'Top'. Each bedspace had an orange box type slatted wardrobe and a kit box, and that was it – not that we had much in the way of worldly belongings in those days. Each leg of the bed stood in a cigarette tin (50 size) containing paraffin in order to stop the bed bugs from climbing up the bed legs and sucking your blood! No windows in the Blocks, but large double doors around the walls leading onto a wide balcony all round the room, and ceiling fans to keep the warm air circulating. Each floor had a 'bearer' who cleaned your shoes, buttons and cap badge for a nominal fee. Our bearer was called 'Minga' and he was very proud of his bicycle, which had numerous feathered birds attached to the handlebars and crossbar. He squatted at his spot on the balcony, surrounded by pairs of shoes and an enormous pile of forage caps. If you required your shoes and cap before he had delivered them around the room, he would run his hand round the pairs of shoes and pick out yours, then he would run down the pile of caps and out would come yours. I don't know how he managed to do this, because the shoes and caps all looked the same, except those belonging to the Engine Fitters – theirs were all solid with oil and grease!

It was less than 3 years since I had finished the final stage of my apprenticeship at St Athan. The journey to the mysterious Orient had taken me via Pembroke Dock, Leuchars, Benson, Bassingborn, Warton, the Mediterranean, Suez Canal and the Indian Ocean. I had finally arrived on my first overseas posting and would not be seeing Blighty again for another 2½ years – but that is another story.

7. The Victory Parade

Ken Cook

It's 60 years on and I'm not quite sure how we got there, but I think it was a combination of 3 tonner and troop train. We didn't have luxury coaches in those days. It was best blue, SD hats and 'blue' webbing belts – white blanco came later. We had to carry a filled water bottle attached to the belt and I dread to think about the standard of hygiene in those water bottles, as they had been an unused part of our kit layout for 'yonks' and I'm sure many of us had never swilled them out, let alone sterilised them. I wonder if any member of the public was given a drink from one and then became a 'legionnaire'?

Having arrived at Clapham Common, we were taken down in lifts to the deep air-raid shelters where we were to spend the night on the eve of the 'Big Parade' on June 8th 1946, two years after 'D-Day'. We were allocated wooden bunks which looked just like Auswitz and smelled fusty; together with blankets which were also smelly. Some of us were to spend Saturday nights in those air-raid shelters in the months later on, when we couldn't get into the Union Jack Club or the other Service clubs on 'gash' weekends. We found that the shelters were used as 'doss' houses for all sorts of 'weirdos' and tramps. We settled in and I don't think we were allowed out that evening. The highlight of our over-night stay was the sight of Chiefy Thomas in his 'shreddies', as he had to 'muck in' with the rest of us.

The next morning it was all hustle and bustle and into the 3 tonners. Our job was to line the route of the parade at regularly spaced intervals; keep back the crowds and give succour to anyone who needed a drink from our bottles of 'suspect' water. Some of us were positioned along the Thames Embankment, facing Scotland Yard, with our backs to the river.

After what seemed ages, the parade band music could be heard in the distance, and the crowds were by this time quite dense and restless, craning their necks and jostling for the best viewing places. Then a great cheer as the Household Cavalry, or it might have been mounted military police, came into view; they were in wartime khaki dress, no shiny breastplates or plumed helmets. They were followed by the Royal horse-drawn carriage containing the King and Queen, the Princesses and Winston Churchill.

Following on came more V.I.P. carriages and contingents from the three Services, with the RAF party being led by the goat mascot. Then came umpteen Commonwealth contingents and our allies in World War 2; the Aussies and South Africans with their bush hats; the Gurkhas with their 'pill box' hats and kukris, all very smart and impressive. The most amusing for me were the Greeks in their 'noddy' hats, ballerina skirts and pointed shoes with large pom-poms.

I began to wonder how many more were coming, because the tramlines in the middle of the road seemed to be merging and I felt a bit dizzy. There were endless columns of bodies with bagpipe and military bands. Then there was a fly-past, and just as it started to rain, the order came to stand down; 'blessed relief'. We were told to cross the road and have a break in the police canteen of Scotland Yard. After a desperate visit to the bog, we found the bar, and there we were, aged 16/17, in the heart of the British Constabulary, drinking beer under age!

8. The Lighter Side of RAF Bomb Disposal

Brian Creasey

I am a careful sort of bloke, always safety and quality conscious. I never volunteered for Bomb Disposal, particularly as I was medically unfit due to deafness caused by gun and aircraft noise. I was just not supposed to be put into an excessively noisy environment, so the Air Force sent me on a Bomb Disposal course!

It was in 1973 when I received preliminary warning that I was being posted to RAF Germany, with the supplementary position as Command Bomb Disposal Officer. I hated the Bomb Disposal Course. There are several ways of making life more bearable when forced to do something we think is unfair. The first is to pull rank, the second to pull superior knowledge and the third to be just really inquisitive to the point of infuriation. So Bomb Disposal, apart from the noise and the digging for supposedly unexploded bombs, with equipment not available in the field, was pretty much an intellectual 'No No', but pleasantly diverting and I drove the course Flight Sergeant wild. Would you believe it? After taking up post at RAF Bruggen, the Flight Sergeant whom I had plagiarised was posted in as one of my Warrant Officers. I was very kind to him and never asked him to do anything with Bomb Disposal. Besides he might just have got his own back!

On posting, the experience, in a place where the IRA might like to make a scene, was a bit more realistic. My first real 'Call out' was to Station Headquarters, where they had received a bomb warning and I experienced my first Bomb Disposal 'Call out' dilemma. Sixty percent of common sense departed. The first rule of controlled evacuation did not, fortunately, include my trousers (!), but, on my advice (By-the-Book), everyone had moved out. The Key Orderly had locked up when everyone was out of the building, and then gone to lunch with the keys. We, the Bomb Disposal Team, could not get in! When the keys were recovered, we started a search. Plastic explosive can be hidden in all sorts of places and can make a tidy mess when detonated, either by time delay or disturbance. Being partially deaf does not make the detection of a ticking clock very easy! The Waaf's had, against all feminine sense, left their handbags behind. Not only were they in a trauma without their make-up and fags, but we were in a trauma of having to inspect and examine every handbag as a potential bomb. To this day I do not know how these females crammed so much into such a tiny bag. The biggest shock was finding a 5-gallon petrol Jerry can in an office of a paper pusher. Now this was ideal for a bomb, but was fortunately empty. On the whole we found nothing, and apart from keeping the Station safe from interference from Headquarters for a couple of hours, nothing was achieved but experience. This was to prove invaluable later.

The Station was Bomb crazy. We quickly assembled some kit which would help with our job, because nothing was supplied. We commandeered the Dental Section X-ray machine until the Head Dentist asked what would happen if a bomb went off in the Dental Surgery. We commandeered the large X-ray machine from the MU (Maintenance Unit), and with the X-ray equipment we irradiated all kinds of packages and parcels. When the Station Post Office got suspicious of a large round heavy parcel, we X-rayed it and wiped the sound track from the Station Cinema film! We made glass knives for opening suspicious letters and parcels, and generally assembled a 'Do-It-Yourself' bomb disposal kit. The one thing we had in plenty was access to explosives and detonators. If we didn't like it, we demolished it. Much safer. Better to apologise than be dead. We used pain killer spray to make envelopes transparent. (The things people write to each other! We could have sued for indecent exposure). If only they knew that a simple pain spray makes envelopes transparent long enough to be read, and when it dries there is no evidence of tampering. We made a case to Command HQ, and, much to my surprise, got issued with motor bikes for fast reaction. If we found out about a bomb first, we could be well away on our bikes before it exploded!

We investigated a 'ticking' aircraft. I must admit we were scared by this one. The Phantom had been parked on the Engine Running Pan on the other side of the airfield, after routine maintenance. The ground crew reported a ticking noise like a kitchen timer (the favourite timing device of the terrorist). We searched diligently in the engine bay, methodically moving from front to rear, assessing the noise level of the ticking and searching with torches in the darkness. At one point the Station Commander poked his head through the hatch to enquire how we were doing and was told to 'Bugger off' in no uncertain terms. I am happy to say he did just that. In the end we found an air lock in a fuel pipe, which was ticking to itself just like indigestion. Loosening the pipe joint cured the problem. Incident closed.

Then we had the case of an attaché case, left in the Officers Mess Reception. We had it all wired up with cortex, (a high explosive in cord form), and were about to blow it open when the owner returned. It got him a dressing down by the CO and we did not get the satisfaction of a controlled explosion.

One Christmas, the RAF Police reported a parcel making a ticking noise. We arrived and confirmed the noise, evacuated the building and declared a safety zone of 50 yards. Nothing was to enter or leave this area. The Police Headquarters happened to be at the junction of all roads into and out of the camp, including the road to the Officers Mess. It was lunchtime and we declared that, for reasons of safety, the area was sterile for at least 2 hours. We then went to lunch, which is more than the Mess Boozers who liked to top up their 'Blood Sugar' could do at this time. After a solid lunch, the Bomb Disposal Team returned. We entered the building and edged ourselves into the room. The parcel was still ticking. Taking our life in our hands, we carefully attached a line to the parcel with Sellotape. Retreating to a safe distance, we took cover and pulled the cord. Nothing happened. In cases like this you pause for at least half an hour in case a timing device has been activated. We then returned to the room. The parcel was on the floor. The ticking had stopped and had been replaced by the sound of "Mind the doors, plenty of room upstairs". The damn thing, which had brought the Station to a halt and cancelled solid and liquid lunch for all the Camp, was a model of a London Bus, which some fool had sent as a Christmas present and left the batteries in!

There were distractions from the run-of-the-mill false alarms. The MU, which dealt in wrecked aircraft recovery, had a problem. The method of dismantling a crashed aircraft was to cut it up, using cutting discs. Now, cutting discs make sparks and cutting through fuel tanks could be fraught with danger. We were asked to conduct a trial of dismantling a Canberra with explosives. We got the aircraft drawings and found the strong points – those places which were held together with bolts. We then laid out a plan of action. We would use plastic explosives and hollow charges to sever the main securing bolts, and dismantle the several parts. We took our time to start with, and each controlled explosion resulted in a part of the aircraft falling apart as a complete bit. The tail plane, the fin, an undercarriage and a wing were taken apart within a week. Now we got cocky, (never the right thing to do). We decided to take out the remaining undercarriage and wing from the fuselage in one go. The charges exploded. The wing fell off but the undercarriage stayed put. This was now hazardous. We could lose face and ask the MU to provide support jacks, or we could take a risk. After all, we had been successful with one undercarriage, so why was this one still attached, and, in particular, by how much? Taking our life in our hands, we went under the suspended wing and placed double the explosives we had used on the other parts. Needless to say, on detonation, the wing and undercarriage parted company. We had taken a Canberra apart, reasonably safely within a week, using about a pound and a half of plastic explosive. A task which normally took the MU team of 10 men over a month, using cutting discs. As usual, the Air Force took no notice. Lets face it, these were the people who sent a medically unfit person into Bomb Disposal in the first place!

Apart from the fun of the motor bikes and a perfectly good excuse to be 'Not at work', there was a serious side to our work. Firstly there was the disposal of Black Listed and Red Card explosives. All the major demolition of the Command stock of unsafe explosive took place at RAF

Nordhom. I do not know what they did at RAF Nordhom, but I do know they were bored out of their very intelligent skulls. When the Bomb Disposal Team arrived, the Station held a party. The Officer i/c of Bomb Disposal had his own flat for himself and his wife. The accommodation for the team was reported as palatial. The NCO i/c Bomb Disposal did not want an officer round his neck when preparing the unserviceable explosives, so the first afternoon was free. Work started on the morning of Day 2 when the Demolition Ground was prepared and the first batch of explosives detonated by the Officer i/c. After this, the Officer i/c would retire until the next day when the next batch was prepared and despatched. In the meantime, an excuse for another party had occurred to the Station Commander. This meant the Bomb Disposal Detachment Commander and his wife had to catch up on much needed sleep before the next round of excesses. After 5 days of preparing and blowing up unserviceable explosives, together with 5 nights of partying with the Station, one was very pleased to be on ones way home, to spend 6 months in normal life before the next batch of unserviceable explosives needed to be despatched to 'explosives heaven'. What did they do at Nordhom?

Occasionally things got serious. We got a call about seven one evening. The information was that there was an unexploded bomb at the Army Explosives Depot 5 miles to the north of RAF Bruggen. Calling on the NCO i/c, we loaded the Land Rover with all we could think would be useful. We included an index of World War ll weapons dropped on Germany. This was 30 years after the conflict, and explosives tend to deteriorate into much more volatile compounds after this length of time. We drove to the Army Depot to find we were the first ones there. We established the site. We found the Army had been installing a new lightning protection system of earthing strips, and, during the installation, had come across an aircraft bomb. The device was exposed on its upper surface. Reference to our manuals identified it as an American 250 lb 1939/45 weapon. We identified the fuse pockets and carefully excavated the surrounding ground to expose the fuses. At this time an Army Bomb Disposal Officer arrived. Between us, using the RAF makeshift tools, we removed the fuses which we could see, but suspected there were more under the bomb. We therefore started to excavate under the device. At this point the ex-Commandant of the Bomb Disposal School arrived. Without more ado, he stepped into the trench, lifted the front end of the bomb and dropped it onto the ground with the remark "Well that's the bump and jerk test done". The Army and RAF Bomb Disposal Teams departed at a rapid rate of knots, leaving the Major in charge. At the end of this call-out, our conclusion was that this was a probably a sand filled practice bomb which had been discarded, BUT, one cannot be too careful!

My last experience before I left Germany, and shortly after that, the Service, was to reinforce the lesson that explosives are potentially lethal. A Phantom Squadron was disbanding from Bruggen and they intended to go out in a big way with a fly past, dropping simulated bombs. In the event they were too drunk to fly and sober enough not to not try. The Bomb Disposal Team were not to know this and prepared simulated explosions to give the impression of bombs. To make a simulated bomb drop, one needs an empty 5 gallon oil drum, buried in the ground, a couple of pints of oil and a detonator, suspended about 2 inches over the surface of the oil. When the aircraft flies over, the detonator is fired, causing the oil to evaporate and an oily ring to ascend into the sky. All very impressive. I insisted that all cigarettes, matches and lighters were deposited at the Detonator Exploder site. I also insisted on staying with the Detonator Exploder whilst the charges were laid. On the return of the Warrant Officer and the Airmen, I went to inspect the charges, leaving one man at the Exploder with strict instructions not to touch anything. On returning to the Detonator Exploder, I noticed the cigarettes, matches and lighters were gone. On enquiry, I found the Warrant Officer and the airmen smoking in the explosives wagon, which contained the tea urn and the remaining explosives which we had not used. My last explosion in the Air Force will be long remembered. We blew the 'bombs' because this was the safest way of disposing with them, and I then blew the Warrant Officer and airmen into a quivering heap before leaving the site!

I left Bomb Disposal and its terrors behind me when I left Germany. Very shortly after that I left the Air Force. Well, I gave it a fair trial for 30 odd years, found I didn't like it, collected my clearance chit and left.

9. No Fault Found

Jack Wetherell

My tour in Aden was from August 1951 to August 1953. I arrived on the troopship Devonshire and landed up at RAF Khormaksah. I found Aden to be a nice sunny spot – we didn't have winter frosts or any snow! In fact, a very pleasant place to be if you didn't suffer from prickly heat.

I found myself in the Aircraft Servicing Flight (who didn't?) working on Brigands, Valettas, Ansons and Austers. However, about halfway through my tour, Ginge Odom of the 52nd, who was in charge of the

Hydraulic Bay, was due to become tour-ex. Now, I reckoned that I could just about handle that job. It was in another hangar which was virtually unused and didn't get much in the way of visitors. The long and short of it was that I got the job and Ginge returned home to the UK. So it was "Put your feet up Jack, and enjoy life". Some hopes!

I don't suppose I had been in the job a month, when one of the Bristol Brigands did a 'wheels up' landing. Apparently the emergency system failed to operate. "Find out what happened Wetherell" said the boss. "Who, me?" said I. So I started to look busy, but soon another Brigand did another 'wheels up', so things kinda 'hit the fan'. Anyway, Bristol's decided to send an engineer out to have a look at the problem. He was a nice old boy, but a bit long in the tooth for Aden, and apparently he was a structures engineer which did not help matters. Bristol's may have decided that he wanted a holiday in the sun. He didn't, so we worked all day and half the night trying to find out what had caused the problem. At one stage, he got soaked in hydraulic oil when a line from the engine driven test rig parted. I ducked! We didn't decide anything and he hightailed it back to Bristol's. We later got a letter from them to the effect that Bristol hydraulic components would not meet the requirements as laid down in the relevant RAF Air Publication for testing their components on the Standard Hydraulic test rig as found in Station Hydraulic Bays. Consequently it was decided that instead of testing at 1,800 psi, an expansion chamber would be fitted to the test rig and the test pressure would be increased to 4,000 psi (the 'expansion chamber' used was a Brigand undercarriage jack, sealed at each end!). So I fitted a jack to the rig and pumped up the pressure to 4,000 psi. Have you ever seen paint cracking as a hydraulic jack expands? It scared me to death and I told them to get some other idiot (or words to that effect) to do the job.

We never did find out why the aircraft pranged and soon nobody cared, for the Brigands were replaced with Vampires. One good thing came out of it for me. I was taking my Cpl Technician board and my specialist subject was 'Bay Servicing of Hydraulic Components'. The Engineering Officer, who had happened to be looking after the Brigand accident enquiry, just said "I don't think I need to ask you anything on that subject Corporal. Its an ill wind".

A couple of years later I was promoted to Sgt and posted to the ATDU (Air Torpedo Development Unit) at Gosport, where I found myself as the only SNCO Airframe Fitter. We had four Brigands and found them to be great aircraft and I did a fair number of hours flying in them. One day, when flying up to A&AEE Boscombe Down to collect a tailplane sling for one of our Canberras, all was not as it should have been. On the approach to Boscombe Down, I heard "Red undercarriage light" over the RT. Looking over the pilot's shoulder, I saw that we did indeed have a Red light. But that is another story and I am still here to tell the tale.

10. The End of an Era or the Demise of the V-Bomber Force

Sandy Sanders (568) – Ex-Crew Chief – 55 Sqn

On Friday 15th October 1993, I travelled to RAF Marham, and on the way picked up Taff Lawrence (38th) at Great Shelford near Cambridge. Taff and I were the two Crew Chiefs allocated to XH 588, Victor Mk.B.Mk.1A, when 55 Squadron reformed at RAF Honington on 1st September 1960, but it was some 18 months later before we were able to collect it from Handley Page at Radlett, where it had been undergoing a conversion from a Mk.B.Mk.1 to a Mk.B.Mk.1A (ECM). After its flying days were over, it was last heard of at RAF Machrihanish being used for fire fighting practice (sob, sob). The reason for our journey to Marham was to witness the disbandment parade of 55 Squadron and the handing-over ceremony of the Squadron's Colour to a Standard Party of 55 (Reserve) Squadron equipped with VC10's. As the Squadron marched off, so ended the era of the V-Bombers, 55 being the last Squadron to fly the Victor tanker.

It all began some 46 years earlier – in January 1947 – when the Ministry of Supply invited the six major British aircraft manufacturers to submit tenders for a replacement for the Avro Lincoln bomber. Specification B35/46 called for an aircraft with the ability to carry a 10,000 lb bomb, over a range of 3,350 miles, at a cruising altitude of 45,000 ft at a speed of 500 knots, with the facility of radio countermeasures. The crew to comprise of two pilots, two navigator/bomb aimers and a radio countermeasure operator. Submissions were received from English Electric, Vickers, Shorts and Armstrong-Whitworth, in addition to submissions from Avro and Handley Page. The first four Company submissions were considered either to be too adventurous a leap into the unknown of aerodynamics, or judged not to be sufficiently advanced. This left the Avro 698 (later to become the 'Vulcan') and the Handley Page 80 (officially named 'Victor' on 2nd January 1953). It was said that it took 14 meetings of the Air Council to come to that decision! Even these designs were unlike anything that had gone before. The Avro with its delta-wing configuration and the Handley Page with its crescent-wing design, so in August 1947 Air Staff issued Specification 14/46 as an intermediary between these two. This resulted in the Shorts ('Sperrin'), a four jet engined aircraft with the engines mounted in two vertical pairs on the wings, also the Vickers 660 (later to become the 'Valiant'), which was already in the design stage to meet Air Ministry Specification B9/48.

On 18th May 1951, the Valiant made its maiden flight, three months before the Sperrin, and, because of its better performance over the Sperrin, the Shorts aircraft was cancelled after only two prototypes had been built. The Valiant came into service early in 1955, with the final delivery in September 1957 after a total of 194 production aircraft had been built, covering three roles – bomber, long range strategic reconnaissance and tanker. The Valiant scored two firsts – on 11th October 1956 it dropped the first British atomic bomb over Maralinga, Australia. The aircraft, from 49 Squadron, was piloted by Sqn Ldr E.J.G. Flavell. The following year, on 15th May 1957, a Valiant under the command of Wg Cdr K.G. Hubbard, dropped Britain's first hydrogen bomb over Christmas Island. The Valiant aircraft were authorised during the summer of 1959 to refuel other aircraft of the V-Force, and in June 1960, using air-to-air refuelling, a Vulcan made a non-stop flight from Scampton to Australia in 20 hours 3 minutes. The V-Force reached its full strength in 1962, but two years later on 6th August 1964, a Valiant tanker suffered a main spar failure in flight. Fortunately the crew were able to land the aircraft, but on examination of the other Valiants the same defect was found – metal fatigue. It might have been possible to re-spar the aircraft, but because of the cost it was decided to scrap the whole fleet.

The development of the Vulcan was continuing with many changes, especially to the pure delta design. It was changed to a layout with a conventional nose and a single dorsal fin and rudder. The Avon engines were replaced with the more powerful Olympus 100 Series, these engines producing 50% more thrust. The maiden flight took place on 30th August 1952, two years after the initial order was placed for 25 production models. The first production aircraft flew on 4th February 1955 and the Vulcan B.Mk.1 entered service in February 1957. With the availability of the Olympus 200 Series engines, the Vulcan wing was redesigned to accommodate this engine and the span increased by 12 ft, plus other changes. The aircraft became the Vulcan B.Mk.2, its performance exceeding the original specification – top speed of 0.98 Mach at 55,000 ft with a ceiling of 60,000 ft, and a bomb load of 21 x 1,000 lb bombs. Three Squadrons of Vulcans were modified to carry the Avro Blue Steel stand-off missile. The Vulcan, after all the years in readiness in the nuclear role, was destined to operate in the conventional role and in a totally unexpected part of the world, when Argentina invaded the Falkland Islands in early 1982. Five Vulcans, aircraft that were only 3 months away from being scrapped, were modified and deployed to Wideawake Airfield on Ascension Island. Just before midnight on 30th April 1982, two Vulcans took off to bomb the runway at Port Stanley airfield, each carrying their maximum bomb load of 21 x 1,000 lb bombs. One Vulcan returned soon after take-off with a cabin pressurisation fault, the other carried out its mission with the air-to-air facility being provided by 11 Victor tankers of 55 and 57 Squadrons, which enabled the Vulcan to create the record of the longest bombing raid, some 8,000 miles. A total of five Black Buck missions, as they were known, were carried out. On one such raid, 3rd June 1982, the Vulcan's refuelling probe was broken whilst refuelling on the return journey some 400 miles off the Brazilian coast and the aircraft was forced to make an emergency landing at Rio de Janeiro. September 1993 saw the last flight of the last Vulcan, XH558, which had been used at flying displays throughout the country since the Vulcans were taken out of service. It is now at Bruntingthorpe, Leicestershire.

The development of the Victor was taking place at the same time as that of the Vulcan under the watchful eye of Godfrey Lee, Handley Page's Research Engineer, ably assisted by Sir Frederick Handley Page and Gustav Victor Lachmann, a former German Air Force pilot. The plan was to have the first aircraft airborne in March 1951, but it was not to be and the target date slipped to the Farnborough Air Show 1952. Then, at the last minute, the Ministry declared Radlett airfield to be unsuitable for the maiden flight, so the first prototype had to be dismantled and taken to Boscombe Down to make use of the 10,000 ft runway. The 90 mile route was surveyed and two critical T-junctions were temporarily by-passed. The fuselage was mounted tail first on a reinforced bus axle and towed by a powerful tractor. Some fertile brain in Security decided that it should be disguised, so the whole load was encased to resemble a ship's hull, with the name 'GELEYPANDHY – Southampton' painted on the side! The 'flying boat' set off on 24th May 1952 along the North Circular (A406) and down the A30 to Boscombe Down. After reassembly, various faults prevented it from being flown at the Farnborough Air Show. Eventually, on 24th December 1952, WB771 took to the air, flown by the Company's Chief Test Pilot – Sqn Ldr Hedley George Hazelden. It was airborne in less than 1,500 ft, which was a quarter the length of Radlett's runway, which showed that somebody had been over cautious. The first production Victor B.Mk.1 (XA917) flew on 1st February 1956, with the RAF receiving its first Victor on 28th November 1957. A total of 50 Victor B.Mk.1's were produced, powered by four Sapphire 7 engines, with a maximum thrust of 11,000 lb, giving a maximum speed of 0.93 Mach, all up weight of

185,000 lb and a bomb load of 35 x 1,000 pounders or the nuclear bomb. In the late 50's/early 60's, 24 B.Mk.1's were flown to Radlett for the fitment of ECM (Electronic Counter Measures) equipment and renamed B.Mk.1A. With the failure of the Valiant main spar in 1964, the programme to convert the Victors into tankers was speeded up, and, starting on 24th May 1965, six aircraft were delivered to RAF Marham as two point tankers – B.Mk.1A (K2P) – with a Mk.20B refuelling pod on each wing. A further 24 B.Mk.1's were converted into three point tankers K.Mk.1 and K.Mk.1A. In addition to the wing pods, a Mk.17 Hose Drum Unit was fitted in the bomb bay. This conversion programme was completed in June 1967. In 1975, the Victor K.Mk.1's and K.Mk.1A's were retired to be replaced with the Victor K.Mk.2's. 24 had been converted into tankers from 8 strategic reconnaissance (SR) aircraft and 21 bombers (B.Mk.2's). The Mk.2's, of which 33 were built, were powered by four Conway engines producing 17,250 lb of thrust, an all up weight of 223,000 lb, with drop tanks and a speed of 0.92 Mach, making it superior in power to the B.Mk.1's.

At 14.45 hrs on that bright sunny October afternoon in 1993, with the last public fly-past of three Victor K.Mk.2's in tight formation at approximately 200 ft, the curtain finally fell on the era of the V-Bomber. Also, after 77 years, 55 Squadron, motto 'Nil Nos Tremefacit' ('Nothing Shakes Us'), was no more. All that was left for me to do was to jump into my car and head home to Basildon to reminisce on my 9 years as a member of that V-Bomber Force.

P.S. In the February 7th 1997 issue of the RAF News, there was an article about Vulcan XH558 which said – "In March, Vulcan XH558 will have been privately owned for 4 years. To celebrate this anniversary, it has been decided to form a Vulcan XH558 Club at Bruntingthorpe. The launch date is scheduled for early April 1997 and members will receive privileges, including Club days at Bruntingthorpe and their own magazine. Membership is £12 for an adult/family and £10 for under 16's and OAP's. For further details contact Colin Mears, 25 Pinewood Avenue, Sidcup, Kent DA15 8BB Tel:0181 302 5197".

P.P.S. Ben Mitchell was serving his time at A & AEE Boscombe Down 1955-57 and recalls each of the three V-Bombers coming in during that period for their initial Service trials. He was the Sgt i/c the Instrument Bashers in the Weighbridge hanger and the aircraft acceptance procedure was to carry out a Primary Star servicing check. The first Victor arrived for trials and as CSDE hadn't got their finger out to produce any servicing schedules for the Victor, he was given a Valiant schedule and told to 'improvise'!!. The Victor went up on air test after the acceptance check and the pilot landed with the parking brake on! It was the usual practice for all the erks to stand out on the strip to watch the take-off and landing of any new aircraft and what a sight it was. Having worked on Sunderland's at Pembroke Dock, Ben had witnessed the picturesque sight of a Sunderland landing on the water between PD and Milford Haven. The Victor gave him a repeat performance, with clouds of white smoke simulating the spray thrown out by the Sunderlands when they landed!! The aircraft naturally burnt its brakes out and a good deal more, but other than slewing off the runway, there wasn't too much additional damage as Ben recalls – but he reckoned that the pilot had a red face!

P.P.P.S. Sitting on the airfield at Southend is Vulcan XL426, in the capable hands of the Vulcan Restoration Trust. It's condition is such that it was able to do some engine runs during the Southend Air Show in May 1997. It is hoped to get it airborne in the future, but this will be a huge task considering the large amount of money that will be required.

P.P.P.P.S. A Vulcan Force reunion for ground and aircrew is to be held on Sunday 17th August 1997 at Wellesborne Mountford airfield, Warwickshire, where Vulcan XM655 will be taxying and performing a full engine ground test run. The XM655 Association has been formed to ensure the active future of the aircraft and details can be obtained from Nigel Pearce on 01328 856657.

11. We Were There

Robbie Roberts

You must all be familiar with the Remembrance Day 'celebrations' at the Albert Hall every year; incidentally this year (2004) one of the back stage 'somebodies' has managed to turn it into a shadow of its former self. It used to comprise demonstrations from all three Services, ranging from military bands to PT displays, before the representatives marched into the arena with their Standards to form up on the stage, followed by the performers who had provided the 'entertainment' returning to the arena for the religious service and the falling of the poppies from the roof.

Well, in November 1945, whether you remember it or not, some of the 51st Entry provided one of the Service displays – together with the Pipe Band and Flight Sergeant Lewis. For the uninitiated, Lewis was a large white goat who was normally tethered at the rear of the cookhouse near the Band Hut. I seem to recall that Ted Tout, who had been the 47th Entry mace basher, was brought back to resume his duties for this event. I'm not sure if we provided the whole of the marching party, or just a part of it, but we were there.

Our participation consisted of a display of marching and counter-marching within defined limits, which corresponded with the size of the oval display area in the Albert Hall, and we were rehearsed on the Henderson Square at Halton for what seemed to be weeks beforehand. Eventually, at some ungodly hour in the morning, we were transported (by bus) to the Albert Hall for rehearsals on the spot. I do remember that Squadron Leader Ralph Reader (he of the Gang Shows) was the Director of Service Participation, and when it was our turn, we all had to assemble in the circular corridors below the arena so that we could come up the stairs which provide four (?) entrances round the periphery of the arena itself. We then had to go into our rehearsed display before disappearing down the holes again to the corridors beneath. We had to return later for the religious bit. Otherwise we were largely left to our own devices, and, during rehearsals, some of us took great delight in wandering about all over the Hall. On one occasion, about five or six of us were up in the Gods when we were called for another rehearsal. Mr Reader was not amused by the length of time it took us to get back down.

On the night itself, when we came up into the arena, the place was packed to the roof and the King and Queen, and all the then Royal Family, were in the Royal Box, with the Pipe Band formed up beneath, with Ted Tout, the goat boy and Lewis at the front, all looking very smart indeed. The display seemed to be received reasonably well and lasted what appeared to be a very short time before we were back down below to await the call for the final parade. Incidentally, Lewis *did* disgrace us all in front of His Majesty! The falling of the poppies and the "Three cheers for His Majesty the King" were very moving and have stayed with me to this day. It was sixty years ago you know!

So there it is, a short, if vague, memory of a unique experience shared with lots of others. The following year, the display was an apprentice wheel of marchers, with the spokes going round one way and the rim the other – but I wasn't part of it – as punishment for some minor misdemeanour I expect!

It was also about this time that the buglers (trumpeters?) of the Pipes and Drums played reveille at the Cenotaph, but you had better ask young Harris or Mold to write a piece about that.

12. From the 1947 Diary of 582491 A/A Hoskins F D, Aged 17⅛

Fred Hoskins

Saturday 4th January 1947. Back to the old routine. Up late though. Rotten breakfast. Flight cleaning and F.F.I. After F.F.I. I went with Curly to Smoky Joe's for dinner. Couldn't stand the thought of RAF dinners. Took some photos in the afternoon. Went to see "Pardon My Past" this evening, good film.

Sunday 5th. Church Parade. Derek has some roller skates which we tried out in 328. Went to P.G. (Printers' Guild) in the afternoon, and round the NAAFI fire in the evening.

Monday 6th. Started to snow today, very cold. Started tech again today. Dobby started R1084 and superhet principles. Went to NAAFI again. They started a new scheme in the cookhouse. Everybody sits down and one table at a time goes to the servery, to stop doubling I suppose.

Tuesday 7th. Snow on the ground. Wore gumboots and two pair socks. Not quite so cold or windy. Nothing much doing. New lot of cadets in civvies. Naafi again.

Wednesday 8th. Snow pretty deep today. Started to thaw later. Went to P.G. in afternoon, rest of flight snow shovelling. Saw "3 Wise Fools" (sobby).

Thursday 9th. Thawed today. Still wearing gumboots. Rumours of having to book out from the block.

Friday 10th. Froze overnight. Started to thaw again. Flight cleaning, was on scrubbing. Payday, 8/- half pay.

Saturday 11th. Snow nearly all gone. Murphy came round after inspection and inspected us himself. Flight cleaning and Inspection by M. next Tuesday. Excused, good kit. Went to Smoky Joe's for dinner, spent 4s7d. Saw "Son of Monte Cristo" (pretty dim).

Sunday 12th. Church Parade. 'Sermon' a pep talk. Waste of 1¼ hours. Went to Smoky Joe's for dinner (2s3d today. Only had one dinner today). Walked back with Curly along Roman Road (Ermine Street) the Brauncewell Road and over North drome. Saw "The Strange Mr Gregory" and "Come out Fighting" (the East Side Kids).

Monday 13th. Short Flight Cleaning.

Tuesday 14th. Murphy let us off flight cleaning and inspection as we had a good room today. Went to baths, life saving classes. Plenty of cocoa and chat in drying room. And so to bed.

Wednesday 15th. Was in lab today. Got signal 1st time on IV detector. Added R F stage, duff, repeat next time. Had a tech test. Went to P.G. this afternoon and evening. 0M1's went to Halton today.

Thursday 16th. Nothing eventful today. PT boxing. Been windy lately, but not cold, in fact rather pleasant weather.

Friday 17th. Payday! 15/-. Impromptu circuit test in basic, 51% for tech. Flight cleaning tonight. Derek got his hook today, also Ack, Jud and Bill. Joe Smith, Mac and Geoff Souch got their 2nd's.

Saturday 18th. Usual Sat morning. Wing Parade. Boobs right and left. Went to P.G. in afternoon. Went to flicks "Maltese Falcon" and NAAFI. Poor old Jud, on Joe first day as hook. J has started working for his!

Sunday 19th. Church parade. Had to make our beds up. Went to Smoky Joe's for dinner and then walked around drome, over assault course, played with rugger ball. L/A/A Ross moved in and I took on job as kitboy.

Monday 20th. Were in Jeep labs twice today and were in Receiver labs, didn't get much joy. Flight cleaning.

Tuesday 21st. Nothing special. Webbing check tomorrow, blancoed webbing. Pressed Jock's blue.

Wednesday 22nd. Webbing inspection, unsatisfactory. P.G. this afternoon, ran off some locker cards. Re-blancoed webbing.

Thursday 23rd. Went up to dock to see Dave. Several light falls of snow and a heavy one.

Friday 24th. Snow on ground. Flight cleaning tonight, a lot to do.

Saturday 25th. A.O.C.'s inspection. Went to flicks tonight to see "Masquerade in Mexico". Early to bed. Broke, -1d. Snow.

Sunday 26th. Snow. On square for church parade in snow storm. Went down P.G. in afternoon and evening.

Monday 27th. Took some shipping telegrams in comms today. Snow again, very slippery. Went to P.G. tonight. In Tx lab we were transmitting from Miller osc in one room to W1117 in the other.

Tuesday 28th. Snow. Blizzards all day. Went with Curly to W/O Wildman's house for supper, very nice.

Wednesday 29th. Snow. Went to P.G. in afternoon and evening. Not much heating in pipes.

Thursday 30th. Snow, no signs of a thaw. Cold. No PT. Went to NAAFI. Did most of tomorrow's bull.

Friday 31st. Snow. Finished valve base. Soldering test job in shops. Started snowing again. Bull night. Gave up kitboy job for Ross, back on floorpads.

Saturday 1st February. No school parade today. Slight thaw. Full kit. Murphy – "It stinks, not too bad for 8M9s" etc. Ross – "Flight cleaning this afternoon. Full kit by Dalziel at 1800"! Opinion divided. We decided to obey orders, do as little as possible, and send Ross to Coventry. Squeak and Gand went to Lincoln. Good kit on inspection. Took liberty of going to second house flicks, not caught. "King's Row", good film.

Sunday 2nd. Snow, thawed quite a bit. Church parade in ankle deep snow. 09.15 On parade, 09.45 Markers, 09.55 Advance, 10.15 March off (didn't march off until 10.25). Went to flicks, "Candlelight in Algeria". Snow and rain. Early to bed.

Monday 3rd. Snow, rain, thaw. Went to see "Lives of a Bengal Lancer". Short Flight Cleaning. Ross has gone, got his C/A/A after 2 weeks as L/A/A!

Tuesday 4th. Woke up to find deep snow and no electric light, not even in cookhouse. Coal shortage. Rumours of being sent home. Had a letter, Dad home from Ceylon. Grantham station reported snowed up, roof in.

Wednesday 5th. Deep snow. Usual tech. Changed my boots. P.G. in afternoon, snowballing.

Thursday 6th. Deep snow. Went to see about weekend, 12.00 tomorrow.

Friday 7th. Went home. Waited for bus until 2.00, just caught 3.07 from Grantham which was 30 minutes late. Arrived home 9.40 pm. Had a good supper, ham, egg, fruit etc, delicious!

Saturday 8th. Went to collect car with Dad, then to Chichester for petrol coupons. Went to Gosport in afternoon. Windscreen wiper went for a burton in snow on way back. Had to lean out of window and work it with my bootlace.

Sunday 9th. Had a lie in. Chicken and ham pie for dinner. Left 1.30, caught 2.30 from Portsmouth, 4.45 King's X. Arrived Grantham 8.00, 1 hour late. Back in camp 9.30. Mac told me I had my hook, found it true. Moved in to 9M9 'E' Flt, C/A/A Joe Smith and L/A/A Ackers.

Monday 10th. Up early. Outhouse drain blocked, dorm flooded. Had to stay behind and supervise mopping up operations. Flight cleaning, had to sew my hooks on. Got 397 Jones for my kitboy. Good bod. 2 special sick.

Tuesday 11th. Nothing much today. Jones altered my hooks and eagles. Saw "In Old Sacramento".

Wednesday 12th. Parade at 13.00 in denims and gumboots. Marched to Rauceby Road, struck up the Rauceby Road and across fields to railway. Supposed to clear railway. Nothing for us to do, line clear for 3 miles where 'B' Sqn were. Dismissed. Walked back with Willy, Ack, Joe, Ted Norman and Dave Chaffey to see Sam Hill (comms instr) in Cranwell village. Saw Terry and Pam Jarrett who asked us in for a cup of tea. Saw "Come Back to Me".

NOTES:

1. **10th & 17th January.** Pay was 1s 6d per day, with 12s paid each fortnight and the rest deferred until going on leave. Presumably pay got out of phase, hence 8s and then 15s only a week later.
2. **11th January.** The Murphy referred to would be F/S Murphy of the RAF Regt who, on taking charge of the squadron said "I will make this squadron a happy squadron even if I have to put the whole squadron inside". That was probably the only thing he ever said that amused us!
3. **11th January.** 'Smoky Joe's' was the café at Byard's Leap. It is still operating. A serving of beans on toast in Smoky Joe's at that time cost about 8d, so to spend 4s7d, or even only 2s3d indicates a great hunger!
4. **18th January.** I can't recall who 'J' was who was working for his hook.
5. **19th January.** Ross was an 8M3, a piper and a boxer. Dalziel, a fellow Scot, was a 7M9.
6. The 'P. G.' was the Printers' Guild. Members of this club met in a hut where we had a printing press and associated equipment to produce leaflets, programmes and other small items. In the hut there was a stove and we had a kettle and the makings of tea. It provided a few of us with a place of relative comfort and privacy where we could get away from the barrack blocks.
7. At Cranwell NCO apprentices were known as 'hooks' as opposed to 'snags' at Halton. It was though the 'hook' came from the naval influence, Cranwell having been a Royal Naval Air Station before 1918. Another hangover from the naval past was that tables were known as 'decks'.

8. The cinema loomed large in importance in our lives – together with the NAAFI and food. A ticket to the Station Cinema cost 2d. To avoid incurring this expense, some A/A's volunteered for cinema cleaning and free admission. A cup of tea in the NAAFI cost 1d, while coffee was 2d. Still lemonade cost 1d for a ½ pint glass. Rock cakes were 1d (or was it 1½d?). Luxury items such as 'iced tarts' or 'fly pies' were 2d. It might be thought that 12s a fortnight would go a long way at those prices, but money was needed also for blanco, polishes, soap and razor blades. Thus it was not unusual to hear requests for the loan of as little as a penny or even a halfpenny, as well as "Lend me five bob, and I'll pay back ten on deferred"!

13. Canada, Here I Come

Eric Mold

I am frequently asked how I came to leave the RAF and join the Royal Canadian Air Force. Well, it is a bit of a story which may be of interest, so here goes. I was a sparkling new Flying Officer, just coming to the end of a tour on Vampires at RAF Gutersloh and RAF Wildenrath in 2nd TAF in Germany. The world was my oyster, as they say, but suddenly it was shattered. Brian Boundy, our Squadron Adjutant came in and handed me a piece of green paper. It was my next posting. To my utter chagrin, I was posted to the Central Flying School at RAF Little Rissington. Every pilot I knew dreaded the thought of being posted back to Training Command. After all, we had only left the Command as graduating students a couple of short years ago. Besides, once you get in, there is no getting out. I'd met dozens of chaps who had spent their whole service in Training Command. But still, there it was, I had to report to CFS for an interview with the Commandant. The dreaded day rolled around all too quickly and I found myself, together with two others of the same ilk, dressed in best blue, with my log book on my knee, sitting in the CFS Adj's office. We were waiting for the *Air Commode* who wanted to meet us and welcome us personally. Apparently he was in bed with flu, but was going to get up especially to come and meet us and welcome us personally. Eventually *His Holiness* arrived and we were ushered into his office, and we sat on three chairs opposite the desk. I shall never forget his opening remarks – "It's very gratifying, seeing chaps like you, volunteering to be flying instructors". Just a minute I thought, I didn't volunteer, there's something wrong here! When I finally had the opportunity to say something, I pointed out as tactfully as I could, that I had not volunteered for anything. "But you would like to be a flying instructor?". "Wouldn't you?" he continued. I stuttered something about not knowing enough about the game myself yet, certainly not enough to be able to teach others. He went on about how they were going to teach me to fly with precision and accuracy to within a degree. I replied that I could already fly with precision and accuracy. "What do you mean?" the now irate *Air Commode* barked. I said "If you check the assessments in my log book, you will see that I have several 'Above Averages' in aerial gunnery. You have to fly within a ¾° to be good at that". "But that's only one instance" the red faced senior officer replied. "Yes sir", I said, "But in my business, it's the instance that counts". With that, my log book came flying across the room, accompanied by the words "Get out! Get out! You are going to be blackballed for the rest of your days in the RAF". I picked up my log book and scampered out of the room. I even forgot to salute as I left. I was pretty shaken up I can tell you. In the outer office the Adj asked me how things had gone. I told him the gist of the story, to which he replied "Em, I see". A little while later I was told I had better go home and await further posting instructions!

 I drove back to my dad's place to await my fate. My dad was surprised to see me there when he got home and he obviously sensed my feelings as I recited my sad tale of woe, so he took me round to the local to cheer me up a bit. My days 'in waiting' stretched into several weeks. I was beginning to think the RAF had given up on me completely. Eventually, after almost a month, the dreaded telegram arrived. I was posted to RAF Benson. Wow! Not the Queens Flight? No, it turned out to be the Long Range Ferry Squadron, considered by some as the repository of many of the RAF's career deadbeats; most of them brilliant pilots. Lads, like me, who had blotted their copybook over some stupid thing and had been posted to this career backwater. My fellow pilots on this Squadron were much older than me and all very experienced flyers; current on a dozen different aircraft types or more, from Spits through jets to Lincolns. They thought nothing of jumping into a Vampire and dashing out to RAF Kai Tak in Hong Kong and bringing a Spitfire back, or picking up a Mosquito at RAF Changi in Singapore and ferrying it back to some Maintenance Unit the UK. They were all great chaps, but my sojourn with them was a short one.

 A few days after I arrived, the Squadron CO, Sqn Ldr Bennett, arrived back from a ferry trip to some distant part of the Empire and called me in for my arrival interview. I shall never forget his opening remarks either. "You've crossed someone, haven't you laddie?" I admitted that I had had a run in with the Commandant at CFS and recited my sad tale again. "I thought as much" he replied, "You're no bloody good to me, it'll take years for me to train you, you should be with (Sqn Ldr) Cole's outfit". This was 'A' Squadron in the hangar at the end of the flight line. The Squadron, made up of transport and fighter pilots, was about to start ferrying 450 F.86 Sabres, which the RAF had recently bought from Canadair Ltd in Montreal, across the Atlantic to the UK. It was the dream posting for all fighter pilots in those days; a good exciting job that would surely lead to another tour on a Sabre squadron in Fighter Command or 2nd TAF after it was over. "Would you like that?" the Sqn Ldr asked. I just could not believe it. "Yes sir, I'd love it" I stammered. With that he picked up the phone, dialled a number and soon began to speak. "Hello sir, Bennett here", he said. "I've got another one of those awkward chaps here, he's had a run in with the people down at CFS". A brief pause while he listened. "No bloody good to me; take me years to train him. He should be with Cole and his boys ... he'd love that". Another pause while he listened. "OK sir, I'll tell him ... thank you". He hung up the phone. "You are posted to Sqn Ldr Cole's Squadron. Go down there and I will give him a ring to let him know you are coming. The paperwork will catch you up in a few days". I was stepping on air as I walked down the flight line to the hangar at the far end. However, I was quickly brought back down to ground level when a voice, the likes of which I had not heard since I left Halton, bawled "MOLD!!!". I turned round and saw Sqn Ldr Bennett leaning out of his office window. "Can't you read laddie?" he said, pointing to a large sign that read 'No Unauthorised Personnel Within 25 Yards of the Queen's Flight'. I saluted and nipped as smartly as I could to put more distance between me and Her Majesty's aeroplanes!

Things went pretty well on the Beechers Brook Squadron, as the Ferry Unit was known. The fighter types had quite a time teaching the transport bods, usually the Flight Commanders and Section Leaders, how to fly. We had several exciting trips, low fuel states, bad weather and the odd dose of frozen controls; and a couple of chaps *augured in* etc. We did the acceptance flight testing and shakedown flying out of St Hubert, in Montreal, and then leapt off in balbos of 20 or 30 kites for Goose Bay – Bluie West One (in sunny southern Greenland, the Florida of the North) – Keflavick and then Kinloss or Prestwick. It was nothing to have 50 or 60 aircraft on the route at any one time. About half were ours, the rest RCAF or USAF. It was not unusual for our CO to have us in the fjord at Bluie West One testing our immersion suits, with extra brownie points going to the idiot who stayed in the water the longest! We all had difficulty in spending our one dollar overseas allowance, which we were given because the cost of living in Canada and along the route was so much higher than in the UK.

I was still under 25 years of age, so received no marriage allowance, consequently Vera and I found it difficult to make ends meet. Fortunately my dad was very generous and helped us to buy a caravan. Gp Capt Dudgeon, the RAF Benson CO at the time, thought caravans were ideal for young couples like us, so he created a nice little trailer park, right on the Station, for the few of us that lived in them. When Beechers Brook was over, I was posted to RAF Linton-on-Ouse, the first wing in Fighter Command to have Sabres. This was a nice job, but Gp Capt Pedley, the Station Commander, thought trailers were strictly for gypsies and would not allow them on the Station, so we had to park ours on a farm nearby. The flying with 92 Squadron was great fun, but by now my heart was in Canada – it was where I wanted to be. I had to get there somehow.

Purely on the spur of the moment, when I was in London one day, I walked into the offices of the Canadian Joint Staff and asked to speak to the Recruiting Officer. After a short talk with him, I was told that they would take me into the RCAF, at the same rank and seniority, however, they would do nothing to help me get out of the RAF. After much thought, particularly about what the Commandant at CFS had said, I decided to take the plunge. I brushed up on Formal Official Letters and wrote to the Air Council requesting my release from my present engagement to emigrate to Canada and join the RCAF. I did not hear a thing for months and then one day I got a call from the Adj. "CO wants to see you, get up here sharpish". I wondered what it could be about as I dashed up to SHQ on my Corgi. I was ushered into the CO's office and handed a signal which I read and could hardly believe. *"582726 Fg Off Eric V. Mold is to report to the RCAF Recruiting Officer at 66 Ennismore Gardens, South Kensington, London, on 4th December 1954 for attestation into the Royal Canadian Air Force for a tour of engagement of not less than 5 years. His release from the Royal Air Force will become effective on the day following his attestation into the RCAF"*. When I had read the signal, I looked up and Gp Capt Pedley said "Don't you dare mention this to anyone else around here or I'll have a queue outside my office of people wanting to do the same thing". That's the end of the story, but only the beginning of the next one!

14. The Aden Protectorate Levies

Junior Roots

Following the Entry's 'improver' year at RAF St Athan, August 1948 to August 1949, a posting to my first 'proper' Unit, RAF Odiham, only lasted for one year before I applied for an overseas posting. At the tender age of 22, I rather fancied a tour to a sunny spot before seeking a life of married bliss. Malta and Gibraltar were top of my list. Well, I got the hot spot all right with a 2-year tour to Aden. Nobody at Odiham seemed to know very much about Aden, other than that there was a flying Unit at RAF Khormaksah.

On 5th November 1950, with kitbag at the slope, I set off for Southampton and boarded the troopship *Empire Ken* with a mix of RAF and Army fellow boarders. The Services were separated far below deck, with accommodation having double-decker bunk beds rather than hammocks. Fifteen days later, after an uneventful cruise involving one short stop in Port Said, we docked in the port of Aden, named Steamer Point. At that time, Aden was a British or Crown Protectorate, largely comprising an Eastern peninsular with the Arabian Sea to the East and a Western peninsular, called Little Aden, with the Red Sea to the West. Little Aden was the site of an oil refinery. A tarmac causeway led North to the Arabian mainland where RAF Khormaksah was situated. Nearby was Sheik Othman where the main body of the Aden Protectorate Levies (APL) was located, together with the Aden Levy Hospital.

On disembarking from the Empire Ken, a coach took we new arrivals to RAF Khormakshah. A large Arab, holding a card with my name on it, grabbed my kitbag and took me in his Jeep some 3 miles North on the causeway to the Singapore Lines, some halfway between the port and Khormaksah. Singapore Lines was the base for the MT Workshops of the APL. 66 Sqn RAF Regiment were also at this location. Accommodation comprised thatched long huts and included a cookhouse staffed by Arabs, a small Naafi and huts for the SNCO's. A separate area of better accommodation was on site for the officers.

The APL main body of Arabs, trained as a small uniformed Army, was based at Sheik Othman. The Singapore Lines element serviced and repaired all vehicles from both sites. We were only about 20 strong and comprised MT Fitters, Electricians, Sheet Metal Workers for body-work repairs and a couple of drivers. The vehicles involved were 3-ton Bedford QL lorries, 15 cwt trucks, GMC armoured cars, Willy's jeeps and Vauxhall Vanguards. The workshops were tin-roofed shed-like structures and extremely hot to work in. An Arab officer, with a good command of English, acted as liaison between the tradesmen and Arab drivers.

Halton trained its Electricians in both Ground and Airborne equipment and systems but in 1951 we had to choose which to follow for future years. This was due to the introduction of ever-more complicated ground equipment and aircraft, requiring specialist training and expensive courses. Having spent a year fixing vehicles, I elected to convert to Electrical Fitter (Air) and was sent to Khormaksar for a trade test. Having passed that, promotion to Junior Technician soon followed and a few months later, promotion to Corporal. Even so, I had to complete my tour with the APL rather than have a replacement sent out from the UK. On promotion, I was promptly given a Secondary Duty: NCO i/c Library! At least this gave me first sight of any new books which came in.

Outside work, entertainment was limited on site to cricket and football against the RAF Regiment, and indoor activities in the small Naafi – one elderly snooker table and a decrepit dartboard! However, a daily truck run was available to Steamer Point. The large Naafi there had an area of the harbour wire-fenced for swimming. A small freshwater pool, complete with high-diving and spring boards was nearby. In town, a reasonable range of shops, mostly owned and staffed by Indians, catered for our needs, especially at duty-free prices. Overlooking the town was No.7 RAF Hospital, perched on a hill, and on the way to the hospital lurked a small building called 'Roses Cottage' where personnel were treated for illnesses created by those of ill repute!

Among the hills on the Arabian peninsular was one named 'Shamsan'. About 500ft high, it provided some challenging exercise to climb in our spare time. In one of the valleys, was a series of once derelict water tanks, discovered in 1854 when they were completely hidden by rubbish and debris from the hills. The tanks were opened out and repaired by the British Government. The aggregate capacity of all the tanks exceeded 20 million Imperial gallons! Quite a tourist attraction.

Towards the end of my tour, I went as convoy Electrician with a force of Levies into the Southern hinterland of Arabia, but after a couple of weeks in rough country I was taken ill and flown in an Anson back to base. There, a diagnosis of amoebic dysentery put me into No.7 Hospital for 10 days and I watched my designated troopship depart for the UK! A short spell of sick leave in the Lines, and then I caught a Hastings aircraft from Khormaksah to Egypt. Four days in a tent there was followed by a flight to Malta, and on to Stansted airport and another dose of sick leave.

Now known as the capital of the Yemen, I wonder what Aden is like today?

15. Feat(s) of Clay – or How to Dodge the Column for 24 Years and Still Get a Pension

W.G. (Bill, Mick, Sam – take your pick) Clay (514)

First thing, the man said, never volunteer, but, after you have volunteered, get in the band. He was right! The Military Band was a route to better things at Halton – down to the bandroom on GST, sports afternoons and Saturday mornings, with tea and stickies laid on by No.3 Wing Sgts Mess (Jock the Bandmaster was a cook there) and off to the Red Shield Club on Sunday mornings while the rest were on Church Pararde. A few days jolly under canvas in Kensington Gardens for the Victory Parade in 1946, (much better than Clapham underground), and we went to the Windmill in the evening after the parade. We did the Festival of Remembrance in the Albert Hall, the Lord Mayor's Show and all sorts of other junketing. Yes, I know the Pipes & Drums did the Royal Tournament and we didn't, but we did nearly everything else, including Lloyd's Bank Sports Day with all those delightful young lady clerks!

After Halton, the good things continued. All those odd little dance band jobs here and there (very curious some of those were too!), and always of course the formal jobs, like the time in Porthcawl in Battle of Britain week when a certain drum major took a left fork instead of to the right. We ignored him and we led the band in the correct direction. His words as he galloped back through the ranks, were very descriptive, if somewhat inaccurate. I got the blame for that little lot, just because I was in the middle of the front rank, playing trombone. (You had to be versatile in voluntary bands!)

No.3 FTS at RAF Feltwell was my first posting after RAF St Athan. It had a Military Band which seemed to get a steady trade in funerals! The Harvards and Prentices fell out of the sky with great regularity, and, as I was playing cornet, I got rather used to the Last Post and Reveille routine. On one memorable occasion, one of the firing party had a hung round on the first volley which went off as he reloaded, and made a mess of the bloke in front of him, who took the wad in the back of the neck. Incredibly the man stayed on his feet, then, as I marched round to the front to do my bit, there was a clatter as the erk who had shot him fainted.

I spent nearly 8 years at Feltwell. One Stationmaster (CO) refused to allow us to play the Royal Air Force March, instead we played 'Sussex by the Sea'. As he said, the troops sang rude words to it as they marched – but at least they stayed in step! Being in the band there got me into trouble at least twice, the first time being when I was detached to RAF

Uxbridge for another Albert Hall Remembrance job. Feltwell was providing the display that year, the climax being a complete airfield layout with Glim lamps in the arena – the old Drem lighting layout. (The Electricians will know what I'm talking about, even if you others don't!) There were a couple of hundred lamps to be sorted out and the Flt Sgt offered me the job, pointing out that I could have a week living at home, which was only about 3 miles from Uxbridge. Naturally enough I jumped at the chance, but when I got to Uxbridge the trouble started, all on account of my band badge, which was the usual sort, a lyre worn on the left arm. At the time, I was a J/T (Junior Technician), and as Uxbridge was the home of the RAF Central Band and the Advanced Drill Squad, the only other J/T's on the Station were either bandsmen by trade or medics from the hospital. Central Bandsmen wore crowned lyre badges on both arms, and medics wore little collar badges, so to the eyes of every keen and eager Snoop for miles around, I was improperly dressed. There were hundreds of Snoops all over Uxbridge, so I collected more F.252's (charge reports) than a Boy Entrant's number!! The post mortem after I got back to Feltwell, when all the documents arrived, was somewhat hilarious. I think the grand total of offences were 22 improperly dressed, 22 conduct prejudicial, 6 or 7 not standing to attention etc, 4 for insolence and one for not having my motorcycle registered on Camp. The Boss, after he stopped laughing, was a gentleman about it all. He handed me the lot and ordered me to get rid of them. No, he was not the Band Officer!

My other bit of trouble was rather silly really. I had reached the exalted rank of Corporal and we had a Sgt running the band, but one Saturday morning there was a parade, the Sgt was on leave, the band was shorthanded (as usual), so I was conducting with one hand whilst playing the cornet with the other. The SWO (Station Warrant Officer) decided he didn't like the pace we were setting, so he rushed over and started waving his arms about, whereupon I absent-mindedly stuffed the baton in his fist and fell in at the rear, still blowing away merrily on the cornet. The felony was well compounded because unlike most Stations, where the band was at the rear and well out of sight, at Feltwell the band was positioned behind the saluting base. I reckon 90% of the parade saw the whole thing and of course they all fell about laughing, but oddly, I was never charged over it! Strangely however, I did find myself down to do the Hereford square bashing course shortly afterwards!! I never actually went to Hereford because in the meantime I had got my time in for my Cpl/Tech, and having inverted my tapes, was immune from such nonsense. Shortly after, the SWO had a lot of trouble getting his electric kettle back from my workshop, he having been unwise in putting it in for repair! (Spares were always dodgy!)

RAF Jever in Germany was my next Station, but I had a brief spell at RAF Stanmore Park, where Henry Ford was in the Fighter Command band. As I was only on detachment, I couldn't get into the band, because I was waiting to go back to Halton to do a Works course in Aylesbury. I'll draw a veil over my second spell at Halton. It hadn't changed much, even though I was in the Sgts Mess. I got into a bit of trouble over my car permit – I suppose putting 'Bloody Immaculate' against the bit on the form which asked for 'Condition of Vehicle' was a bit daft, even if it was a Lanchester. By then Bill Bond was the civvy in the Bedding Store, Dinger Bell (not our Chairman, but the PTI) had the inside bunk and Wilbur Udee was a rock-ape Warrant Officer with no sense of humour and had his sticky fingers into everything, so I made hurried arrangements to live out in Harrow, despite the travelling.

To Jever, with no Station band, but we soon got a little dance band going. Having a young family and working shifts, it quietened things down a bit and the tour went quite quickly. Tour-ex and we soon found ourselves at 2,000 ft over the Channel in a Bristol 'Frightener'. Rough as it was, it was smoother than down below. It was December and rather choppy, the white horses on the wave tops looked more like elephants! When we landed, we got an object lesson in upsetting the Customs from the driver of the other car on the plane, an Aston Martin complete with a willowy blonde. He was a very superior person, from the Household Cavalry or somesuch, and he insisted to this quiet little Customs bloke that we would have to wait because he was only on a short leave and wasn't prepared to hang around behind the RAF. Well it didn't really work. As we drove off having cleared Customs, the heavies were removing the Aston's door trims with a dirty great screwdriver, whilst the blonde stood by tapping her foot and the driver chewed the tarmac!

We arrived at RAF Chivenor for the New Year (1960). There was a band, all drums and trumpets, and once again versatility triumphed. I became the man with the big bass drum until I managed to recruit a few like-minded people, then we became a real band with instruments and music, and even a Band Sergeant from the Regional Band at Locking. (He and I are still in touch and he was at our Ruby Wedding party recently.) There were plenty of local bands in the area, so we were quite chuffed when Ilfracombe got its new lifeboat and asked us to play for the launching ceremony. It was quite a party. After the ceremonial bit we went for a slap up tea, then had a trip out in the new boat. Very interesting – especially as it was blowing half a gale at the time!

I was posted to RAF Gan in the Indian Ocean in 1968 and I took my trumpet along. It got lost on the way but turned up a week later, the VC10 having done a circumnavigation, so the old trumpet has probably flown more yards than it has blown notes! I swopped a little James motorbike for it while I was at Chivenor and I've still got it some 30-odd years on. Not bad seeing as I only paid a tenner for the bike in the first place! We had two parades on Gan that year. It was the RAF's 50th Anniversary and there was Remembrance Sunday as well, but the highlight for me, (apart from coming home), was when the FEAF Band came over from Singapore to do a week of concerts on the island. Their Musical Director was good enough to let me do the jobs with them. I had approached him to ask if I could sit in whilst they practised and his reaction, after we'd had a blow together, was "If you've got a bow tie and dark trousers, why not play with us", so I did. We had a dance band there too, with lots of guitars, mainly Caribbean style, a piano, drums, accordian, clarinet and me. It was a lot of fun and certainly helped the tour along. Apart from leave, I took the Rifle team to Singapore, but that's another story!

Finally I was posted to RAF Benson. Not much of a posting, but convenient as a departure point for Civvy Street. During my months there I ran a Brass Band in Wallingford, and also went on loan to RAF Abingdon when their band needed a hand. It all came to an end for me in September 1969, when I pointed the car in an Easterly direction and figuratively shook the dust of Oxfordshire from my boots after a somewhat acrimonious farewell session with the Stationmaster, who seemed to think I was one of his Riggers! As they used to say in the News of the World, I made my excuses, or rather my comments, and left hurriedly!

The bands hadn't finished with me though. Next year I bumped into Henry Ford again, we were living within 3 miles of each other and have been in close contact ever since. Being Henry, he's got me into more bands than enough, but I've largely run out of puff now, although if I save it up I should be able to cope with the 51st reunion at Bromsgrove next time round!

16. Much Ado about Nothing – or Come Back Eric Mold, All Is For Given

Toddy Hood

We were on the lookout for a gift to send home, but behind the glass of the gift counter were just a few stuffed seals looking the worse for wear.

Around us, sharing a makeshift building, were some hundreds of US Servicemen also in transit. The two Icelanders, serving stale sandwiches, were the only signs that we were in Reykjavik, Iceland. It was late August 1951, and we had been diverted by bad weather from a Stratocruiser flight from Heathrow bound for Montreal. (Remember the Stratocruiser? A double decker with a lounge bar on top!). Most of our kit was to follow us when we had a permanent address. Rumour had it that No.1 CANS Prince Edward Island (Spud Island!) was full and a new Navigation School was to be opened somewhere on the prairies. About eight hours later we made it to Montreal and then by North Star to London, Ontario, where we began a two week acclimatisation course before Nav training proper.

Fire Picket took on a whole new meaning. Clocking in points on each floor of a very large tinder dry wooden barracks, each hour of the night. Having a crafty fag meant setting off the 'fire alarm' in the nostrils of patrolling Royal Canadian Air Force erks and a public dressing down. Drill in the RCAF meant being counselled not to stamp our feet during turns and on the march – didn't know that such stamping damaged our spines! (You didn't tell us that Chiefy!!)

Wine bars down town (bars were for men only!) where for the price of a drink you could spend an hour or two being entertained and insulted for nothing. The resident pianist/comedian's stock in trade being good-natured jokes about Limeys. A memorable trip to Niagara Falls in September, with delicious sweet black grapes from roadside stalls, unending tiny settlements based on a filling station and a drug store, the names reminders of old Crimean and Boer War battlefields, with the London Underground thrown in for good measure. Brilliantly coloured barns with the farmers name in large letters. Railway level crossing lights, which could be seen for miles. Then to Toronto for the train out West en route to RCAF Winnipeg. Cowcatcher on the front of the engine, a caboose at the very end (useful for putting latecomers in who had supped too much ale in the city), Negro porters who magically converted daytime seating into double bunks. In two days we only passed through about three settlements, thousands of lakes and an uncountable number of pine trees. Finally we arrived at Winnipeg where tea, cookies and fags awaited us, handed out by the wives and families of "The Wartime Pilots and Observers Association". To the North of us were parallel lakes 300 miles long and to the West of us were hundreds of miles of prairies ending at the Rockies. To the South, about 60 miles away, ran the US border where North Dakota meets Minnesota.

Several weeks later, Princess Elizabeth arrived for a Royal Visit in October 1951. By then the city was living up to it's name – 'Windy'. The citizens were in parkas and hats, but our issue of Canadian parkas were not deemed to be smart enough to be seen by the Princess, so we dressed in Best Blue without greatcoats and we were soon blue all over as we lined the steps to the Provincial Capital Building. Our deep-sea kit was apparently still on the high seas (as we found out later) addressed to 'Portage la Prairie' – an abandoned base well West of Winnipeg. Some people never saw their kit again, it ended up in Korea! Portage la Prairie, in large letters, became corrupted to 'PORT AGELA PRAI RIE', which was assumed by some shipping clerk to be the Royal Irish Engineers! The troops must have been glad of all those Burberry greatcoats!

A mile away from RAF Winnipeg was the trolley bus terminal, which ran right into the city centre. The driver had an anthracite stove by his side, which he stoked occasionally to heat the pipes, which ran round the bus. There were two other smaller towns near Winnipeg and then little else until many miles West. St Boniface was the French-speaking town; the other was the railway township of Transcona where the railway network was serviced. It was there that my grandparents had lived prior to the 1914-18 war. I paid a visit to some Scottish friends there. I don't believe the town had altered much from those early days. There were still wooden sidewalks and stores with batwing doors. The Scots family had an ancient wooden house, which they had bought from some Ukrainians. It was complete with a huge tiled Russian stove, which stood in the centre of the open plan ground floor. There were seats built into the surround and cooking could be done on the top like an Aga. The central heating consisted of vents above the stove to the upstairs bedrooms. I could imagine my grandfather in a similar house and what it must have been like for them in that bitter climate, when his burnt down. He told tall stories about his days as a brakeman on the Canadian Pacific Railway, places with a ring to their names like Moose Jaw, Medicine Hat and Kamloupe, and using an axe handle to prevent hobos from boarding and robbing the freight as the train slowed on the steep inclines of the Rockies.

On the Base was a huge wooden hangar in which all physical and social activities took place. You could play basketball or even, as they tried to teach us, the moves of American football. On the side was a 10-pin bowling alley, which, as it was manual, counted as PE! At one end of the hangar was an all ranks canteen, which stayed open until the end of the daily flying, so we could get a toasted ham and rye before bed. Once every month, any profit was blown on an entertainment night – a bit reminiscent of a 'do in the tank' (Remember those at Halton?). Tea, sugar, meat and eggs, were still on ration back home and the Hudson Bay Co ran a 'food parcels for Britain' scheme, so I sent in orders for

Thelma to receive at home. Nothing was sent from Canada. As they were export orders, the items never left England. Talking of food, it was the breakfasts which I remember. Egg and bacon every morning, pancakes with maple syrup, with lashings of rye toast and butter. The Canadians had opened their Nav Schools on behalf of NATO. The French hated the food and sat, as they do, dipping crusts of bread into their black coffee, mumbling about a country of savages with no culture. Never mind the culture, "Taste the food" was our motto! The only two exceptions were a couple of French Navy 'old sweats' who took up two bunks in our barrack room. They had more fun with us they said, and anyway they wanted to improve their English. (Their closest neighbours were an Ulsterman and an ex-brat called Puffers, who was a Scot and lisped!)

The winter weather, with the exception of a few heavy snowfalls, consisted of clear blue skies with sunshine. The sunny days however were very deceptive, as one keen cross country runner on our Course found out. In early winter he lined up in a pair of very short running shorts and sped off before any of the Canadian PE staff could grab him. We followed dressed in overalls, woolly hats and boots. He was eventually caught and taken into hospital with suspected frostbite in the 'crown jewels'. Night flying was sometimes quite awesome with the winter night filled with stars and even they were dimmed by the Northern Lights dancing and flashing. When standing in the astro dome, it was difficult to concentrate on star shots.

Local radio stations were in abundance and Country & Western music was the main diet. While tuning in the radio compass, the lyrics sank in and I can still recall the words of "I'm going to Montana to throw the Hoolahan". Not surprisingly, in view of the greenness of the navigators, few pilots flew anything other than their own headings and heights to prevent getting lost! We just plotted their headings and made the best of it. We were supposed to use the radio beacons for bearings and not to home on to, but unfortunately two ex-brats and their pilot homed to a beacon South of Winnipeg and were all killed. After that, the pilots at least flew our heights! There was a singular lack of bull at RCAF Winnipeg. The RAF contingent was completely integrated with the Canadians. There was no marching about and you could book in and out of the guardroom at any time of the day or night. The French would not allow their men this privilege and so had a large parade on Saturdays to do extra drill after catching culprits climbing the wire! The French, Belgians and Danes had their own officers and marched everywhere in large flights. Only the Belgians and Danes chose English as their language of instruction and seemed eager to adjust to Canadian life.

One day, our Course Leader, Sandulak, a great bear of a man of White Russian descent, arrived at lectures spitting fire. "Goddam Limeys!" Apparently a new Flt Lt had been posted in to handle discipline, and he was ex-RAF. He had button-holed our ex-Bomber Command CO and convinced him that a station parade would be just the thing. By this time it was late winter, with hard packed snow underfoot – the only possible parade ground being the tarmac apron. About a week later, a Chinook wind blew downhill all the way from the Rockies. The slightly warmer air formed dense fog which rolled across the prairies. No flying – a rare event. And a completely new event – a station parade – was announced. Oh dear, we could see the first shadows of 'bull' appearing. After breakfast, the new Flt Lt strutted round making snide remarks as we formed up. "Wait till I get you on parade, I'll smarten you up". In the fog we slithered in our overboots on the hard packed snow. Warmly wrapped in our issue parkas, we lined up in flights in front of a brand new saluting base. RAF, French Navy, French Air Force, Belgians in two groups (Flemish and Walloon – they loathed each other!), then the small flight of Danes alongside the very reluctant Canadian staff. The CO was on the saluting base looking very grim, and behind him a beaming Flt Lt (known to all as Flt Lt Snide). About 50 yards from them, barely visible in the fog, was the new flag pole and a lone bugler (we found out later that he had been co-opted from the station jazz band – and no – it wasn't Eric Mold!). The CO was passed a piece of paper by our favourite Flt Lt. "Parade, stand at ease!" "Bugler, sound the still". Not a sound. The CO looked at the piece of paper again – had he got it right? Try again. "Bugler, sound the still". No movement. Look at paper again. Try something different. "Bugler, sound the alert". Not a sound. In the fog, the whole parade was getting very restless and on edge. By the time the CO had gone through the whole thing once again, he was a VERY ANGRY MAN. "Sergeant Major (SWO), arrest that man". Tramp of feet, fall in two men. Brief exchange of words with a quivering, embarrassed bugler. "What are you waiting for?" roared the CO. "Sir" said the Sergeant Major. "Goddam it, don't Sir me, I said arrest him" roared the CO, very red in the face. Bravely the Sergeant Major called back "Sir, he only knows how to play the General Salute". Stunned silence. Then a roar of relieved laughter came from the fog hidden English speakers. There then followed, at intervals, more laughter as it was translated into French, Flemish, Walloon and Danish. The CO was a big man in every way, and he drew himself up very straight. "Parade – Attention" he roared. "Sergeant Major, take over". He and a somewhat shaken Flt Lt marched away and there seemed to be a very one-sided conversation taking place. We never had another station parade!

17. Hardships

Gus Thorogood

I was stationed at RAF Wyton, and it was in August 1950 when I was informed that I was being posted to RAF Heany in Southern Rhodesia. On arrival at the Preliminary Despatch Centre (PDC) at RAF Warton near Blackpool, I discovered that my fellow 51st Riggers – Geordie Haggar and Tom McHarry who had come from RAF Topcliffe – were also on the same draft for Heany. We were told that we would be sailing on the Union Castle liner, Llandovery Castle, and not a military troopship, which sounded fine to us. So in October 1950 we boarded the liner at London Docks and set sail on a 28 day sunshine cruise to Cape Town, calling in at Las Palmas, Ascension Island and St Helena en route, and arrived in Cape Town in mid-November. Conditions on board were very good, including waiter and cabin service, swimming pool and moonlight dances on the deck with the female passengers. Talk about hardships! We even took part in the 'crossing-the-line' ceremonies. As there were only 10 of us in the draft, we quite easily mingled with the passengers. On arrival in Cape Town, we had two days sight seeing before boarding a South African railway train for a 3 day and night journey up to Bulawayo. Once again, waiter service plus sleeping accommodation was provided, and the train stopped at lots of places for four hour periods. These included such places as Mafeking and Kimberley, where we met a couple of drunken diamond miners in a bar and we nearly missed the train! It was a case of panic stations to catch the train, because the next one wasn't due for another week!! On arrival at Bulawayo, we came back to earth again with a 20 mile ride in the back of a 3 tonner to RAF Heany. I suppose to contemplate a journey like that nowadays would cost thousands of pounds – and we did it for free. I ended up on the Flying Training School, which operated Tiger Moths and Harvards; Geordie went to the Maintenance Unit at Heany; and Tom went across to Kumala, which was another Maintenance Unit some distance from Heany. Every time I got in touch with him, he seemed to be always rebuilding an Anson. I must ask him one of these days if it ever got airborne.

During my tour I met up with many of the Entry who had volunteered for aircrew and did their initial training there – Pete Ashby, Don Bessant, Tony Carlyle, John Chapple, Don Ellis, Geoff Glanville, Bob Kelly, Ivor Lee, Skate Lee, Andy Magness, Kipper Morton, Vic Parker and Slim Pocock. Others – Geof Bradshaw, Johnny Jones and Roy Sherriff – did their flying training at RAF Thornhill, not so far away near Gwelo.

On completion of our tour in December 1952, the three of us returned together from Livingstone in Southern Rhodesia, this time by air in a Dan Air York that had been used to ferry coal on the Berlin Air Lift. Before we took-off, the aircraft had to have a mainwheel change and every time we landed, we had a layer of coal dust drop down on us. The clapped out aircraft became unserviceable at such places as Entebbe, Khartoum and Wadi Hulfa (now the site of the Aswan Dam), including a stop at Benghazi in order to do a harness change on the engine. We eventually arrived at RAF Lyneham in the middle of the first snowstorm of the winter. That journey took 10 days – now I suppose you could do it in 10 hours! Those were the days!!

18. Nothing to Do With Me Chief!

Ginge Mushens

Messrs Roach (Rhino) and Coleman (Derek) turned up one Sunday afternoon as I was trying to digest what was laughingly called Sunday Lunch. What you did was to lie on your extended Macdonald, (for our non ex-brat readers, please see the Glossary at the end of this story. You will need it, because this story contains a few 'strange' words!), until the gas in your stomach exited and all rumbling stopped, then it was safe to move. If one ignored this ritual, then a trip to the thunderbox could result and inspection of the deposit was necessary to allay any fears of damage.

"Well lads, what's on?" sayth I. Both proceeded to empty a sidepack and produced what can only be described fully if one was the munitions expert for the SAS! There were masses of stick cordite, detonators and various shells. Some quite large, by that I mean bigger than .5 inch, and one in particular which seemed to me to be able to sink the Hood.

"Are they live?" queried I, hoping that it was some leg pull.

"Of course they are" both stoutly affirmed, "You don't think we went to all this trouble for duds!".

All thoughts of my stomach contents vanished.

"And what are we going to do with them/it?".

I couldn't think of the correct gender.

"We are going to set them off" says Roach, with Coleman nodding in agreement.

"Where?" says I, hoping it was going to be about 6 miles away.

"Here" they chorused.

Of course anyone with half a brain would have envisaged alfresco, and me with a full brain, thought maybe if they were careful, somewhere yon side of the woods. How wrong can one get?

"Here means at the end of your bed!".

I felt myself visibly go sick. "You must be bloody mad. What happens if we get caught?" I said. Thoughts of getting killed hadn't registered yet.

"It'll be alright" said the duo, "We know what we are doing. We are trained armourers".

This really did my confidence a lot of good, as my next thought was what excuse could get me out of this and away to somewhere safer. Before I could make a move, Coleman asked me to locate and fetch the bumper weights from the other end of the barrack room. Meanwhile, they were jamming the wooden benches behind the hot water pipes at the end of the room near the window. Back to my bed space and they thought it would be a good idea if we turned my bed on its side and got behind it, with the biscuits as a cushion.

The selected shell was balanced on one weight, and the other weight was put on top of the shell as a retainer. The shell was aimed by our experts to hit the benches, thereby not causing any real damage as they proceeded to tell me. "The benches are thick pieces of wood and will absorb any shock".

Gullibility does not enter the equation! Roach and Coleman next laid a trail of cordite from the position in we were sheltering, to the percussion cap of the shell. They then rechecked the angle and elevation, and having satisfied themselves that all was in order, lit the cordite with the usual Swan Vesta. I say this in case there are any royalties pending! The cordite, I remember, burnt very fast and before I could cover my ears there was an almighty bang! I couldn't believe I was still in one piece, as the whole room was full of fumes and my ears were ringing. I checked all my vital parts, whilst the two protagonists whooped with exhilaration. I say this advisedly, as I am sure there must have been some relief on their part that we didn't end up dead. Anyway, we hurried to the far end of the room to inspect the damage and clean up before the 'Snoops' arrived, which surely they must considering the noise. One bench was split from end to end and the window didn't look too clever. There was very little damage to the wall and none to the pipes, which I thought was rather fortuitous, as I don't think we could have explained that away so easily. The bench was quickly replaced from an empty room in another barrack block, and traces of the occurrence cleaned away. By this time, the guardroom mob were buzzing around trying to locate our escapade. I'll rephrase that – to the terrible twins escapade – as I was an unwilling volunteer and was too busy thanking my lucky stars to claim involvement. The door of the room burst open and two Snoops, with vicious looks on their faces, demanded to know who was responsible for this transgression of RAF regulations. They obviously must have been new boys to think that anyone would give them the slightest hint! We said we were also puzzled at this terrible bang and wondered if it was a breech of the sound barrier, or had someone lit a firework in the woods. They must have been really green, as I could still smell cordite fumes, and the new bench was a different colour to the other one. Maybe they thought all apprentices smelt funny, as the thought of washing regularly, to most of us, was still a long way off – it being an unnecessary chore! On Monday, with the return of Chiefy Thomas, there was no escape. He knew we had been up to something, but I think he knew that if he delved too deeply he may have to initiate serious charges and his boys would end up in the Glasshouse, so a word of warning was conveyed in our direction. Needless to say, we were never considered for any promotion and we were all still A/A's at the end of our training.

GLOSSARY

A/A's	Aircraft Apprentices.
Biscuits	Three square mattresses which are put onto the Macdonald bed.
Bumper Weights	A heavy lead weight to put on the bumper which was used to polish the lino floors.
Glasshouse	Military prison.
Macdonald	A two piece metal framed bed – one piece sliding under the other.
Snoops	RAF Police.
Woods	A copse which ran along the back of the barrack blocks.

19. An Honorary Aussie

Jack Smith

As some would no doubt remember, I had some standing as a rugby union footballer at Halton and then, at St Athan, I learned the Welsh rules – "Bugger the ball, get on with the game!" By 1952, I was playing first class rugby for the Saracens and played for them up to the Saturday before I left for Australia on the following Tuesday in February 1958.

In January 1955, I was stationed at RAF Upwood as Cpl i/c Instruments on 214 Sqn (I think), when I was posted sideways to do the same job on 148 Sqn (again, I think). My counterpart took my place on 214 Sqn. Why the change? Don't ask me, Air Force bloody-mindedness I supposed at the time. However, I found out why shortly afterwards. 148 Sqn was off to RAF Tengah in Singapore with their Lincolns for a three month detachment. I was less than pleased, as I had only been married for five months. I complained of course, even officially, but to no avail. So off I went in a Hastings on a five day flight to Tengah, leaving my poor Aussie wife, who had been brought up in the Mediterranean climate of Western Australia, to freeze in the bleak Fen country with the winds straight off the North Sea. Fortunately the school in Ramsey where she was teaching was sympathetic and gave her a classroom with reasonable heating.

Two days after I arrived at Tengah, the pennies began to drop. I was ordered to report to the Station Sports Officer and who should it be but a man I knew, having played against him in London. He was my counterpart No.8 for the London Irish and an Irish International to boot.

"Hello Smithy, did you bring your boots? You're playing for Tengah tomorrow in the Singapore Cup!"

I soon found out that there had been two other aircrew ring-ins, one of whom played with me at Upwood, and both first-class club players in England! Another part of the Tengah team was supplied from the members of the No.1 Bomber Squadron, Royal Australian Air Force, normally based at Amberley in Queensland – a noted rugby state. As a rugby player with an Aussie wife, I was soon made an honorary Aussie and invited to 'events' in their quarters. Pay-nights were a riot and the two-up schools made cards in Room 16-3 at Halton look like an elderly ladies whist club! Of course, with such talent, Tengah went on to win the Cup and the Singapore Sevens, and I was lucky enough to be selected for the Combined Services Far East for a tour to Hong Kong.

Using the swimming pool at Tengah after dark was not permitted, but this never bothered the Aussies, especially on pay day. Usually nothing was said, but on one occasion the snoops (RAF Police) must have been told by an officious Orderly Officer to put a stop to it. The snoops arrived and the Aussies just grabbed their towels and ran, starkers and in bare feet. Bare feet was no big deal for them, because most Aussies wander around at home in bare feet for a good part of the year, and I even garden in bare feet in the warmer months of Western Australia. But for a poor Pom, running on gravel with no shoes on was impossible, so I hid behind a hedge and got away with it while the snoops chased the Aussies.

On the trip to Hong Kong for the rugby tour, we flew up in a De Havilland Dove and overnighted at Clarkfield, a USAF base in the Philippines. The NCO's and erks in the party were given one US dollar to spend in the PX. I think there were three Aussies from Tengah plus me, a couple of Fijians from the Fijian Regiment then stationed in Penang, one Army guy and I think a sailor. It was a warm evening and we all sat outside round a big table. Up comes a burly black gentleman in uniform with arms covered in chevrons, some pointing up, the others down – a top sergeant waiter, I ask you!

" Hi guys, what's you-all want?"
" What's you-all got?" says one of the Aussies.
" Waal, they's hamburgers 'n stuff like that".
" What about beer?"
" We got Buddweiser 'n, Coors 'n, Millers 'n…..".
" How much is a hamburger?"
" Tain cents".
" How much is a beer?"
" Tain cents, mos' everthin' is tain cents".
" We'll have one hamburger and nine cansa beer!"
" One hamburger n' nahn cansa beer! Is you-all gwine drink all that beer?
" Too bloody right mate".

I thought it was a pretty tall order, especially as the Fijians were teetotal, but, in the event, the Aussies knew what they were doing, because they had done the run before and knew that you couldn't buy a can of beer in Honkers for ten US cents. The hamburgers were enormous and the amount of beer horrifying. I think maybe we drank a couple, had one more for breakfast and got on the plane a lot heavier than when we got off!

Talking of breakfast, they were also enormous, with everything one usually gets in an English cooked breakfast, plus other stuff which I didn't recognise. I saw one US airman load his plate with what looked like thick pancakes, pile a huge heap of scrambled eggs on top, along with a couple of slices of fried ham, and then proceeded to pour maple syrup over the whole lot! Fortunately I had almost finished by then! It wasn't real maple syrup of course. I tried a teaspoonful of it and it tasted like a liquid fudgey caramel.

Afternoons at Tengah were usually free – siesta time, but one afternoon I wandered down to the Aussie lines for a spot of socialising. Walking past one of their Lincolns, I saw a very sweaty grease-stained fitter working on an engine under the shade of a canopy. Just as I arrived, an Aussie Flt Lt pilot walked up, and after acknowledging my very smart RAF style salute with a wave of the hand which might or might not have resembled a salute and a "Gooday mate", the following conversation took place:-

"How's she comin' on?"

There was a moments silence while the fitter withdrew his face from the guts of the Merlin and then said:

"Oh for crissake, 'aven't you bastards got nuthin' better to do than askin' f…..g stupid bloody questions? Can't you see I'm f…..g busy 'ere getting your f…..g kite ready for you to go f…..g swanning around droppin' bloody useless f…..g bombs on the poor buggers in the jungle!"

Oh dear, thought I, expecting any moment to hear sirens wailing with a paddy wagon arriving to take the offender away to be court-martialed.

"Orright, orright, I was only askin' " said the pilot as he wandered calmly off.

What an Air Force! Where do I sign on?

Nevertheless, despite all this excitement, I was glad to get back to Upwood (in the belly of a Lincoln!). Shortly after that, I was off to Halton, which is where we came in.

20. Two of Our Aircraft Are Missing

Roy Manington

I was stationed at RAF St Eval in Cornwall at the time when two Shackleton Mk.2's disappeared during a sortie from the Station. On 11th January 1955, two Shackleton's of 42 Squadron took off on a search and rescue exercise south of the Fastnet Rock off Southern Ireland. The exercise was to last for 15 hours. Piloting one of the aircraft, WG 531, was Flying Officer Georgie Board – a FllE of the 51st, the other by a Pilot Officer Len Wood. Some 10 hours into the flight, radio contact with both aircraft was lost, and two hours later another Shackleton in the area was diverted to carry out a search for the missing aircraft, without success. For three days, aircraft and vessels carried out a thorough search of the area, but drew a blank, and the search was finally called off. 11 years later, one of the engines of Len Wood's Shackleton was trawled up off the Southwest Irish coast. The Court of Enquiry found no evidence on which to base a reliable conclusion and apportioned no blame. It cited collision as the least improbable cause.

I was the duty NCO i/c Airborne Lifeboat loading party for that week. The lifeboat was a Mk.II, and we loaded it on a Lancaster borrowed from RAF St Mawgan to help in the search for the missing aircraft. The Mk.III lifeboat, designed for the Shackleton, never got past the trials stage, and, from all accounts, the Mk.III trials would have made a good subject for a 'Carry On' film.

The lifeboat was kept in the Safety Equipment Section on an adapted Type 'F' bomb trolley. The Lancaster had a bomb release slip, Type 'H' (?), mounted on an inverted pyramid shaped tubular rig attached to four bomb release points. A piece was cut out of each bomb door, to allow them to close over the rig with just the slip showing. The lifeboat was hoisted through the aircraft floor (No.15 position) and the centre tube of the rig. This meant that some poor sod (the smallest member of the team), had to be hoisted aboard the lifeboat to ensure that the mechanism had engaged correctly with the boat hoist point and then to disengage the hoist cable. He would then be pulled out of the lifeboat through a panel 12 by 18 inches in the side of the boat, usually a tight squeeze! The lanyards of the parachutes were attached to the aircraft before hoisting. The last thing before hoisting, and the first thing after lowering, was to disconnect the battery.

On a previous occasion, after a practice hoist, the lifeboat was being returned to the Safety Equipment Section by a 'careful' Bomb Dump tractor driver. There were rainwater puddles on the perimeter track, and outside Air Traffic Control he went through a large one. The water hit the Mercury Immersion switch, firing the three rockets (Buoyant Line Carrying). The forward facing rocket just missed the tractor driver, the port facing rocket hit the rear wall of Air Traffic (a wooden structure) and the starboard facing rocket went through the Wingco Flying's office window. Batteries never again travelled connected!

The lifeboat had never been cleared for night release, so it had to be loaded first thing in the morning, around 08.15 hrs, and lowered just before dark, which at that time of the year was around 15.30 hrs. In any case, the battery had to be changed after 12 hours. We did the loading and off-loading for the 3 days of the search for the missing Shacks, and to my knowledge we were the only team ever to put the lifeboat up with intent.

Unfortunately, nothing was ever seen or heard again of the two Shacks, and the Lindholme Gear came into use shortly after this and the Airborne Lifeboat became history.

21. Stand by Yer Boats, 'ere Comes the Air Chief Marshal

Eric Mold

When I retired from the Royal Canadian Air Force in 1974, Vera and I and our two boys had Solaris Superstar built for us at White's Shipyard on the River Hamble. She was a 43' catamaran yacht, built to Lloyd's highest specifications, with two Mercedes diesels for auxiliary power and comfortable accommodation for nine people. Our plan was to cruise around by ourselves for a while, to learn the ropes and then take charter guests.

We sailed from the Hamble at midnight (to catch the ebb tide) on 16th August 1974, bound for Gibraltar and the Mediterranean. We had no specific destination in mind, but when we eventually fetched up in Port Grimaud in the South of France, we liked the place so much that we decided to spend the winter there. Port Grimaud was the dream of Francois Spoerry. A dream that sprang from a model he had seen of a lagoon village in a museum when he was a young boy. The boy grew up and became an avid yachtsman and architect. He eventually combined his passions and made his dream come true. He built this delightful 'old' fishing village which has often been described as a 'three dimensional work of art'. Port Grimaud was said to be the second most visited tourist attraction in France, second only to the Eiffel Tower itself. A fact which turned out to be very fortuitous for us.

The winter of 1974/75 turned out to be one plagued with postal strikes. Canada Post shut down for about two months, only to be followed with a similar work stoppage by the French Post Office. In those days, the only economical way to conduct international money transfers was by postal transactions. The result was that we were unable get our pension through. In spite of the incredible generosity of the locals, we were desperate for cash.

Then suddenly our luck changed. I was standing on the dock one day when someone said, "I know you! I know you! I'm Munier, remember, Munier?". The little Frenchmen with a smiling face and pointed goatee rushed up to me. He can't mean me, I don't know anyone around here, leave alone any Munier I thought...it went right over my head. "I'm Munier" he persisted. "I do caricatures. I did you and your wife....in Germany....remember?" We certainly had had our caricatures done while we were stationed in Germany. I was beginning to remember, the name Munier was starting to ring a bell in my brain. He could see I was still mystified, so he started to explain. Munier made a living doing caricatures. He did the rounds of the NATO Officers Messes. Sitting in the bar, he would sketch everyone that came and went. If you liked yours, you could buy it for a few dollars. Several years before he must have been at the RCAF Base at Zweibrucken and had 'done' Vera and me. The happy little guy with the goatee said, "I never forget a face, it's my job".

When not up in Germany working in Officer's Messes, Munier said that he and his wife and their many young children, took a cottage on the French Riviera. He would pay a small commission to be allowed to sit in the bar of the more swanky hotels and do caricatures of the guests. "How interesting, and what a pleasant way to make a living" I said. "How nice to be just cruising around in such a lovely boat" he replied. It did not take us long to explain that we were not just cruising around. This was a venture that we hoped would pay off. We hoped to get paying guests to charter our boat, we explained. "Ah!" Munier exclaimed, "I might be able to help you". He went on to explain that Philip, the head barman at the Hotel La Pinede, where he was currently sketching, was often looking for someone with a nice boat. Many hotel guests asked if he knew of anyone who could take them out for the day. After our encounter with Munier we never looked back.

One evening, about a week later, there was a 'tap tap tap' on the side of the boat. I looked out of the window and saw two very shiny black shoes, topped off with the bottoms of a pair of immaculately pressed pin striped trousers, which disappeared into the bottom of a khaki trench coat. I went outside to see who the visitor was. He introduced himself as Philip, the barman at La Pinede. I welcomed him aboard. He said that Monsieur Munier had told him that we had a nice boat and wanted to take people for trips. He wished to look at the boat and see if we could work something out. He said he often had customers who were looking for a day's outing on a boat. We settled on a deal which worked out at $30 per person, of which we would give him $6 for each client he sent us. We would not take more than eight people at a time because we wanted to maintain an exclusive standard.

Our daily routine went something like this:-

Each evening we'd call Philip and find out how many passengers there would be for the following day. Early next morning, Amery would hose off the boat and chamois her down. I would go to the winery, on one of the bikes, where they would fill my 5 litre bottles with vin rosé. Later we would put the wine into a large, German, 'wine spender', which we set up on deck to provide our guests with chilled wine throughout the day. Vera went to the market to buy fresh bread, pastries, cheeses, patés, fruit and flowers, etc, with which she made a delicious and attractive buffet on the saloon table. By 09.00 hrs we would be on our way, out of the harbour, heading for the jetty at La Pinede.

It was a nice 2-hour cruise to Tahiti Plage, where we anchored for lunch. Our guests would swim and water ski. Sometimes the more adventurous would go ashore to view the sights, which at Tahiti Plage, were something to be seen. At the Northern end of the beach, it was just topless girls, which are quite commonplace in the South of France. As you wandered further along it became nude girls, further still it was nude girls and guys, further still....nude guys and guys....quite a revelation to most.

Our guests would either swim back to the boat or else they would signal from the shore and we would pick them up with the dinghy. When they stepped aboard, Vera's delicious buffet would be awaiting them. After lunch and a glass of wine, it was invariably a siesta in the sun for an hour. This gave us a chance to tidy the boat and do the dishes. Then we would sail back. If the sailing had been fast and we got back early, we would throw in an extra little cruise around St. Tropez harbour. The first time we threw in this 'extra', we almost got into trouble with the gendarmes. Two policemen were standing on the quay shouting "Madam...s'il vous plait....Madam....s'il vous plait". I wondered what they were shouting about until I realized that the female members of my ship's company were still 'topless' and here we were, coming into harbour. A quick 'cover up' satisfied the police.

One evening, after a long day charter, we tied up our boat, outside the 'Capitainerie' at Port Grimaud. I guess we were either too tired or too lazy to go in to the inner harbour to our regular berth. Early next morning I was on deck, chamoising off the dew that had formed overnight, when I noticed a rather distinguished looking gentleman watching me. He seemed very interested in *Superstar*. "Good morning" I said. "Good morning" he replied in perfect English. Thus our conversation began. We had been chatting about the boat for a few minutes when I smelled the aroma of coffee brewing below. I asked my new friend if he'd care to come aboard and have a coffee and a look at the inside. An invitation he readily accepted. After he'd looked around, we sat on deck talking and drinking our coffee. During the conversation, something about me having been in the RAF came out. It frequently did, for it was something I am very proud of. As our guest was leaving, he asked Vera and I if we would care to join him and his wife that evening for a drink. An invitation we were pleased to accept. "Fine" he said, "Our boat is called *Astra*. She's tied up in the visitor's berth in the Place d'Eglise. See you at about six?" he said as he stepped ashore.

That evening, prompt at 18.00 hrs, we presented ourselves at the gangplank of *Astra*, a beautiful Scottish built trawler yacht about 65 ft long. We were welcomed aboard into an elegant saloon, where we were offered cocktails and hors d'oeuvres by our charming host and his gracious wife. We had a very pleasant couple of hours with them. In situations like this, in fact in most situations, I talk too much. It is a weakness I know, but I lack the patience to listen. Vera is always telling me about it. So after telling our hosts just about all there was to know about us, I forced myself to ask, "What was your line of business?" – and I was determined to hold my tongue and listen while our host and hostess had their say.

I shall never forget our host's opening remarks. "I was in the RAF, too" he said, "You may have heard of me, John Grandy. I was Marshal of the Royal Air Force. Now I'm the Governor of Gibraltar" he continued. They just don't come any higher than Marshal! I was awe-struck to say the least. Sir John and Lady Grandy, whom I had heard of but never previously met, were kind and gracious hosts. As we stepped ashore they made us promise that we would 'drop in' and see them at The Convent, as the Governor's official residence was called, when next we passed through Gibraltar.

22. A Memory of the 51ST, by an Outsider

Air Chief Marshal Sir Michael Armitage KCB CBE (56th Entry)

As a member of the Junior Entry in 'C' Squadron of No.1 Wing at the time when the 51st formed the Senior Entry, I have many recollections of the characters who inhabited Blocks 15 and 16 in 1947 and 1948. Not all memories of those days could be published without a certain amount of embarrassment to the principals, but one printable event does stick in my mind. In what must have been early 1948, I was a newly qualified trumpeter in No.1 Wing Drums, a splendid band and one that had attracted all sorts of skates into its ranks, including this one. Two of the other and very senior reprobates in the Drums were Ted Willis (side drum) and Eric Mold (trumpet). Members of the 51st will recall Eric Mold's habit, when Duty Trumpeter, of sounding his own version at 'Lights Out' of various melodies, notably, I seem to remember, 'Cheery-Berry-Bim'.

This rendition was always received with acclamation by audiences leaning out of the barrack block windows, and once I was reasonably proficient with the trumpet, I resolved to emulate Eric's performance. So one evening at 22.30 hrs, as Duty Trumpeter, I sounded several gash tunes after the routine 'Lights Out', including a rather weak attempt at Eric's 'Cheery-Berry-Bim'.

This turned out to be a mistake. The next evening I was summoned by Ted and Eric to their eyrie in the far reaches of Block 16, as a result of which I was obliged to deliver each of them a non-standard cup of tea at 06.30 hrs every morning for a week. This humiliation involved not only a very early rise, but also impressing on the reluctant cook the urgent necessity of the task, then actually making the tea – with plentiful sugar and condensed milk – and delivering it piping hot to the authors of the routine. It was a real pain in the elbow!

In later years, as OC 17 Squadron at RAF Wildenwrath and then later again as Station Commander at RAF Luqa, I always made a habit of scanning the lists of new arrivals on the Unit so as to identify old acquaintances. It would be satisfying to be able to claim that these two characters eventually turned up under my summary jurisdiction to receive their own humiliation, but it was not to be. Ted is sadly no longer with us, and I can no longer pull rank on Eric Mold; but when I next bump into him it will certainly cost him a couple of pints.

23.   Conversion – Piston to Jet

Dave Williams

The following tale might not be terribly exciting, but perhaps of interest to some. It concerns the early days of transition from piston to jet. Or rather, *my* transition from piston to jet.

Those of us of the 51st Entry, who, for whatever reason decided to fly for a living, did so at one of the most fascinating and rewarding junctures in the history of aviation. In my case, from Mosquito to Vampire. Test pilots and others have always been required to read Pilots Notes, then 'get in and fly it'. But perhaps the first jet flight was a little different? Perhaps? Definitely so for your ordinary run of the mill flyer such as me.

My first solo happened at Cardiff Flying Club on July 15th 1949, while stationed at RAF St. Athan, aka 'Stalag Luft 32'. Whilst there, weather permitting, I would spend most Saturdays at Cardiff Flying Club flying Tiger Moths, as did a 51st Halton guy at the same time, but I simply can't remember his name. Perhaps we shall meet-up some time? Who knows? (Since we published this story, 643 Andy Andrews got in touch with us. It was he who started his flying career with Dave and they have been re-acquainted with each other.) The aviating was £3 2s an hour (£3.10 in 'new money'), not greatly removed from our fortnightly wage packet, which was 4/6p a day if I remember correctly (about 22p).

On leaving St Athan, I was posted to the CFS (Central Flying School) at RAF Little Rissington to practise my trade of Air Radio Fitter. Little Rissington is only a few miles down the road from where I am typing this, and where, in the village church, my No.2 daughter would be married 30-odd years later. At the end of 1949, I was posted to an ATU

(Aircrew Transit Unit) at RAF Driffield. and, 3 days later, with everything catalogued and sorted, it was south to No.1 ITS (Initial Training School) at RAF Wittering, where we expected to stay for the Course duration of 5 months. Here it was all 'book larnin' as I recall, except for Morse Code (8 wpm) and marching to schools wearing flying helmets with oxygen masks fully buttoned-up. This was to get us used to wearing them I suppose. Our expectation of 5 settled months did not come to pass, as the Air Ministry, for their own good reasons I suppose, decided that No.1 ITS should relocate to RAF Jurby on the Isle of Man. To achieve the move, everyone was involved in loading everything onto a long line of lorries, and that took a few days to accomplish. Then off to Jurby, where we were fortunate to be for one of the annual TT Races which 'they' were good enough to let us loose to attend. I soon met a young lady, Joan, who lived with her parents in one of the Island's lighthouses and had a 350cc Triumph on which she used to whiz us to and from various parts of the Island – me on the pillion of course.

July 17th 1950 saw my first flight with the RAF as a Cadet Pilot. This was at No.3 FTS (Flying Training School) at RAF Feltwell, in Norfolk, (now a 9-hole golf course I am told), and the plane was the Percival Prentice, a most odd and useless machine which didn't last very long as the RAF's primary trainer. On January 22nd 1951, I had my first flight in the ubiquitous and much-loved Harvard, and on June 15th that year came my FHT (Final Handling Test) under the eagle eye of Sdn Ldr Trent VC, a truly professional and charming man. I felt singularly honoured to be tested by him and to have him congratulate me on a 'very good performance'. Too bad they didn't have pocket voice recorders in those days! A spot of leave before reporting to RAF Swinderby, which was No.204 AFS (Advanced Flying School), to get to grips with the redoubtable Mosquito. I was the only member of 48 Course to actually *want* to be on night fighters (NF). Finding aircrew for that assignment was normally a job for today's equivalent of a 'Press Gang'! I loved the idea of being a loner and was not madly enthusiastic about formation flying and horsing around the sky at 35,000 ft. Had I been so, it would have meant being posted to a jet AFS on Meteors or Vampires, and I was desperate to get one or two 'Merlins' in my hands. Also, I was a bit of an ace at instrument flying and loved it, another incentive to opt for NF. What a remarkable machine, the Mosquito. There were more than 40 different Marks of the aircraft, ranging from the trainer version, the Mk.3, to the late Mk.30's. They were the early Multi-role Combat Aircraft, flying in an astonishingly wide range of roles. I was trained on the Mk's 3, 6 and 36, trainer, fighter bomber and night fighter respectively, and the Mk.36 was the interceptor radar-equipped version (AI).

What all the Marks had in common – as well as the well known fact of their wooden construction – was the Rolls Royce Merlin engines which, oddly and occasionally embarrassingly, drove enormous propellers in a clockwise direction as seen from the cockpit. Both of them! There was doubtless a good engineering reason for this, but whatever that was, it proved to be occasionally tragic, often frightening, and, to those on the ground, occasionally amusing! The average power output of the Merlins was about 1650 HP and some awesome more when the superchargers kicked in, all that being delivered to those whacking great props. After 60 or so flying hours on the Mk.3 and Mk.6, came the final training posting to No. 228 OCU (Operational Conversion Unit) at RAF Leeming, where, on the night fighter version of the Mosquito, the Mk.36, we learned to use the plane with its AI radar as the offensive weapon it was. At some time during the Course, a Sdn Ldr Boyle arrived in the smartest, most highly-polished aircraft I had ever seen. All of it was pristine and seductively attractive and I fell for it absolutely 100%. It was a Vampire Mk.10, the two-seat night fighter, and, as Boyle was recruiting for his re-forming Squadron, No.151 at RAF Leuchars, I had no hesitation in 'signing up'. I should have been joining a Javelin Squadron of course. Books have been written about the unconscionable delay of that plane (7 years), not all without rancour or worse. The Air Ministry, seeking a stopgap, ordered the transformation of single-seat Meteors and Vampires into the Mk.11 and Mk.10 respectively, endowing both with rather bulbous noses and lowered performance.

Just before leaving Leeming for Leuchars, I was called to the RAF hospital at Nocton Hall for some long-delayed minor surgery. Just before discharge, a signal arrived at the hospital ordering me to RAF Chivenor for 'Conversion to the Vampire'. My arrival there at No.229 OCU, a Vampire Mk.5 (single seat) Ground Attack Unit, did not augur well for the immediate future. The OCU Commanding Officer was not pleased with me. Not pleased at all, and delivered himself of such an angry torrent of words that I almost went AWOL. His job, he yelled at me, was to run a Ground Attack OCU and not to convert odds and sods, such as me, to anything! I recoiled from this onslaught and only slowly recovered. He regarded me, apparently, as the personification of the nitwit at the Air Ministry who had brought about this admittedly odd situation which had no precursor in his experience, and he made *me* suffer for it. He kept me waiting for 2 weeks for a Vampire to become available, during which time I had all but worn-out a borrowed set of Pilots Notes. In those days of course, there was no two-seat trainer version. Had there been, the twitch factor might have been much reduced !

A Sgt Pilot Instructor assigned to me was most anxious to impress on me, to burn into my mind, that on fully opening the throttle for take-off, the evident lack of 'push' would disappear and that all would eventually 'come good'. The little plane *would* get airborne he assured me. He had many Spitfire hours and was used to the Merlin-driven prop grabbing great parcels of air in immediate response to the throttle opening, and knew that I, used to *two* Merlins, might well find the slow reaction rather off-putting. Apparently, it was not unknown for some pilots with my lack of experience to assume an engine problem and abandon take-off with occasionally depressing consequences. To my eye, the Mk.5 Vampire looked ridiculously tiny with the cockpit floor so near to the ground that I felt I might be expected to pedal! The Mosquito was more than twice its physical size, and, being a 'tail dragger', the Mossie cockpit was 'way up there' in comparison.

Came the day! Harry, my mentor, encouraged me into the cockpit which, when I was connected to oxygen, seat and radio, felt so claustrophobic that I all but went AWOL again. But Sgt Harry (who always called me 'Son'), clucked over me encouragingly, and, for the thousandth time, went over 'everything'. 'Everything'? There was nothing to do! The pre take-off checks in the Mosquito were remembered with the letters 'TTMPFFGGIHL'. The Vampire equivalent seemed to be 'Burning? Turning? Brakes off? Then go!' The engine starting procedure seemed ridiculous. I can't recall too much of the actual gadgetry, but I think it was a matter of pushing a lever and pressing a button! With a hearty "Off you go then lad" and a slap on my helmet, Harry left me. "So here it is then," I thought, "The big day". The engine-start routine worked and I could not only see the RPM indicator building up, but could hear the engine-whine going up the sound scale. Everything settled down as advertised and I released the brakes. Nothing happened. I opened the throttle a little and she began to move forward, again as advertised. Brakes 'ON' and she stopped. So *they* worked anyway! And so, with no excuse for any further delay, I called for and received permission to taxi to the run-up area alongside the duty runway. During my cautious journey, I began to feel a little less apprehensive. The pre take-off checks done, I got the OK to enter the active runway, followed by the OK for take-off. Lined up, I tentatively advanced the throttle and released the brakes. Nothing happened. Dropping the tentative bit, I opened the throttle fully and the mini-plane started to move – slowly. Eventually it got into its stride and gained speed, and I realised that I was beginning to be a little apprehensive about getting off the ground before running out of concrete. I recalled Harry's reassurances and eventually eased the stick back and we were off the ground. My first jet flight! Once airborne, I think my heart rate decreased to near normal from anything *but* normal, and I was soon discovering how the little beast behaved. If this account were part of a Hollywood film script, I would here relate how I looped and rolled the tiny jet, and chased my shadow through the fluffy white cumulus valleys. But it's not, and I did as I had been briefed by Harry to do, which was "An area recce, followed by a barrel roll (one) and return to Chivenor to do two overshoots and a landing stop". The approaches and overshoots were routine, all things behaving as they should, but the final approach to land was different. I got things right for finals – three green lights (indicating that the undercarriage was locked down), full flap and correct speeds.....and held off about 5 ft too high! No slight bump as I touched the runway I noted, and immediately assumed that I had forgotten something, and, keeping my eyes on the runway, went to slam the throttle open to go round again – at which moment the jet's main wheels gently touched the concrete and we were down. I had forgotten Harry's words, so oft repeated...... "When your ass is about to drag, you're there". I had four more trips over the following 2 days, by which time I was hamming it up 'a la Hollywood' and had learned to delight in the little Vampire.

Much later, whilst at RAF Leconfield on an aerial gunnery instructor's course of 3 months duration, the Flight Commander of a Spitfire outfit there readily agreed that I could borrow one of his aircraft for an hour. He was happy to allow this, as I had quite a few hours on the 'Bull-nosed Mosquito' as he put it (he was a Czech). This meant that I was used to coping with the 'can't see ahead' problem which was the main worry for a pure jet man. Well briefed by Jan and the F.700 seen to, we had strolled out to a Spit parked just near the hangar doors and I was listening carefully to Jan as he went over the cockpit procedures for the nth time and issued a few caveats. He helped with the straps and was saying something like "Enjoy your trip", when a car horn sounded and the Wg Co Flying drew up near the Spit and asked Jan what was happening? Jan told him and to my astonishment – and to Jan's – he just said..... "I don't think so Jan". No explanation, nothing, and that was the end of that. I almost wept and had never felt such an emotional blow in my life. I had always dreamed of flying a Spit and to get *so* close to doing so. A sad day for me indeed. Those in the know reported that the Vampire and the Spitfire were very similar to fly. The slightest movement of the stick and the Vamp responded instantly as did the Spit. Aerobatics in the Vamp were a joy to perform, and yes, I *did* fly down the cumulus valleys and yelled with delight as I did so. I went on to fly the Vampire NF.10 for about 600 hrs, then on to the Meteor NF.11 for about 1,000 hrs. And *they* paid *me*!

24. Food, Glorious Food

Fred Hoskins

On the way to the 1999 Cranwell reunion, I was leafing through some old copies of the Cranwell Magazine owned by a fellow traveller on Tom Olliver's bus, and I believe it must have been in one of these that I saw the following tale. I do not know what the copyright position may be, but I offer the author my apologies, particularly as I am writing from memory.

One evening the teller of the tale was working in the cookhouse (presumably on jankers), when the cooks were preparing breakfast for the following morning. Suddenly, one of the cooks rushed over to a steaming vat of porridge, leaned over and began fishing around with his ladle. After a few seconds he straightened up and was seen to have a cat on the ladle, covered in porridge. Expertly flicking the cat off the ladle and towards the open door, the cook muttered "Stupid cat! It did exactly the same thing last night!"

This brought back recollections of other memorable cookhouse incidents, but I will leave it to others to tell us about those at Cranwell, if they will, and I will merely relate a few moments I recall from days in Borneo during the Indonesian Confrontation in the late 1960's. Our Whirlwind helicopters of 103 Sqn, were based at Kuching to support Army operations in the First Division of the State of Sarawak. Having received tasking orders by signal during the previous evening, we would usually set out from Kuching at about 07.30 or 08.00 hrs and might be away until 16.00 or 17.00 hrs, or even later. During that time we would have been flying between Army locations and various landing sites, moving men and supplies, doing what had to be done and refuelling from drums of avtur stored around the place. Often it was simply not possible to calculate how long crews might be away from base. Strangely, we never took any food with us. I cannot remember any official reason for this and no doubt rations would have been available if we had asked. However, I think we simply became accustomed to being looked after by the Army.

Almost everywhere we landed, the soldiers would offer us at least a drink of the lemonade made up from crystals and usually termed 'jungle juice'. I was told that early on, before they had got used to the novelty of RAF helicopters, the Gurkhas used to offer mugs of rum, but jungle juice or tea were the usual refreshments. I remember one occasion when, working all day with the Durham Light Infantry, we shut down for a break after a few hours and the RSM, a very large man, approached and asked quietly and civilly if we would like something. When we indicated our grateful acceptance, he turned slightly away from us and in a real parade ground voice, roared "Private Gallon! Double away and fetch the gentlemen a drink!". No doubt it was the name of the soldier, which has made this stick in my mind, because a rather small soldier appeared within a few seconds, running, and carrying a large cookhouse dixie which must have held, literally, several gallons of jungle juice.

At a battalion headquarters in the little town of Bau, there was a permanent staff of locally employed labourers who virtually ran the landing site. The senior one had been given an RAF beret and was always known as 'Number One at Bau'. Not only could he be relied on for tea, coffee or jungle juice, but he supplied us with 'egg banjos'. I have never been able to establish the connection with banjos for these popular food items, which were merely two slices of bread with a fried egg in between. Number One would hand them up to the pilot while the rotors were turning if there was no time to stop. Payment was never required and I assume that Number One had a good contact in the Army cookhouse. Egg banjos were also the stock in trade of the Pakistani vendors, always known as 'Pop', who had permission to set up mini-canteens on the airfield and elsewhere. Coffee and tea from Pop always came very sweet and milky in pint glass mugs. Obviously, Pop's goods had to be paid for.

Landing and closing down at a Gurkha location at the right time could mean a good chance of a curry, and so perhaps it is really not surprising that we did not ask for RAF flying rations. However, this ploy misfired on one occasion. After a long and busy morning, I landed, well into the afternoon, at Padawan, which was home to a Company of Gurkhas with whom we were on particularly good terms. We were ravenous and looked forward to a good plateful of Gurkha bhat; at the very least some rice and dhal, we thought. Unfortunately, the Gurkhas were all out on patrol, but Padawan was also home to a detachment of Royal Artillery with two 105 mm howitzers. So I approached the young 2nd Lieutenant in charge of the gunners and asked if he could offer any refreshment. He pointed out that it was mid-afternoon and his men had eaten more than 2 hours ago, but he promised to see what he could do. There were four of us, from two Whirlwinds, and we followed him through the sandbags into the gun position and seated ourselves around one of his guns. The gunners cookhouse was also within the same sandbagged bunker, and as we sat and chatted to this very pleasant young subaltern, we could hear some clattering and banging going on. We waited, but no appetising smells accompanied the clattering and banging, only some muttering and grumbling from the cook, whose afternoon we had presumably ruined. At length, out came the cook, a surly sort of individual, who produced two tin plates, one piled high with thick doorsteps of bread and jam, and the other piled with slices of luncheon meat. Disguising our disappointment, not to mention our distaste, and hunger getting the better of us, we tucked into this watched by the young officer. After a while he could contain himself no longer and said "Heavens! That looks so good it makes me feel hungry. I think I'll have some myself!".

One kitchen supplied all the Messes at Kuching. The food was not greatly appreciated and many of us went into town virtually every evening to eat in the open market. The food was cheap and delicious, but sometimes had unwanted effects on the system. One morning, when flying, I was subject to an urge which would not be denied, so, landing at an Army base at Tepoi, I closed down and jumped out. Tepoi and Padawan were only a few miles apart, and both were about a mile from the border with Indonesia. On making my requirements clear, I was shepherded through the barbed wire into the Army fort, which was built around the summit of a small hill, and shown the way to the top where the Company Commander had his quarters. Clearly, the Gurkhas decided that I should have the facilities provided for the sahibs, whereas in my state anywhere reasonably private would have been adequate. I ran up what seemed a very long path with steps made of ammo boxes and sand bags. At the top of the hill I was ushered to what, in the 18th century, was termed the 'seat of ease' (and a better euphemism could surely not be found!). It was amazing! Directly beneath the seat was a shaft lined with empty fuel drums with the tops and bottoms cut out, and falling to a pit about 40 ft below. The 'convenience' was spacious and situated to the side of, and just below, the summit of the hill. It was not brick-built, but constructed of sandbags and corrugated iron, with what I can only describe as a huge unglazed picture window. The view from the 'seat of ease' was to the West, where range after range of the mountains of Indonesia receded to the horizon, the colours changing from shades of green to shades of blue, gradually getting paler and greyer with the distance. It was all so tranquil and beautiful that it was hard to realise that men were ranging those hills intent on war. I believe it must have been one of the most magnificent views possible from such a facility and the experience was almost worth the pain! The things one remembers!

25. Whoops!

Eric Mold

I shall never forget the Sunday morning church parade at Halton when I put a half crown into the collection plate by mistake. Most Sundays after church parade, I used to nip off home for the day – my Dad lived in London. It just cost 2/6 for the train ticket from Wendover to Kilburn Street Station. I got off there to avoid any possible encounter with the Snoops that hung around the station at Baker Street. From Kilburn, I took a number 36 bus to my Dad's home. After a nice Sunday lunch and possibly an afternoon matinee, my father would drive me back to Camp, dropping me off behind No.1 Wing HQ, just in time for 'by your beds'. Well, this particular Sunday, I was singing away boisterously, thinking about the roast beef and treacle pudding yet to come, when the collection plate came my way. I thrust my hand into my pocket to get the two pennies I had earmarked for the collection. As I let the coins drop into the plate, I noticed that one of them was silver in colour!! I quickly thrust my hand into my pocket again and felt the smooth edge of the only other coin I had ... it was a penny ('one dee' to you ex-brats). Well, that was it. I had blown my day at home for this weekend. No Sunday roast, followed by an afternoon at the flicks, and no cake to put in my kit box for next week. As the service wore on, I got to thinking that maybe the padre would understand my plight and take pity on me? So as soon as we were 'fell out', I rushed back to the chapel and caught the padre just as he was locking up. He listened patiently as I explained my problem and how much the half crown (a substantial sum in those days!) meant to me. Finally he poured the contents of the little money bag, which held the collection, onto the table. There amid the pile of pennies, half pennies and a couple of tanners, was my big half crown. I was allowed to change it for the penny I had in my pocket. "Hi Dad, I'm home!"

26. We WAAFs Were Not All Angels

Lee Downton

I regret to say it, but one of my prime memories of my time at RAF St Athan in 1948/49 was being on jankers, mostly for missing curfew, which was at 11pm for the Waaf's. But it was worth it. St Athan was where I first met up with the 51st lads and I have vivid memories of tearing around the country lanes on the back of Stan Downton's (my husband-to-be) motorbike, along with Beaky Leach and his pillion rider. Not having previously been a motorcycle enthusiast, I was not aware of the consequences; I remember that the first long ride we took was to Weston-Super-Mare and we stopped at a restaurant for refreshments, had our nibbles, and it was not until I retired to the washroom that I discovered that my face was pitted with dead flies. Disgusting – and the three guys never said a word! On future trips, the ladies room was my first stop!

I also remember trips to the local village, Llantwit Major, for visits to the pubs of course, and also to the one restaurant which we always visited on payday. It was on the right as one entered the village. And of course the cinema. I wonder how many of the 51st will remember that was where we first saw Jane Russell in 'The Outlaw'? The walk back to camp could be quite hilarious. I remember Stan pulling me down off the memorial when he caught me trying to turn the 'stone' pages! Another memory was Fred Saunders climbing over a hedge into a field and riding some farmer's cart horse! It was OK for the blokes, they just had to turn in. No jankers for them!

It really was a good thing that 'poverty was no disgrace', as pay was poor. Waaf's only got 10 to 15 shillings a week, and after buying one's essentials i.e. make-up and soap, there was nothing much left for the NAAFI, so we always had huge mugs to take to the NAAFI so that the penny cuppa's could be shared – and do you remember how sweet that tea was?

I worked in the Signals Headquarters and often did 'late' and 'night' shifts. After coming off shift, we would walk to cookhouse, and on the 'late' shift we would be treated to ham and egg's. "Quite yummy", so there was an advantage of working odd hours. Then to me the highlight was walking from the cookhouse back to the Waaf billet, usually cutting across the parade square. It seemed that every billet was listening to the music played on the Camp radio, mostly requests and Camp favourites. Guys, do you remember how frequently you heard Vaughan Monroe singing "Ghost Riders in the Sky"? It was quite an experience to stand by the flagpole and hear the music echo around the Camp. Sometimes if there were a group of us Waaf's returning to the billet, we would have a little parade of our own to whatever music was being played, and I am sure that whoever appeared on the parade ground first on the following morning would wonder where the egg and bacon sandwiches, which they saw on the ground, came from. Well, they dropped out of our battle dress tops! We were taking them back to billet for the other gals to have a nosh. Nothing was ever said about it, so maybe the night creatures stuffed their tummies.

Now, I do have one naughty memory, and can still blush when writing about it. One of our adventures kept us out late, and it would mean getting into trouble if we were caught, and I had just come off jankers and couldn't afford another session. Along with another Waaf, Cynthia Comben, we decided on a scheme. It would have been perfect had it worked! As many of you may remember, the ground floor windows of the barrack blocks were mighty tall and high off the ground and difficult to scale. However, we knew (at least we thought we knew!) that the Corporal who had the back room behind the stairwell always went home at weekends and she left her window open at the top by about 6 to 8 inches. Well Cynthia happens to be over 6 ft and I a full 5 ft 2½ inches. We went for Plan 'A'. Cynthia would hoist me up and I would pull down the window, climb in and lower the window so that Cynthia could haul herself in. Also we were busy watching for and expecting the duty guard to turn the corner of the Block. So all in haste and dead silence, Cynthia gave me a push up and she was whispering as loud as she dare "Hurry up, I think the guard is coming". I was too petrified to make any comment. You see, I had trouble with getting my leg over the top of the window. Those windows were quite deep and I was feeling with my foot for the window ledge or the bed below. Suddenly a hand grabbed my ankle, and what was my reaction – being a female I wet my pants! Believe me, there is nothing more painful than wet, course, flannel, battle dress pants and a very aggravated Cpl to cope with. I forget how many days jankers I got for that, and how Cynthia got away with it. But why not, she didn't do the dirty deed. That was one of my not so happy memories of St Athan.

But life went on, and the 51st moved on with it. As I had decided to wait around for Stan, I decided to leave the Waaf and move to London and work at the American Embassy, which was a smart move. But I have to admit, I missed the Waaf and the comradeship quite a bit. But because Stan stayed in the RAF and was posted to RAF West Raynham in Norfolk, for a while I was able to enjoy life on Camp living in married quarters. When Stan left the RAF, we went on our adventuresome trots living in various parts of Canada and the USA, and finally settled down in Oceanside, California, but we are now pleased with our contact via 51st Entry newsletters and the reunions. It will be their Diamond Anniversary of joining up this year and I hope to get to one of the two reunions which they have planned for the year, and I know that Stan will be over for the HAAA golf meeting in June.

So tally ho you bods, here is one airwoman that has not forgotten, and fond memories to one and all.

27. Flying Training – Rhodesia Style

Geof Bradshaw

In September 1952, along with my fellow u/t pilots, I stepped down from a Central African Airways Viking onto the tarmac at RAF Thornhill, near Gwelo, in the middle of Southern Rhodesia.

Fresh from ITS (Initial Training School to you non-aircrew wallahs!), we were unconcerned when a Regiment Sgt formed us up in threes and marched us away. We had no illusions about our brand new Acting Pilot Officer status! Fifty yards ahead, a Regiment Officer appeared and shouted, "Double those men, Sergeant" and when we came to a halt, we asked him why we were late! Well, what would you expect from a rockape? So, while we waited for our baggage to be off-loaded, we were put through 15 minutes drill!

The customs check was a bit fierce, they even found a sheath knife strapped to one fellow's leg. *A sheath knife...on his leg?* Oh well, I suppose this *was* Africa! Most of us were retreads, so the FFI which followed (Free From Infection if you have forgotten that one!) didn't bother us and our Flight Commander seemed a reasonable chap when he welcomed us, but we began to wonder just what sort of place we'd come to after the Padre gave his little talk. Sanctimonious and self righteous were two of the kinder terms which sprang to mind, and his exhortations to go and see him if we had any problems fell on deaf ears, at least as far as I was concerned. It was all a bit hectic and by the time we'd been allocated rooms in the hutted Mess, paired off on an alphabetical basis, there was little time left for lunch if we were going to make our appointment with the CFI (Chief Flying Instructor) in the anteroom at 14.00 hrs. There was talk of voluntary suspensions.

After a quick bowl of indifferent soup served by a couple of surly waiters, we rushed into the anteroom to be met by a bunch of cheerful chaps who ignored our babblings about the CFI and thrust drinks into our hands. It took a few moments for the penny to drop, and we realised that every one of our tormentors from the morning had been a member of the senior course in borrowed uniform, even down to the waiters. And, indoctrinated by ITS, not one of us had suspected a thing. A cheerful afternoon went by including a display by one of our number up on the bar of the DA (dead *rs*) painted on his backside with gentian violet ("Bit of sweat rash there old chap"). After that welcome, the next 9 months could only be a breeze, couldn't they? Incidentally, 3 years later I did the Pilot Attack Instructor course with the "Padre".

Rhodesia was (is) a beautiful country and Thornhill a very pleasant Station. The weather factor was excellent and since we worked tropical hours there was always the afternoon in which to make up time if we fell behind schedule. This happened now and again, sometimes due to the gutie (spelling?), when a low cloud which could appear very suddenly, or occasionally when we found ourselves walking to work ankle deep in running water. The instructors were a friendly approachable lot and on 16th September Lou Cody (Sir, as I called him) led me up to a Chipmunk.

I was slow to go solo, couldn't get the landing attitude right, and one Friday I got the impression that Sir was reluctantly considering me as a chop candidate. During a long session of Egyptian PT that weekend I gave it a lot of thought and on the Monday produced three good landings on the trot, followed by one more to prove I wasn't cheating. I remember thinking as I climbed away on my own for the first time, that what goes up must come down. I never saw Sir standing by the caravan waving frantically for me to land further away. I was never actually airsick but I became very familiar with that cold sweat as we practiced aerobatics and spinning. Sir was quite sympathetic and would open the canopy while I took off my mask for a few gulps of fresh air before the next spin. By the time of my mid-Chipmunk phase check, I could admire the scenery whichever way up it was, but it didn't matter because my examiner, the Squadron Commander, was suffering from a hangover and was quite content to go and wave to his friends from the night before.

Most people seemed to aim for South Africa for mid-course leave, but four of us decided to visit Victoria Falls. I think the train took 12 hours to Bulawayo and then it was another 18 to the Falls. We arrived at about 06.30 and enquired prices at the Victoria Falls Hotel, then the only one there and quite swep'up. Somewhat discouraged, we walked off down the road to some chalets the receptionist had suggested. Even more discouraged after looking at them, we walked back to the hotel and negotiated a price for four of us in one room. In the four or five days we spent there, we "did" the Falls pretty thoroughly. Walking round a rock at the bottom of the western end I came face to face with a crocodile. It was a good *18 inches* long, possibly even *2 ft*. Anyway it took one look, said, "**** one of Trenchard's lot" and jumped into the water and disappeared. I can only assume it had been washed over the Falls, because even a passing acquaintance with Tarzan films would indicate that the seething maelstrom it leapt into was not crocodile habitat.

Another time my friends went off ahead of me, a man has to do what he has to do, and it was a good job I had because I rounded a corner in the path to find a troop of baboons browsing across it. Check, left, right, left, forward and a strategic withdrawal was in progress. I gave them a few minutes, then cautiously investigated. They'd left so I pressed on. There was a grunt and a straggler leapt out of the grass and started after *his* mates. I caught up with *my* mates, managing to stop before passing them, and we proceeded down to the river, well below the Falls. There, on the bank, was a paw print, definitely not of the domestic pussycat variety. We didn't think it was that fresh and anyway we'd made enough noise coming down, so the others quickly stripped off and into the river. I didn't like the look of the current and eddies and let them get on with it. Besides, they hadn't seen my crocodile!

Back at Thornhill I was introduced to the Harvard. Again I had trouble with the landing attitude, but Sir, Wilky Wilkinson to his fellow instructors, got me proficient enough at tail down wheelers to risk sending me solo and the course progressed. I enjoyed flying the Harvard to the extent that a couple of years later I jumped at the chance to fly it again on low level anti terrorist recces in Malaya. But pride goeth, etc, and as I actually achieved a three point landing at Kuala Lumpur, the dreaded ground loop syndrome occurred and the aircraft swung smartly for the side of the runway. Stick hard back, full left rudder, sweat, and brake, and we were travelling down the runway again. The corporal in the back said he thought I'd decided to take a shortcut. On the subject of low flying, Rhodesia was the place to do it; there was nobody to complain. Following a railway line (perhaps I should say *the* railway line), I came across a work gang who hurled themselves off the track as I approached. Don't know why, because our minimum allowed height was 250 ft!! A bit further on I met one of my colleagues going the other way. Fortunately we were obeying the rule of putting a line feature on our left, so we passed happily and I suppose the work gang thought I was having another go at them.

The four of us bought a car, a beat up old Graham, although we didn't have a full driving licence between us. We used it to get around the area, but the bloke had seen us coming and we finally sold it at a big loss for scrap, driving it into Gwelo with no brakes at all. The town wasn't exactly Piccadilly and we managed to judge the one set of traffic lights just right. I said "we" but I have to confess that I was the steerer.

The local people were very friendly and three or four of us spent Christmas Day with the Du Toit family on their farm about 17 miles out into the bundu. The rest of the holiday seems to have been spent at the Bata (shoe company) Club in Gwelo, one of my cronies having become friendly with the manager. Many afternoons were spent at the town swimming pool, although there was one on the Station where there were also other opportunities for those with sporting tendencies. Having carefully avoided anything involving chasing a ball around since leaving Halton, I only became involved with the inter-wing shooting match and later went to Kumalo, HQ Rhodesian Air Training Group, near Bulawayo, to take part in the Inter-Station competition.

Time moved on and in May 1953, sporting my brand new brevet, sewn on by Mrs Wilkinson, I stood once more on the tarmac waiting for the Viking to take us to Livingstone, where we would join our colleagues from RAF Heany to catch the Skyways York for home. We never got to demonstrate our histrionic abilities with a new course, because the course ahead of us was not replaced owing to the imminent closure of the Group. Our next stop was an acclimatisation course at RAF Feltwell, where our reception and treatment was reminiscent of our reception at Thornhill, only it wasn't play acting. I realised how lucky I'd been to do my training in Rhodesia.

28. Trains – or You Can Only Fool Them Some Of The Time!

John McLaren

As we all were for most of our time at Halton, especially on ten bob a fortnight, funds were always low or non-existent. To supplement this and to assist in departing for weekends to the London area, the more cunning erks latched on to a scheme colloquially known as ;Fiddling the Railways'. I recall, amongst various methods, the best and most used one was carried out as follows:-

A return ticket to Amersham was purchased from Wendover. Why Amersham and not Great Missenden was used I never discovered. The Metropolitan Line, as it was in those days, went to Baker Street, but by alighting at Finchley Road, one avoided such encumbrances as ticket barriers and ticket collectors. You then proceeded through into the Underground, and, in my case, onto the Northern Line to Tooting Broadway. On arrival at the ticket barrier, the pockets were searched and "Sorry guv, I've lost my ticket", followed by proffering 2d (two dee to those who can recall our days at Halton) which always got me through OK. Whether or not the ticket collector believed we'd come from Trinity Road or not is a matter for conjecture! The return journey required a 2d ticket from Tooting Broadway to the next station, then back through the tubes and onto the Aylesbury flier to Wendover. The return ticket half was carefully 'Vee' clipped using a razor blade, all ready to be offered to the man on the gate at Wendover and then to leg it up the road to

Camp. Mind you, there were some POSB (Post Office Savings Book – a reference to those who didn't spend their money) bods who wouldn't even expend this pittance. They either left the train whilst it was still in motion and vaulted over the low fence into the allotments on the left, or alternatively, they would run back down the platform slope, risking life and limb by crossing the lines, up the embankment beside the bridge, over the wall, down the road and back to Camp. This system worked very well and to the advantage of the cash strapped apprentices for many years – until one day it all went wrong.

One dark and rainy night, we were gleefully and carefully cutting Vee's in our tickets en route to Wendover. Off the train, over the footbridge to the exit and handed our carefully doctored tickets to one of the four ticket collectors. Hang on. Four ticket collectors. Strange! Not for long. All 'Vee cut' ticket owners were steered firmly into the large Waiting Room and there sat, resplendent in his immaculate WO uniform, WO bull on the table in front of him, sat *Wog Warner*, the i/c Snoops from the Maitland Guardroom. A marked loss of humour overtook us all. "Tickets" he grated, "Wrong shaped clip". He held up a ticket with a moon shaped clip. A brat behind me blustered out that he'd lost his ticket. "Tell that to your Flight Commander" said Mr Warner. Another half a dozen dishevelled reprobates were pushed into the room by a couple of Snoops, having been 'collected' from the allotments. The Snoops had had a busy night and it didn't take long for us to admit all. Number, Rank, Name, Entry, Wing, Squadron, Room, was taken and noted. We were then allowed to leave and left to ponder, with some trepidation, our future fate. Warner's parting words were "The war is over. This type of fiddle is dead and buried".

We received scant sympathy from our Wing WO Boggy Marsh, but I suspected a touch of admiration from Chiefy Thomas. Up before the Flight Commander a few days later, 7 days were handed out (no fines in those days) and the Flight Commander's parting words were "I don't know how you thought you would ever get away with such an obvious fraud as this". Some of us hardened 'railway children' managed a quiet smile. After all, nearly 2 years of very cheap rail travel hardly amounted to 'not getting away with it', did it? Shortly after this harrowing event and along with several others, I bought a motor bike – but that's another story!

29. My 16 Years as a Navigator

Peter Blackman

No.2 Air Navigation School – RAF Thorney Island

I commenced navigator training with twelve other young lads in November 1950, flying in the slow, comfortable Anson. Initially, confidence in the air and map reading were the initial important lessons to learn. Landmarks like rivers, railway lines, towns and roads must be identified and used for homing, timing and fixing purposes. All those mystical words – 'Babs', 'Rebecca', 'Sarah' and 'Eureka', had special significance to us all on the course. After about 15 hours of familiarisation flying, we did our first 'Navex'. My first exercise took place on December 29th 1950. Base-Oxford-Okehampton-Alton-Base and lasted 2 hrs 45 mins. The trip went quite smoothly – maybe this navigation business wasn't so bad after all.

Through January and February more Navex trips, usually finishing with a 'Rebecca' homing and 'Babs' let-down onto the runway at Thorney. We learnt to use radio bearings, get position lines and acquire three position line fixes by transferring position lines along track. This is not too difficult when you can see the ground.

Night flying started in February 1951. Things got a bit more complicated then. The first item on the agenda was Met Briefing, which took place about 2 hours before take-off. Half-an-hour for briefing, then winds and temperatures were made available for flight planning. This took about an hour, as radio beacons and diversions had to be plotted on the charts, Gee chains selected and routes marked on topographical maps in case of electrical failure. Next, a short walk out to the aircraft waiting on the pans and eventually airborne. Usually a trip of 3 hours followed, and after landing a short de-briefing. Roughly, a 3 hour trip covered about 8 hours from initiation to completion. During the 6 months to May, I logged just over 100 hours and started to get the hang of the profession of navigation – or so I thought!

I commenced flying on Wellingtons on May 2nd 1951. The first twelve flights were bombing practice at Theddlethorpe and Wainfleet in The Wash. Three trainee Navs were carried on each flight. We would each find the current wind velocity, then drop eight bombs each, re-adjusting the wind as necessary. Quite enjoyable, just like playing darts!

After the pleasant interlude of target practice, it was back to the serious business of navigation. Anson flying had meant flying around the countryside for about 3 hours in a nice comfortable aircraft at 10,000 ft, without too much pressure. 'Wimpey' trips were a different proposition.

Even walking out to the aircraft was harder. We students would be loaded up with Nav bags, parachute and harness, and a bulky sextant banging against our legs. Ahead was a 5 hour trip in a draughty, smelly, rattly and sometimes very cold aircraft at 12,000 ft. The worst trips for me were the 'Astro' trips. At times we were not allowed to use radio or radar aids, but had to rely on the stars only for navigation. This entailed taking 2 minute readings on three different stars, converting them into position lines, then obtaining a 'fix' from these lines. Quite possibly a cloud would obscure the star in the middle of the sighting, so a new star would have to be found. While this was happening, the staff instructor or the pilot would be asking stupid questions like "Where are we?" or "What time do we get to the next turning point?". Astro navigation definitely was not my forte. Nevertheless I managed to complete the course and obtained my Nav's brevet in October 1951. Half the course passed out as officers and half as Sergeants. I was one of the Sergeants, mainly because I damaged a bit of property in the Officers Mess – nuff said.

One item merits a mention before I leave Thorney Island. The day before I departed, an Anson crashed just behind the Mess. Naturally we all dashed out to see this partially disintegrated aircraft on the rear lawn. Sitting dazed in the wreckage were two of the crew. Two of us dashed into the wreck and pulled them out, then I returned to my room, cleaned up and went on leave. When I returned I discovered that my fellow rescuer had been recommended for a decoration. I suppose I should have stayed for recognition as well and probably got my commission. Looking back everything turned out for the best, as I shall explain later.

After graduating as Navigators, we were posted to various Commands and I was lucky enough to get Fighter Command, so off I went to Yorkshire for a conversion course.

228 Operational Conversion Unit – RAF Leeming

Radar interception air-to-air. This was the purpose of 228 OCU – to train night-fighter crews to work in conjunction with ground stations in order to intercept and destroy enemy aircraft by day or night. The aircraft was the Brigand, which carried three trainee 'Nav-Rads' and one instructor. The equipment was AI (airborne interception) Mk.10. This comprised two scopes, one giving azimuth and range of a target, the other giving elevation (as on a clock face). The ground station would vector the hunting aircraft as near as possible, at the same time passing as much information about the target as it could regarding height, speed and heading. When the hunter acquired the target on the airborne equipment, it would take over the interception and complete the 'kill'. Sounds relatively simple, but at closing speeds of about 700 mph, evasive action by the target and some radar sets with a maximum pick-up range of less than 3 miles, it could get very 'hairy'. Of course the instructor was there to abandon the intercept if necessary. During the 3 months course, I carried out about one hundred PI's (practice interceptions).

A typical interception would go something like this:-

"*Target sighted, 45 degrees off to the right, about 6 miles range and about 3,000 ft above. We'll be turning onto his heading shortly, meanwhile go up 3,000 ft. Turn now to 095 – harder, go up another 100 ft. Almost there, level out, about one mile ahead. Hard port, (turn noticed), go down, (descent noticed). Level out now, closing fast, throttle right back, turn left, about 500 ft ahead. Twelve o'clock/15 degrees, 250 ft, hard starboard, 150 ft*". By now, to put it mildly, we were in close proximity to the target, travelling at about 400 mph. About then the pilot would transmit – "*Murder, murder, set us up for another PI please*". Then off we would go again for another nerve wracking practice. We poor trainees probably lost about five pounds in weight during each of these sessions, but it was all worthwhile as in March 1952 we got our postings to operational squadrons.

141 Night Fighter Squadron – RAF Coltishall

141 Sqn were in the process of converting from Mosquitos to Meteors, so I was detached to RAF West Raynham to fly with the Radar Interception Development Squadron (RIDS), while my pilot-to-be was converting to his new aircraft. RIDS, as the name implies, experimented with various types of radar to evaluate their worth in different aircraft. The systems were installed in a Bristol Wayfarer and tested by experienced pilots and navigators (I was just along for a little experience of course) against other aircraft. Quite interesting of course, but I was quite happy after 3 months to return to Coltishall and commence my training on the sleek Meteor. I crewed up with Flt Lt Gordon Cammell and over the next 3 months we flew Sector Recees, NFT's (night flying tests), camera sorties, and generally got familiar with the aircraft. From September to November 1952, Gordon was away on a course, so I flew with other pilots and had a short detachment to Leeming where I flew with Sqn Ldr Stewart. Quite honestly I believe that my technique needed some polishing. Apparently I finally came good and back to 141 Sqn in October. My new pilot was Flt Sgt Dick Turton and I crewed with him for the next year.

Here I must digress from military to romantic matters. It all started about June 1953. I visited the station cinema one night and saw *HER*. This gorgeous little Waaf, with the beautiful black hair and marvellous figure, ran down the right-hand aisle to join her mates. I thought to myself, what a little darling she was and why couldn't I have a girl like that. Not much chance of that happening, me being awkward with girls and not exactly Errol Flynn. Still, some lucky fellow is in for a treat – back to the film.

A few weeks later, Sgt Charlie Rees and I were sitting in the Sgts Mess on a Saturday night wondering what to do. We decided to go over to the weekly dance, drink a few sherries and leer at the Waaf's who congregated there, so off we went, ready for a bit of fun, then back to the Mess for some serious drinking and darts later on. When we arrived, who should I see but that dream-girl I saw a few weeks previously. Charlie said, "That's Blossom, one of my Waaf's. I'll introduce you". Over we went and to my surprise Blossom asked me for a dance. Me – dance? I wasn't even sure which was my left foot, let alone how to dance. She soon found out, but more in hope than expectation. I asked her to go to the cinema the next night and she accepted. From this moment I realised that Fate had not been unkind to me when I failed the pilots course, didn't get my commission and wasn't recognized for helping to save those chaps at Thorney Island. If my career had deviated at all, then I wouldn't be here now with 'Blossom'. Gladys (her real name) and I met in June, were engaged in August and married on February 13th 1954. I still cannot believe how lucky I've been to share my life with such a wonderful girl. After our first date we spent many evenings down at the Red Shield Club where we played 'Black Bitch' or darts. I'm afraid her South American temper came to the fore at times, especially when I slipped her 'The Bitch', but we usually made up afterwards. Teaching her to play darts was quite enjoyable. I'd have one arm correcting her aim, the other round her waist, merely to keep her steady of course!

During the 'Dick and Pete' partnership, we flew the normal missions and took part in many large-scale exercises. Lincolns, Shackletons and B.29's were easy meat, but the Canberra was a different story. These sleek bombers were as fast as our Meteors and interceptions had to be executed perfectly to achieve a 'kill'.

One incident rates mention here. The squadron had recently taken delivery of some new aircraft and Dick and myself took WD.740 up for an air test on July 27th 1953. We were climbing to 35,000 ft, and passing through 15,000 ft, when suddenly the hood opened!!! Dick momentarily lost control and we plummeted to about 7,000 ft before he regained full control. We were quite lucky really. If it had happened at 7,000 ft we would probably have hit the ground, and if it had occurred at 35,000 ft, loss of oxygen and pressurisation could have had dire consequences for us. When your lucks in, it's in. Luckily Dick didn't jettison the hood (hinged in the middle) as it might have decapitated me. The cause of the incident was newness and stiffness of a new hood, so we always double checked that it was shut properly after that incident.

Regarding aircraft accidents. 23 Sqn, also based at Coltishall, had three accidents leading to three pilots and two navigators being killed. Their aircraft, the Venom, had only one engine, whilst our Meteors had two, so we could lose one engine and still fly on, whereas they would be in big trouble. It is always a bad moment when your mates go, and that happened a few times during my service, sad to say.

Ground control was from RAF Neatishead, where Gladys was a radar operator. Often, at nights, when we were returning to base, we would inform them – "Escort 60 returning to base", and back would come the reply – "Goodnight Dick, goodnight Pete".

American Sabre squadrons were also based in East Anglia, so if we happened to meet up it was the perfect excuse for a 'dog-fight', instead of doing mundane practice interceptions. Sabres could out-manoeuvre us and were faster, but at least our radar was an asset, and for a few minutes we had great fun. I say great fun, but the poor Nav in the back seat would often 'black-out' through excessive g. The squadron had one Tiger Moth, which was used for communication flights and bombing Martello towers on the coast with coke bottles. Don Coleman (Flash Gordon) managed somehow to crash this aircraft, but not before I experienced the joys of an open-air cockpit. Low level flying was strictly prohibited over the airfield, so every so often a pilot would request a radio altimeter check. If this was approved, we would all go outside the crewroom, ready and waiting. A few minutes later this Meteor would fly down the runway at about 500 mph, a sight always worth seeing.

Dick was posted, and I teamed up with Fg Off Johnny Allison in September 1953, for what was to prove a long partnership. Finally in May 1954, 3 months after my marriage to the 'Argentine bombshell', my tour on 141 Sqn came to an end and Johnny and I were posted to 87 Sqn in Germany.

87 Night Fighter Squadron – RAF Wahn

At last, an overseas posting, always an added plus for those of us who wanted to see the world, and I was certainly one of those. My darling wife was initially left at Coltishall, but soon followed me out and we managed to find local accommodation until we were allocated a married quarter. Two squadrons were based at Wahn, 68 and 87, both equipped with Meteors, and Wahn was also the main commercial airport for the whole of the Cologne/Bonn area. It was near the fabulous Rhine river, and we had many trips on the Rhine steamers whilst we were in Germany. I met up with my old friend Flt Lt Basil Wynell-Sutherland, who was also a Nav-Rad and the maddest individual I have ever come across. Once he climbed up the flagpole in his front yard in Troisdorf and would not come down until his wife called him "Noble and brave Wynell". One day whilst out shopping in Troisdorf, this loud voice came from across the road – "Glad my old clothes still fit you Blackie". No need to wonder who that was. It may have been Wynell who christened me 'Smutzi alt Schwartzi;, freely translated to 'Dirty old Blackie'. Sad to say our fortunes were tragically entwined later as I shall tell you.

Flying from Wahn entailed the usual round of PI's, NFT's and Sector Recces, but we also got to visit places like RAF Bruggen, RAF Wildenwrath and RAF Geilenkirchen, and on our return to base would see the famous twin spires of Cologne Cathedral overlooking the beautiful Rhine. A yearly detachment was made to the island of Sylt, which is one of the Friesian Islands and also marks the border between Germany and Denmark. We would spend about a month, mainly carrying out intensive air-to-banner firing with our 20 mm cannons over the North Sea. For one exercise we flew to Brusthem in Belgium and spent 2 weeks living in tents in a cherry orchard. Unfortunately my one medical weakness, hay fever, reared its ugly head and I was totally incapacitated for the whole of the time spent there.

On August 3rd 1955, another wonderful event took place. Gladys presented me with a beautiful baby girl. Mum decided to call her Giovanna Maria, so that people couldn't shorten her name, so everybody calls her Gee! Life was pretty good out there, brandy was six shillings a bottle and cigarettes ten shillings a carton. As a result, there was plenty of scope for much drinking, smoking and generally having a good time. We aircrew had to be careful, as there's not much scope for making mistakes at 40,000 ft and 400 knots. Which brings me back to Wynell, though I'm not suggesting that over indulgence was concerned in the following episode.

The Station Commander, Gp Capt Jones, often relaxed by flying with one of his Squadrons, and so one day he walked into the crewroom, came up to me and asked if I'd like to fly with him that day (August 28th 1956). You do not turn a Groupy down, so off we went on an NFT and we arranged to fly again that night. At briefing, Wynell arranged to fly, instead of me, with his mate Groupy, so off I went back to my lovely wife and baby. Next morning I went into the 08.00 hrs Meteorological Briefing to be greeted with the news that Groupy and Wynell were both dead, having crashed while landing after completing their sortie the previous night. It would appear that Lady Luck was still looking after me, as Wynell had flown instead of me. Knowing Wynell, he might have been playing one of his practical jokes, but we shall never know. All I do know, is that over the years something or someone seemed to be looking after my best interests.

During our stay in Germany we had a maid provided for us. Her name was Trudy and we became great friends with her husband Josef and their children. When Giovanna was born, Trudy was ecstatic and took her home whenever she could. Conditions were very austere for the locals at that time, but I made sure that Josef never went short of cigarettes or brandy. Germany, at least when we were there, was a marvellous place for eating, drinking and for generally having a great time and one of the highlights of the year was 'Rosen Montag', held in Cologne just before Easter. The climax of 'Rosen Montag' is The Grand Procession through the streets of Cologne and past the famous cathedral. Thousands of people put on fancy costumes and the procession takes hours to pass by. Inhibitions are cast aside and I did hear that after one particularly dance, over a hundred wedding rings were swept up off the floor next morning!

After three great years on 87 Sqn, I was told to pack again – I was posted to No.1 ANS at RAF Topcliffe for conversion to the Canberra.

No.1 Navigation School – RAF Topcliffe

A short refresher course on navigation was the first item on the agenda. Two tours on night-fighters, using mainly radar and radio instant fixing aids, had rather dulled the senses when it came to astro-navigation, three-drift wind velocities and all the other basics of pure navigation. After 35 hours in Varsities and Marathons, I was adjudged competent and off I went to try my skills on the Canberra.

No.1 Bomber Command Bombing School – RAF Lindholme

Another short refresher course on bombing, both visually and using Gee-H, which entailed using radar chains to pinpoint a target. We flew in the Vickers Varsity on this course and little did I know that I would log over 1,000 hours in this one aircraft type. I must mention here that Gladys and Gee were having to live in temporary Service accommodation while I was still moving around and would not join me until I got quarters on my future squadron, so it was in my interests to get there as soon as possible. Next stop was ......

231 Operational Conversion Unit – RAF Bassingbourn

At last – the fabulous Canberra – the bomber that it had been so hard to catch in our Meteors. From January to April 1958, I was busily perfecting my navigational and bombing techniques with my new crew. In this mark of Canberra (2, 6, 15 or 16) the crew consisted of a pilot and two Navs – one plotter and one bomb-aimer. The two Navs changed duties, but I spent most of my time doing the bombing and map-reading. All the crew had their own ejection seat, but the two Navs in the back had one small window to look out of and I found it very claustrophobic, so I always moved down into the perspex nose whenever possible, even if I wasn't using the visual bombsight which of course was there. There was no ejection seat in the nose, so if an emergency ever arose while we were flying at, say 200 ft, I would never have managed to get back to my seat in the rear, strap on my parachute harness and connect my intercom before ejecting. We did practise doing just that, but I would have been history if the worst had happened. Once again fate was kind to me. My pilot on this course was Plt Off Tilsey, and the other Nav was Fg Off 'Tiny' Tew. We all completed the course successfully and though Tilsey didn't come with us, Tiny and myself were posted to our operational squadron.

9 Bomber Squadron – RAF Binbrook

The squadron was equipped with three different marks of Canberra, the T4 trainer, B2's and B6's, both light bombers but capable of carrying a nuclear bomb or 6 x 1,000 lb non-nuclear bombs. My new crew consisted of Fg Off Hurrell (pilot), Fg Off Tew (Nav-plotter) and myself (Nav-observer). In short, I did all the map-reading, visual bombing and the 15 minute checks on fuel tanks and various other gauges around the cockpit. I would normally be sitting in the 'rumble seat' next to the pilot or lying in the perspex nose looking at the ground below, which was anything up to 8 miles straight down. Our first weeks were spent familiarising ourselves with the aircraft, flying lots of 'circuits and bumps' and learning how to carry out minor servicing and refuelling in case we ever found ourselves on an airfield where the local groundcrew were not familiar with our type of aircraft. It was also necessary from a security point of view. On August 18th 1958, we were awarded our 'Combat Classification' and took our place in the squadron. For the next few months we practised formation flying, bombing, cross-country exercises and even got on one individual detachment (hereafter known as a 'Jolly'), to RAF Gutersloh. A 'Jolly' is when one crew go off on their own to another country, spend a few days in this new location, then return to base. These trips are much sought after. New places to see, new crewrooms to visit, and always the possibility for picking up some 'Duty-free'. Longer trips to say Aden or Singapore would take about 10 days and were known as 'Lone Rangers'.

At least once a year, complete squadrons would be detached to bases in the Mediterranean – RAF Luqa (Malta), RAF El Adem (Libya) or RAF Akrotiri (Cyprus), and would carry out concentrated bombing sorties at the El Adem ranges. Sometimes the squadrons would do the bombing in conjunction with an exercise in which all the squadrons would be involved and was arranged so that all the bombers dropped their bombs on the SaD1e target within a few minutes. This meant split-second timing so that each aircraft was over the target within 15 seconds of the specified time. Our squadron detachment came in late 1958, and on November 7th we flew from Binbrook to Luqa, the flight taking 3 hours and 10 minutes. One days local flying then we commenced our bombing exercises at Filfla (Malta), Tarhuna (near Tripoli) and El Adem. Each sortie included a navigational exercise, dropping 23 x 25 lb practice bombs, then return to base. Some days we would fly to El Adem, drop our bombs, land at El Adem, have lunch, load up with more bombs, drop those then return to Luqa. El Adem had a duty-free shop, so I always bought some cigarettes and 'My Sin' (an expensive French perfume) to take back to Gladys, waiting back in the cold U.K. This was all great fun and I was being paid to do it! On November 24th 1958, we took part in one exercise with twelve other aircraft. These aircraft took off from four different airfields around the Mediterranean, each did a long navex and we each dropped a 1,000 pounder on the El Adem target at intervals of 30 seconds. It was the first time I had dropped a big bomb and it was the second nearest to the target. Accuracy of course depends on each member of the crew. The pilot must fly at the correct speed and height, and follow the bomb-aimers commands implicitly, the plotter must find a good wind-velocity and ensure good timing and tracking, and of course the bomb-aimer must do all he can to ensure a good final approach and release. We returned to Binbrook on December 4th in good time for Christmas, looking forward to an interesting New Year, and in our first married quarter. Another 'Jolly' on January 2nd 1959, when I visited Gibraltar for the first time. The trip took 3 hours and 15 minutes flying over France. A very pleasant 3 days including a trip over the border to La Linea, where we visited a club and watched the Flamenco dancing and tried the local wine. One disadvantage of Gibraltar was the scarcity of fresh water, which was only used for drinking. Shaving and washing in salt water is both difficult and painful at times I can assure you. We returned to Binbrook on January 5th with lots of presents for my two beautiful girls. Giovanna was 3 years old now and luckily taking after her mother for looks. February 1959 and another detachment to Luqa. The first attempt led to a quick return to base with engine failure. However, we transferred to another aircraft and arrived in

Malta the same day. The same routine, except that we did get one 'Jolly' to Akrotiri in Cyprus. Stayed only one night, got horribly drunk and saw very little of 'The Island of Dreams', but I did get that chance later. As soon as we landed back at Luqa, we were greeted with the great news that we were off back to the UK in a few days to ferry the T4 back for urgent maintenance. This was great news because it meant spending Easter with the family at Binbrook, and getting home earlier than the rest of the squadron. So, on March 26th, we took off from Luqa and had to return an hour later because of engine trouble. Later on the same day we took off again and landed at Orange in France just over 2 hours later. A quick re-fuelling then off again to RAF Waddington, where we left the aircraft and travelled home by train. At that time it was very cold and miserable weather in England, and we had been sun-bathing in the Mediterranean sun and all had great sun-tans. We really did look out of place amongst all those pale faces.

Squadron life continued through April and May. I even got to fly with the Station Commander, Gp Capt Warne, on 'Exercise Topweight' and recorded a very pleasing bombing result – thank goodness. Low-level exercises over Germany, including a stopover at RAF Laarbruch, and then the best 'Lone Ranger' to date. On May 14th we flew to El Adem, spent the night there then on to Khartoum the next day, transiting at 40,000 ft at optimum speed and height to conserve fuel. The pilot would do a 'cruise climb', that is, he would set the engine settings at the most economical and as the fuel was burnt and the load lightened, the aircraft would slowly climb and eventually level out at about 43,000 ft. An amazing fact was that in a fully fuelled Canberra, carrying fuel in the main tanks in the wings and main body and also in the wing tanks, the weight of the fuel carried was greater than the weight of the empty aircraft. We landed at Khartoum, and because we had made a fast descent from our cruising level, the underside of our wings was covered in ice. The local ground crew thought this was amazing, as the temperature on the ground was about 100° F. Next morning we took off at 04.00 hrs, as with our great fuel load the aircraft would never have lifted off in the heat of the day. On to Eastleigh Airport just outside Nairobi, where the elevation is about 6,000 ft, which makes for quite pleasant living conditions. During our 4 days there we hired a Land Rover and toured the nearby National Park and got some great photographs of vultures, gazelle and zebras, but no lions. Apparently they feed early and were just resting by the time we got there – maybe it was just as well.

After our return to Binbrook, the squadron were re-located to RAF Coningsby in Lincolnshire. While there, Gladys and her mate Freda learnt to drive, so there were two more Stirling Moss's on the roads!

At this time a change in role for the bomber force was decided. When the Canberra was first introduced, bombers still relied on height and speed to reach a target and deliver their bombs, but tactics had to be changed. With the advent of surface-to-air and air-to-air missiles, any aircraft approaching at height would inevitably be destroyed before reaching the target. It was decided that against technically advanced opponents, routes to targets would have to be partially planned at low-level to avoid acquisition by enemy radar defences. By low-level I mean as low as possible, tree-top level if possible, after all if you can be safer the lower you get, you'll get pretty bloody low!

A typical flight profile would be something like this:-

Take-off from base and climb to height, say 38,000 ft. Navigate to 'Go-No Go' point just outside enemy radar cover and wait for the vital signal. If it was to proceed, descend to say 20 ft and proceed to the target by a prepared route. Here I must mention that each crew had two targets, for which we had memorised routes and prepared flight-plans, using winds and temperatures averaged out for each season over the years. Methods of delivering bombs were experimented with, the 'Low Altitude Bombing System' or 'LABS', which I will describe here:-

Flying at low-level along the route, our first objective was to reach the Initial Point (IP). At this point the weapon would be armed (the nuclear core had been inserted prior to take-off), and the pilot would be maintaining a set speed and correcting his heading as instructed by yours truly lying in the nose and map-reading. He would also be watching a particular dial on his instrument panel. At a certain point in the final run-up, a needle would suddenly drop, the pilot would then pull the aircraft into a 3g loop. At a set point in this loop, the bomb would automatically release, we would continue the loop to its apex, do a quick roll, then make for the surface as quick as possible and hopefully make our escape. I would be in the nose during the whole operation, but after a while it became second nature. Quite honestly we would never have expected to reach the target and if we had dropped the bomb, we would not have survived the blast, but that was what we were paid for.

Whilst on Canberra's, I dropped hundreds of LABS bombs, but all practice 25 pounders. I often wondered whether I would have had the courage to drop a nuclear bomb and kill possibly thousands of people – now I shall never have that decision to make. In January 1960, I flew with Fg Off Flash Grindon, but the weather must have been pretty bad that month as we only logged 16 hours flying time. In February 1960 we got away from the terrible English weather and had a very pleasant and warm month in Idris (just outside Tripoli), practising our LABS manoeuvres. Swimming in the crystal clear waters off Tripoli just reinforced my determination to always get my family and myself away from England and warmer climates whenever I could in the future. During April, the CO called me into his office and casually asked how my bombing results were progressing. Modestly, I said they were quite reasonable. "Good" he said, "You are off to BCBS as a bombing instructor".

No.1 Bomber Command Bombing School – RAF Lindholme

I joined No.180 Canberra Course as a student, flew 10 sorties, dropped my quota of bombs and successfully completed the course, and while the rest of the students went off to squadrons I stayed behind as an instructor. The aircraft used was the Vickers Varsity, and besides bombing practice we would fine tune radar approaches and let-downs, emergency drills and radar bombing as well as the visual type. The next 3 years followed much the same pattern, day after day. 'Met' briefing in the morning, out to the aircraft with three students, out to Wainfleet or Theddlethorpe in The Wash, calculate the wind velocity, drop 23 practice bombs, back to base, discuss and evaluate the exercise and hopefully learn how to be more efficient bomb-aimers.

During my tour at the Bombing School, I took part in one large 'Escape and Evasion' exercise. About 300 aircrew personnel were dropped off from lorries in different parts of Yorkshire, given some flying rations and a map and told to reach various rendezvous over the following 5 days. Local army and police personnel were sent out to capture and interrogate us. For the next 2 days my partner and I trekked over the Yorkshire countryside, sleeping by day (not very well) and travelling by night. We reached the first checkpoint successfully, but I was captured on the third night. I was stripped of my clothes, given an overall to wear and a sack was put over my head. For the next 2 days I was made to stand at attention unless I was being interrogated. I believe I was placed in a hut with quite a few other chaps, no talking, no food, just standing at attention and no idea of the time of day or night. After about a day the old thud could be heard as one of us fell to the ground, personally I was determined that they wouldn't beat me, so I kept getting up. We had been trained that, in the event of capture, all we must give the captors was name, rank and number. Glad to say I got one of the interrogators very upset when all I would say to him was "582601 Flight Sergeant Blackman P" over and over again and he had me doubling around the room. Of course, if they had been 'real' interrogators I might not have been so brave. Anyway, the exercise finally finished. It probably taught us a few lessons and I went home with a 5 day growth of beard.

January 1961, my squadron commander and I were allocated a 'Lone Ranger' to Gibraltar. We flew out on the Friday, a couple of relaxing days in the sun and back to Lindholme on the Tuesday. Better than a mundane Monday to Friday job – no wonder some ex-servicemen find it hard to settle down.

A very special event in May – my dear Blossom presented me with a beautiful baby boy. Now I had the complete set – a lovely wife, a gorgeous daughter Giovanna Maria (now 7 years old), and a handsome son Ray Peter, that I could play soccer with in the near future. Talking of soccer, lots of the big clubs were within a few miles of the Station, so I often went off to see my team Ipswich Town play at Manchester and Sheffield. This was an especially good bonus in their championship year, although I was lucky I wasn't beaten up when I got a bit too rowdy in my support at times.

'Mayflight', the annual UK Air Defence Exercise, certainly brought a change of pace to our flying. Our role was to transport aircrew and ground crew to various airfields around the UK, wherever they were required. My log book for 2 days reads as following:-

10th	08.57	Lindholme – Swinderby	15 mins
	09.27	Swinderby – Lossiemouth	2 hrs
	11.41	Lossiemouth – Lindholme	1 hr 15 mins
	14.36	Lindholme – Cottesmore	25 min
	15.47	Cottesmore – Wittering	10 min
	16.07	Wittering – Gaydon	20 min
	16.39	Gaydon – Lindholme	35 min
11th	09.43	Lindholme – Cottesmore	20 min
	11.48	Cottesmore – Boscombe Down	40 min
	12.40	Boscombe Down – St Mawgan	50 min
	13.36	St Mawgan – Cottesmore	1 hr 30 min
	15.23	Cottesmore – Lindholme	20 min
12th		Two bombing sorties at Tweedlethorpe	5 hrs 40 min
13th	16.32	Lindholme – Wittering	25 min
	17.09	Wittering – Gaydon	20 min
	18.35	Gaydon – Wittering	20 min
	19.09	Wittering – Cottesmore	5 min
	19.25	Cottesmore – Gaydon	20 min
	20.00	Gaydon – Lindholme	30 min

The above flights, except for the bombing sorties, all involved landing and either loading or unloading personnel or equipment at various Bomber Command stations around the country. A real high-speed and efficient taxi service and no overtime rates paid!

During my 3 years at Lindholme, I was constantly trying for another operational tour and if possible an overseas posting. I had never liked

English weather, especially after my trips down to the Mediterranean, and wanted to get travelling again. Finally, one day, the Commanding Officer called me into his office and told me that my repeated requests for a posting had at last been answered and I was going to join another Canberra Squadron. So after 970 hours on Varsities, I was off to those sleek bombers again.

231 Operational Conversion Unit – RAF Bassingbourn

I joined 231 OCU's Light Bomber Course in September 1963, and met my new crew – Fg Off Taff Lewis (pilot) and Plt Off Chris Hickson (Nav-plotter). I remained with this crew for the next 2½ years and I could not have wished for a better crew. Taff was a proficient pilot, but not an absolute stickler for the rules (as will be seen later), and Chris was a hard-working navigator who was quite content to sit at his plotting table at the back, while I spent most of my time in the nose or in the 'rumble-seat' beside Taff. Poor old Chris suffered quite badly from airsickness and early on he would fill a brown paper bag on almost every flight. Blossom of course was still at Lindholme in married quarters looking after our two beautiful children, waiting for me to get a permanent posting, where hopefully I would soon get another quarter for them to move into.

Just over 2 months of concentrated flying were spent moulding we three into a competent crew. We flew familiarisation flights, Navexes (high, low and medium level), and about twelve bombing sorties. I incurred the wrath of the Chief Bombing Instructor. We achieved some excellent results, but not by using the strictly laid down procedures. I had dropped so many bombs on my first Canberra tour and during my instructing tour, that I often corrected my aiming point by unorthodox means. If, say after about three bombs, I could see that the bombs were falling a little short, instead of adjusting the bombsight, I would release the bombs a fraction later. When I admitted this at de-briefing, I was cautioned in no uncertain manner. Our average error, converted to 25,000 ft, was 137 yards, which is quite good. After flying 67 hours on 231 OCU, we were given our postings to squadrons and to my great joy we got 32 Sqn at Akrotiri in Cyprus.

32 Bomber Squadron – RAF Akrotiri

Cyprus – that beautiful island in the Eastern Mediterranean. About 200 km long, situated 70 km from Turkey, 90 km from Syria, 250 km from Israel and about 300 km from Egypt. The climate is ideal, never too cold and even if it did get hot at times in the summer, you are never far from a beautiful sandy beach where you can just lay in the sun or go snorkelling. As for history – well at different times over the last few centuries, Cyprus has been occupied by Romans, Greeks, Turks, and of course by the British. At the time of writing, it is partitioned between Greece and Turkey. Population is about 80% Greek and 20% Turkish, and the UK has sovereign control over a few small military areas, including RAF Akrotiri, the largest military base outside the UK. I was ecstatic over my new posting and as soon as I arrived I got my name on the married quarters list, so that the family could join me as soon as possible to enjoy this wonderful place. Then my crew got deeply involved in becoming operational as soon as possible and taking our place with the rest of the crews, ready to defend whatever needed defending!

The 32 Sqn Canberra's could carry a variety of weapons – either 6 x 1,000 lb conventional high-explosive bombs, 32 rockets, an AS30 (a French made guided bomb) or a nuclear bomb. The latter was of course the most destructive weapon, and most of our training was devoted to the understanding and 'delivery' of this bomb. As a crew, we spent many hours learning how to 'arm' this weapon by inserting the nuclear core into the bomb, which without this core was just a few hundred pounds of inert metal. If this insertion process was not carried out perfectly, then the whole mechanism would jam, which was yet another one of many safety precautions. We were allocated two targets in Soviet controlled territory, each crew had two targets known only to that particular crew, and of course we never discussed these targets with other crews. We prepared four flight plans for each target, using 'seasonal' climatic conditions, and then memorised each turning point in case our navigational equipment was destroyed and we had to rely on map reading – guess who would have been lying in the nose travelling at about 400 knots at about 10 ft, trying to pick up landmarks! As mentioned earlier, our method of delivery for the nuclear bomb was using the LABS manoeuvre and we practised this many times in Episkopi Bay or at Tarhuna range. Training for normal bombs was carried out at El Adem. This entailed a four hour round trip. Once or twice I had a problem finding the target, a 100 yard-sided target is pretty hard to see from 40,000 ft, especially if the desert sand is blowing around. Rocket firing was carried out at Larnaca, a few miles along the coast, where we blasted ground targets. Sorties would only take about an hour, so we did three a day.

When my name came to the top of the quarters list I was allocated a quarter, but because of the increasing tension between the Turks and Greeks, my family was not allowed to travel out to join me and I had to wait another 4 months before the ban was lifted. Probably because I looked so miserable, I was given 3 weeks 'Compassionate' (maybe

'Passionate' was a better word) leave and I travelled back to UK by Hastings, got back to the family for three glorious weeks, then back to Cyprus on April 21st 1964. My old mates at Lindholme ferried me by Varsity to Abingdon, where I picked up a Beverley to transport me to Nicosia. This time the taxi service worked for me. Not long afterwards families were allowed out again, so once again we all got together. When we picked them up at Nicosia, all but Ray were pleased to see me – he was just about one year-old and cried his eyes out. Glad to say, it didn't take long for us all to settle down and enjoy the next 3 years in 'Paradise'. As soon as we could the next day, we went down to Buttons Bay and enjoyed the clear warm water. As the name suggests, it is an ideal place for the whole family, with shallow, clear, warm water, and many multi-coloured fish swimming around you.

The tension between the Turks and Greeks was still pretty high and at one time it was possible that Turkey was going to invade the independent island. Only about 80 km separated us from the Turkish mainland, and during February 1964, we were ordered to fly patrols in the straits separating the two countries and watch out for a possible invasion fleet. Taff was away on leave at the time, so I flew with Flt Lt Widdall on one of these patrols. We reached our patrol line, cut one engine to obtain maximum endurance, descended to 100 ft, patrolled for just over 5 hours and returned to base. We had been too low for radio contact during this time and it was assumed that we had 'bought it', as our fuel should theoretically have run out about an hour before we actually landed. It is rather dodgy to fly at low level on one engine and the CO wasn't sure whether to praise him or reprimand him. I was stupid enough not to be concerned at the time, a little bit of danger always set the adrenalin flowing a bit faster, which is probably the reason I went through my flying career without a single injury of any kind.

Our next door neighbours were Bill and Carrie Swain. He was the local schoolmaster and soon took Giovanna under his wing and they became amongst our dearest of friends. Giovanna by now had become an absolute beauty at the age of 8 years. Ray was a real scamp even as a 2 year-old and was always bossing the other kids around. Luckily both of these two treasures had their mother's good looks. Once when I was out pottering around I stepped on a rusty nail, it turned septic, so I went to Sick Quarters where they gave me a few pills. Later, my leg suddenly swelled up to double the normal size, I was rushed into hospital and apparently they managed to remedy the trouble just in time. Obviously my time wasn't due – I had a lot more living to do!

Lots of low-level flying, bombing, LABS and rocket-firing filled in the next few months. Then, in August 1964, the squadron were detached to

Sharjah in the Persian Gulf. This detachment was to get us used to operating in extreme heat, practise navigational techniques over featureless desert terrain and show the flag to the United Arab Emirates, which we had various treaties with. The usual range of exercises were carried out, but our crew did get a 'Lone Ranger' to Tehran in Iran. We landed at Mehrebad on September 10th. At this time the Shah was still the ruler of Iran and a close ally of the Western Powers, so co-operation was the order of the day and we were made very welcome. We toured what can only be described as the 'treasure house' in Tehran. Here, on public show, but very well guarded of course, was a fortune in gold and precious stones. The one item I shall always remember was a globe of the world. The oceans were portrayed in blue diamonds or rubies, and each continent in precious stones of different colours. Goodness knows what that would sell for at Sotheby's.

On September 26th we flew to Halfar in Malta to take part in 'Exercise Fallex'. I remember this exercise because of one sortie we did at night. We took off and commenced climbing to 35,000 ft, with me in my usual place in the nose of the aircraft. All the way up we were in this violent thunderstorm and I witnessed the most spectacular display of 'St Elmos Fire' it is possible to imagine. The perspex nose was literally covered in this blue, crackling fire – quite harmless of course, but what a sight.

November 1964, and the closest I ever came to seeing real action. President Sukarno of Indonesia was flexing his muscles, and, during what became known as 'Confrontation', he threatened our allies in Singapore and Malaya. These two countries were part of the British Commonwealth, so our government decided to support our allies. Various combat units and RAF units were sent out to the area in case fighting broke out. Fighter and bomber squadrons from New Zealand, Australia and the UK were detached, on a rotating basis, to defend the Malay Peninsula. 32 Sqn was given two days notice, then off we went to Singapore. Taff, Chris and myself were flown out by Transport Command Hastings in late November to RAF Tengah on Singapore Island, and on December 1st commenced patrols and exercises. We were allocated targets in Java and Sumatra, which we would have attacked with normal 'iron' bombs. 1965 arrived and my crew carried out one very important mission on January 27th. The Officers and Sergeants Mess, because of a very hectic Christmas period, had run out of duty-free cigarettes and liquor, so some low-level exercises were planned to RAF Kuching in Borneo. We flew to Kuching, had lunch while a rather large amount of the desired supplies were being loaded in the bomb-bay, then flew back to the grateful Messes back at Tengah. All good training and very much appreciated too.

Although we were away from our families, we tried to have a good time in Singapore, and of course we had to visit Bugis Street, which at that time had quite a notorious reputation. My main memory was watching this gorgeous looking 'girl' with the beautiful black hair parading down the street. I thought 'she' was the best looking lady there. Unfortunately 'she' turned out to be a 'he', so I was told!

While the husbands were having a good time in the Far East, the wives back in Cyprus weren't doing too badly either. They all got together for 'Social Days', which were just an excuse to imbibe lots of liquor and get up to lots of mischief. Blossom got very friendly with the CO's wife Beryl Dodds. We had purchased a little Fiat 500 Bambino for getting around the island, and it really was a fun car. It was quite a sturdy little car and it had to be because it came into contact with Beryl's brick wall once and the wall came off second-best. Blossom claimed that she was temporarily unsighted at the time, that's probably another way of saying blind drunk!! To think – we had left our innocent children in the hands of those ladies! Blossom had also caught the eye of Savaas, the local orange plantation owner, which wasn't surprising, as she was just the type the Cypriots went for, dark-haired, slim and beautiful. During our 2 years in Cyprus, we were never short of oranges and they are probably the best in the world.

In February 1965, we left Tengah to return to Akrotiri, and of course we had to do this trip of about 5,000 miles in stages. Our first stage took us to RAF Butterworth on the west coast of Malaysia, then on to RAF Gan in the Indian Ocean. Gan is one of the coral islands comprising The Maldives. It is situated about 600 miles south-west of the southern-most tip of India, and was the main staging post for military aircraft between Africa and South-East Asia. It seemed idyllic at the time, but would get pretty boring after a short stay. Later that day we flew across the Indian Ocean to RAF Masirah, on an island off the east coast of Oman, and the next day completed the journey back to Akrotiri, refuelling in Tehran. In flying time, we were airborne for a total of 18½ hours. We arrived back at base, all ready for a joyful reunion with our families after nearly 4 months away, but it was not to be. Near East Air Force Command decided to have an exercise to see if their squadrons were up to the mark. So for the next 4 days we were confined to the squadron dispersals, sat either in the aircraft or the huts at readiness for 'scrambles'. Finally, on the 27th, we scrambled, flew a 3 hour Navex, culminating with a simulated nuclear weapon attack at El Adem, returned to base, de-briefed and finally got back to 'the wife and kids'. Life got back to normal. Bombing, rocketing and trips down to Buttons

Bay or Tunnel Beach with the family – it was a hard life but somebody had to do it!

April 1965 and we purchased our first new car, a Renault R8 1100 for £496 (£777 in UK), which we eventually shipped back to England and then out to Australia in 1968. On one of our first jaunts around the island we visited Famagusta, the walled and main Turkish city on Cyprus. We always found the Turks very friendly, but got on well with the Greeks as well. We visited the beautiful St. Hilarion castle overlooking Kyrenia. It is said that the castle in 'Snow White' is modelled on this beautiful fortress.

May 1965, and another 7-day detachment to Tehran, where the squadron took part in 'Exercise Shabaz', and we flew three sorties before returning to base.

One particular Navex in June 1965 must be mentioned:-

A Liberator bomber of the American Desert Air Force, 'Lady be Good', failed to return from a bombing raid on Italy on April 4th 1942. No trace of the aircraft was found and it was assumed that 'Lady be Good' had ditched in the Mediterranean. During May 1959, some oil prospectors working in the desert came across the wreck of the aircraft about 500 miles from it's home base at Solluch, near Benghazi. Some of the bodies of the crew were found in the well-preserved wreck and their diaries were recovered and returned to the American authorities. It transpired from these diaries that the aircraft had been damaged by enemy action and attempted to limp back to base. They crossed the North African coast on a southerly heading, but mistaking the smooth desert for the sea kept on going south thinking they would hit land soon, whilst they were actually going further and further into the unforgiving desert. When they finally crash-landed, some set off hoping to get help and some of the crew remained with the aircraft. They all perished and 17 years later, the sad story of 'Lady be Good' was finally told. The dry desert air had ensured that the wreck did not rust away, but just sat there until some prospectors stumbled across the last resting place of a brave crew. Books have been written and films made about 'Lady be Good', and our squadron decided to plan a Navex using this aircraft as a turning point. So, on June 16th, we carried out this exercise at low-level and finally turned onto the leg, which, if our navigation had been accurate, would bring us up to this bomber lying broken but proud in the desert sand. We passed over 'Lady be Good' at about 15 ft and 400 knots, and I took a picture of the broken aircraft with the camera in the nose of the Canberra.

By now I had been promoted to the rank of Master Navigator. To be honest, the promotion was more a reward for time served and good behaviour (?!?) than for achievement, but it sounded great to be called "Sir" and we were respected in the Sergeants Mess, as having reached that exalted rank we must have lots of experience and flown lots of hours. I had clocked about 3,200 flying hours by then, a fair amount considering that many of these hours were accumulated on short trips on fighters.

August 1965 and three of the squadron aircraft were detached to Vahdati airfield for 'Exercise Shahin 3'. Vahdati is on the western border of Iran, near the town of Dezful and a few miles from the Iraqi border. Three things stood out about this detachment:-

- It was very hot, the temperature continually reached 100° F plus, and one poor fellow dropped dead from heat exhaustion while we were there.

- The Iran Air Force officers lived well, but the poor conscripts, who did all the menial tasks, were clothed in little better than rags and slept whenever they could and wherever they happened to be at the time.

- We visited Tehran markets, which are all under cover from the sun and spread over some acres.

I mentioned earlier that Taff was not an absolute stickler for the rules. The official minimum height for low-level flights was 100 ft above ground-level, but at times the temptation became too great. Over the desert or the coast road we would skim above the ground at about 20 ft. This could prove very upsetting for some poor Arab who would be quietly riding his camel along the road to discover 8 tons of metal hurtling towards him at 400 knots and just above the surface – a bit noisy too. Of course if any complaints were received, we all agreed that it must have been somebody else.

On one of our many visits to Malta, we tried the local brew of wine. It was nicknamed 'Screech' and cost 15 cents a bottle, of which I believe the bottle cost was 10 cents! At times I drunk a lot of this concoction – no wonder I was paralytic next morning, and no wonder it was called 'Screech'.

While we were at RAF Idris on one exercise, one pilot had a harrowing experience. He had just lifted off when he flew into a large flock of birds. The force of the impacts was so great that the canopy disintegrated and some of the bodies smashed into the cockpit injuring the crew. Covered in blood, the pilot somehow managed to land the aircraft straight ahead in the sandhills. A very gutsy effort, in spite of his injuries, he saved his crew and the aircraft.

Low-level flying puts a great strain on an airframe and inspections uncovered cracks in mainspars. These cracks were always supposedly repaired and we continued flying the aircraft, but it was often wondered whether some of the unexplained Canberra disappearances of previous years might have been prevented if these checks had been made earlier.

September 1965 and another week in Malta. I had often wondered if Italy was as beautiful as pictured on postcards, so one day we found out. On September 14th (my birthday) we took off from RAF Luqa, flew low-level past Sicily, up the Italian east coast to Rimini, across the country to Verona, down the west coast to Naples, then back to Luqa. There you are – Italy in 3½ hours. I still recall the beautiful chateaux we saw and the famous 'Autostrada del Sol'. Yes – it is a picturesque country. We returned to Cyprus on September 21st, only to have another week in Luqa for 'Exercise Dazzle'. Most of these exercises entailed standing-by at various states of readiness, culminating in a 'scramble' at any time of the day or night. We would then fly a Navex and drop a 1,000 pounder at El Adem with one aircraft 30 seconds behind us and one 30 seconds in front of us. All good training for the real thing and split-second timing essential.

December 1965, detached to Malaya again to keep an eye on Indonesian intentions. This time we were quartered in tents at RAF Kuantan in the jungle. It was not unusual to awake in the morning and find 6 inches of water or a snake sharing your tent. Just off Kuantan lie the wrecks of 'The Prince of Wales' and 'Repulse', warships sunk by the Japanese in December 1941. At low tide these wrecks are visible from the air. This detachment did not last very long and we returned to Akrotiri in time for Christmas.

The next incident worthy of note occurred on January 27th 1966. We had just completed a low-level exercise over the Libyan desert and were climbing up to 35,000 ft when the aircraft lurched to the right as the starboard engine failed. Chris transmitted a 'Mayday', I made my way back to my ejection seat and we carried out the normal emergency procedures. Luckily we were not far from Benina Airport, so we landed there on one engine and sent off a signal to Cyprus informing them of our problems, and arrangements were made to send some groundcrew and a spare engine to us as soon as possible. We spent the next 3 days in a Benghazi hotel, checking on the aircraft and lounging around the beaches. On January 30th we flew back to Akrotiri.

In February I visited another city in yet another country. On the 23rd we flew to Ankara and spent just one night there. The highlight was visiting one of the clubs and watching the famed 'belly dancers' perform. Whenever I hear that kind of music, I remember that night in Ankara. The city itself is surrounded by a range of mountains which trap all the industrial smog, and this dirty haze can be seen miles away. It takes just an hour to fly from Akrotiri to Ankara by Canberra.

March 1966, and my last month with 32 Sqn, but time for one last interesting mission. We were detached to RAF Sharjah again, and one of our allies by treaty in the Trucial Oman States was the Sheikh of Salalah. Apparently he was having trouble with his relatives from the North, and one of his cousins had decided to travel south and assassinate him! His would-be assassins had to travel about 300 km across the desert to reach Salalah and there was only one waterhole on their route south. Each day our squadron carried out patrols to this waterhole and reported back to base if we spotted any groups of Arabs in the vicinity. The Trucial Oman Scouts would then investigate and take any action necessary. This waterhole was just that – a hole in the ground and very difficult to find. We had to fly about 200 km over flat featureless desert to reach it, but we did find it and I have a great picture taken at about 10 ft off the ground approaching a bunch of Arabs and camels at a high rate of knots. A split second after taking the shot, Arabs and camels were scattered all over the desert. After we returned from this last detachment, I was given the news that I really didn't want to hear – "You're posted Blackie – to Air Sea Rescue helicopters at RAF Manston", so we sadly left Cyprus in May 1966.

No.21 Crewman Course – RAF Valley

We travelled to Manston in Kent, where I was allocated a quarter, and after a few days I left for Valley on the Isle of Anglesey to complete my crewman course. Initially the training was done over dry land and this part of the course went smoothly. I would either operate the winch and position the crewman on the end of the cable, or the roles would be reversed. On July 1st 1966, I was dangling on the end of the cable, simulating a rescue, when the aircraft's main rotor failed, causing the aircraft to plunge to the ground. I was thrown to the ground partially dazed and was groggily getting to my feet when I somehow heard a yell - "Get down Blackie" and I did just that. Apparently the tail rotor just missed slicing into my head! After dry-winching, we progressed to wet-winching over the Irish Sea. Sad to say I had never learnt to swim and this fact proved disastrous. At times, when I was attempting to pluck a 'victim' from the cold sea, I would end up in more trouble than him and practically required rescuing myself. We finally realised that Air Sea Rescue was not for me. The instructors commended my efforts, but after a few days I was posted to HQ Bomber Command as Operations 1(E).

HQ Bomber Command – RAF High Wycombe

Although this posting did not involve flying duties, I feel that it was interesting enough to include in my narrative. My job at HQ Bomber Command was as assistant to Air Chief Marshal Sir Wallace Kyle, Air Officer Commanding Bomber Command, and later Governor of Western Australia. The family moved into Married Quarters on the Station, and Giovanna and Ray were both enrolled at Lacey Green School. We spent a pleasant 2 years there, although I missed the flying and the desert.

ACM Sir Wallace Kyle gave many lectures and presentations to NATO chiefs, Station Commanders, MP's and various other dignitaries, and used both films and projector slides in his talks. My job was to prepare these films or sets of slides so that he could enter the presentation area and start talking, knowing that the required pictures or slides would come up at the right moment on the screen. Fairly straightforward, but no room for errors, so I always carried at least two projectors, spare bulbs and anything else that I could think of to cover any eventuality. Often he would only give me an hours notice of his requirements, so I had to be constantly on hand. We often travelled to other Stations to give these presentations. Normally I would travel the night before so that everything would be set up for him when he arrived. I also worked in 'The War-Room', deep in the basement of the Operations Centre. On one wall was a huge map of Europe showing all the targets that Bomber Command, Polaris submarines and SACEUR had targeted in the Soviet Union and their satellites, together with the routes that the bombers would fly to get to these targets. I remember that one seaport was allocated 16 strikes, including some nuclear. The defence systems were also plotted in – Moscow had two rings of SAM sites. Attending one Station Commanders Annual Conference, I learnt that it was planned to do away with all NCO aircrew, so not particularly keen to try for a commission, I started enquiring about a new career. I tried the Rhodesian Air Force and the Royal Australian Air Force, and got accepted for the latter … but that's another story.

Afterthoughts

During the time that I was writing this narrative, I became more and more convinced that somebody or someone had been looking after me and charting my life my life for the best. Consider the facts:-
- My Entry at Halton, the 51st, numbered 189, of which about 60 transferred to aircrew duties. Fifteen of these lads were killed in aircraft accidents, just about a quarter.

- Wynell took my flight with Groupy, and within a few hours was dead.

- If the hood had opened on the Meteor a few thousand feet either lower or higher, we would not have survived. Also if Dick had jettisoned that hood, it would probably have decapitated me.

- If I hadn't just managed to hear the warning shout, I would have had a rotor blade through my head.

On a career note:-

- *If* I had succeeded on the pilot's course, *if* I had become an officer, and *if* I had been acknowledged for helping those chaps out of the wrecked Anson (which would have ensured my commissioning), I would never have finished up with a wonderful wife and two beautiful children.

When you consider those facts, plus the fact that I never even suffered a scratch through my flying activities, I think my nickname shouldn't have been 'Dirty old Blackie' but 'Lucky old Blackie'.

Summary of Flying Hours – 1950 to 1967

Percival Proctor	21 hrs 10 mins
Tiger Moth	40 mins
Avro Anson	91 hrs 10 mins
Vickers Armstrong Wellington	103 hrs 35 mins
Bristol Brigand	62 hrs 40 mins
Armstrong Whitworth Meteor	998 hrs
Handley Page Hastings	10 hrs 15 mins
English Electric Canberra	1,104 hrs 10 mins
Westland Whirlwind	29 hrs
Vickers Varsity	1,114 hrs 50 mins

Grand Total: 3,535 hrs 30 mins or just under 3 months spent aloft.

30. My 'Basic' Career

Jack Smith

When I read about the careers of some of my former 51st apprentice colleagues, I conclude that, in comparison, my time in the RAF was rather humdrum. There were highs and lows of course, but after RAF St Athan it was out into Bomber Command mainly servicing Lincolns and then, in 1955, for the last three years of my time, I was posted back to RAF Halton as an instructor.

My metamorphosis into a Senior Lecturer in Physical Chemistry at an Australian University is probably marginally more interesting, but certainly illustrates the value of the technical training that I received at Halton both as an apprentice and as an instructor. I emigrated in early 1958 with my Australian wife Joan and one son, and my first job was as a technical officer in the Department of Physics at the University of Western Australia (UWA) in Perth. The key to getting that job was Basic with a capital 'B' – filing, fitting and lathe machining. One of the subjects that I had to teach at Halton was Basic Engineering, in the same Instrument Bay where I had myself been taught all those years before. And yes, Mr Roberts, our instructor at that time, was still there!

By the time that I retired from the RAF, I was quite a competent lathe machinist and that was what was wanted at UWA because they wanted to build a big instrument and I was an Instrument Maker, wasn't I? The instrument was a mass spectrometer. I hadn't a clue as to what it was, but I could follow technical drawings and when finished, it actually worked and I soon learned to drive it. The function was to measure the age of some of the rocks in Western Australia.

In 1961, it was suggested that I should apply for a new job in Melbourne with the Commonwealth Scientific and Industrial Research Organisation (CSIRO). I think it's called head-hunting nowadays. The job? To build a mass spectrometer, this time to study taints and flavours in dairy products. No problem, this one worked too! After five years with CSIRO, my boss was appointed to the chair of Physical Chemistry at La Trobe University, a new institution in Melbourne, and invited me to go with him as his Research Associate. He wanted a what? Would you believe – a mass spectrometer! No worries mate, only this time it was to design and build, not just build! However, I did know a bit about mass spectrometers by this stage and we were able to incorporate some really novel features like computer control.

Because I was now a mid-level boss, I could submit my designs to the workshop and here was when my experience with Basic at Halton really came into its own, because I could talk to and understand the technicians in the workshop. My only problem was a rudimentary knowledge of electronics. I was brought up on valve radio – not the new-fangled transistors – so I spent some time ingratiating myself with the departmental electronics expert, a German who had been in the Hitler youth, and perhaps he thought that if he didn't co-operate he might have ended up in the Aussie equivalent of Auschwitz. Nevertheless, we had a good relationship and published a couple of papers together. As to what followed, I remained at La Trobe until I retired in 1988 and with a lot of luck, being in the right place at the right time, a degree of finger and a hell of a lot of midnight oil, I became a Senior Lecturer and can truthfully claim that I taught Physical Chemistry at all levels up to Honours, and successfully supervised Masters and PhD students, without once myself formally studying Chemistry!!

31. A Middle East Safari by Land, Sea and Air

Joe Woodford

The Empire Ken – in the summer of 1951 – en route for Mombasa. It was an ex-German ship, one of three which had been converted to troopship duties, with a speed of around 12 knots. We sailed from Southampton Docks, across a comparatively calm Bay of Biscay, then through the Straits of Gibraltar. I can recall seeing small rowing boats fishing in the Straits and I didn't envy them having to row back to whichever shore they had come from. The Mediterranean was very rough, and according to the matelots on board they had never seen it so bad. Many of the troops on board were seasick, and the Mess Deck cooks recommended greasy bacon and toast for breakfast to combat the seasickness! Anyway, when I went down for breakfast, there were only half-a-dozen of us eating toasted bacon sandwiches and thankfully I was all right. I never did find out if the recommended breakfast was a joke or not.

Our first stop was Port Said, where we picked up the Canal Pilot and his so called 'look-out', who was an Arab who was to be seated in a small box suspended from the bow. While he was waiting to go into his box, he squatted down and heated some opium in a tin lid and inhaled the smoke coming from it. I think he had to be doped to get him in the box! We then sailed through the Suez Canal on to our next stop – Aden. Here I went ashore and found a shop which sold Mah Jong sets (Game of the Four Winds). I bought one for enjoyment on the remainder of the journey. In Aden, I met an ex-brat of the 52nd Entry who I promised to write to. His number was 582853 J/T … and it was then I boobed. I put my name down instead of his! The rest of his address was "3 Block, Top West, RAF Khormaksar. (I have just found that piece of paper with this address on, so can anybody out there help me to find him?) At Aden, two Army chaps joined the ship, one from Rhodesia and one from the Belgian Congo. I soon struck up a relationship with them and they had been fighting the guerrillas in Malaya alongside the Gurkhas. They told us a lot about the war out there which would fill a couple of pages.

Next stop was Port Louis in Mauritius. Here, another chap and I decided to climb the hill, or mountain, behind the town. When we arrived at the foot of it, the other chap chickened out. So off I set and reached the top after brushing through various cactii plants, collecting a few prickly hairs en route. At the top, it was flat with numerous cactii and bushes, so I decided to explore and whoops – within 30 ft the escarpment ended abruptly, with a sheer drop to a fertile valley below. I was very pleased that it was daylight, for there was no indication or barriers. I laid on my stomach to peer over the edge, but not for long as I am not a great one for heights. While at the top I watched the strange looking birds gliding in the thermals. They looked like small magpies, but they didn't have tail feathers, instead they had a long quill over a foot long, which they used as stabilizers. I don't know if those birds were unique to Mauritius or not. I started the descent and when I arrived at the bottom there was a small park with a hut nearby. It started to rain heavily, so I ran towards the hut and went in to find it was already occupied by three or four locals. Whilst waiting for the storm to clear, an old man sitting next to me kept saying "La femme, very young, only 12, you like, I get?" "No, no. Thank you" I said politely and hurriedly departed. Wandering down the main street I heard a familiar sound, the sound of Mah Jong tiles. I went up some steps and found myself in a Mah Jong gaming hall. There were at least a dozen card tables, all with linoleum tops to facilitate the easy movement of the tiles. It was then I realised that it was a gambling den and they asked me if I would like to play. I naturally declined but asked if I could stay and watch them. They nodded and I stayed quite a while and was astounded at the speed in which they played the game and realised how lucky I was in declining their invitation to play. I would have lost!

It was time for me to return to the ship, but not before I stood under a drain pipe from which water was pouring after running off a roof. You know the feeling, you are already soaked from the tropical downpour, so why not get thoroughly wet and cool off at the same time. That night, back on board, one of my companions used my tweezers to remove some of the hairs from the cactii plants from my body. I was covered with them and it took several days to get rid of them all. I now treat cactii plants with a lot of respect! The next day the Army took some of us to a sandy coral reef beach, where as usual there are always some people who want to be first in the water. The trucks stopped and even before the tailboards were lowered, people jumped out with their trunks on and made a dash for the shore line and dived in. Their efforts were short lived – they stood up in the water with their chests spurting blood. The water was only about 18 inches deep with a coral floor! Some of the party went climbing for coconuts, but after struggling to break them open, they sheepishly asked the watching local natives to help them. They did, by breaking them using the edge of a sawn off tree trunk. The Army lads had been trying to break them open by banging them on the flat table of the tree trunk!

Our final port of call was Mombasa, where the following day we were to disembark for RAF Eastleigh, Nairobi. We watched the Army lads disembark first and they headed for the 'cattle trucks' to start their journey by rail. We then asked when were the RAF personnel going to disembark. We eventually discovered that the senior RAF Officer i/c had inspected the 'cattle trucks', which were carriages with wooden slat seating, and he had decided that this form of transport was not up to white mans standards for a 2 day crossing of semi desert to Nairobi. He then phoned RAF Eastleigh and requested air transport for the following day. Fortunately for the Brylcreem Boys, the pongos had already departed and were not aware that we were going to fly! After a night on the town in Mombasa, the following day we flew to Eastleigh and on the way we spotted the train still chugging along! On arrival, we were left to fend for ourselves, to find the Mess, to sort out where to sleep and to search out the Bedding Store. The next morning the CO called us to a 'welcoming' meeting and after preliminaries, and was foolish enough to ask "Any complaints?". In typical ex-brat fashion, I simply mentioned the fact that we had arrived, totally unexpected and had to organise ourselves. At the time, my complaint was answered, and as far as I knew – end of story. A week or two later, the Ops Room secretly let me know that my tapes had been substantiated, because for the past two years I had been paid as Acting Cpl. I thought that was great and waited for the call from the Orderly Room. A week later I received a message to report to the CO's office. "Woodford, you have been posted to the Canal Zone and you will leave as soon as possible". I naturally queried the posting, and he said "I don't like you and I don't want you on my Station, so I have got you posted to the Canal Zone". "What about my stripes Sir?". "Yes, they have arrived, but I am certainly not going to give them to you. They may reach you sometime, somewhere, now get out". I think this was in November/December 1951.

I had an interesting flight up to the Canal Zone in a Dakota, sitting on the floor and using the aircraft fuselage as a back rest. I think we stopped three times en route – Jubba in the jungle, Khartoum and Wadi Haifa on the banks of the Blue or White Nile. The worst take-off was at Wadi Haifa, at least, I think it was Wadi Haifa. The pilot said "Don't worry. I've done this many times" as we raced towards a sheer cliff face at the end of the runway, and, seeing the skyline disappear and the cliff face filling the windscreen, he pulled back on the stick and we just missed the cliff top. He said "I hope you enjoyed that one!". We had a nice stop-over in Khartoum – it was the only place I have ever tasted sarsaparilla – lovely. On arrival in Egypt I went to 107 MU Kasfareet and it was as if the hate campaign against me had followed me, because I was picked on and hassled most of the time. I even studied navigation in case I could steal one of the Meteors on the drome and fly home! I was desperate, then I was picked on once again and that was when I told them in no uncertain terms what they could all do to themselves and the Air Force! Two years earlier they had refused my application to buy myself out, now I was being discharged on medical grounds for free. At the last minute, they asked me what would persuade me to stay in. I told them that many times I had applied for pilot training, so they put this to whoever adjudicated on these matters and the reply came back "If it was wartime, he is just the chap we are looking for, but in peacetime we could not take the risk of trusting him with a few million pounds worth of aircraft!". I flew back to the UK in a York via Luqa, and it was a bumpy ride all the way to Northolt. It was then on to Halton Hospital, and, after seven years to the day, I was set free and went back to college to study as a Mechanical Engineer and graduated in 1957.

32. Travels With A Reluctant 'Pig' Or Never Fear, Freddy's Fixed It For Christmas

Toddy Hood

The Scene: 52 Sqn, RAAF Butterworth, Malaya, early December 1964…

"Toddy, we're off". It was Fred, a recently arrived pilot with a 'happy go lucky' way with him. "We're off to the UK. There's a refurbished 'pig' to be collected on 14th December". "That's a bit tight for Christmas Fred". "Never you fear my lad, your Uncle Fred has been fixing that. The CO says we can go early, do our own air tests and maybe hurry things up a bit. And the Aussie Dak Squadron have a spare crew to come with us. We can do two legs a day if we have to". H'mmm, with a bit of luck we could make it. Anyway, with Fred along, we'd have a few laughs.

10th Dec – At RAF Hullavington, we did a long air test on Valetta 814. In the air she wallowed her way over S.W. England, refusing to trim out to the pilot's satisfaction. She really was a bit of a pig! Anyway, on the 14th we took her from Hullavington to RAF Lyneham. On the 15th, the

Aussies who had been swanning around London, arrived complete with a large Christmas tree. Covered with plastic, they were sure it would be the talk of Penang. At 09.45 hrs we took off for Nice. "I'll get you half hourly pin points" said Alec the Aussie Nav. Some chance I thought, having seen the met chart. Cloud covered the ground the whole way. It was a grim trip, with the clunk of ice bouncing between prop and fuselage – so much for our new paint job! Later that evening we had a drizzly walk along the promenade des Anglais looking at a grey Mediterranean. Roll on Penang, palm trees and blue seas!

16th Dec – Took off from Nice to RAF Luqa in Malta. Cloud cover again, Elba appeared, our first view of the ground. At Luqa it was wet and cold, just in time to pick up some cheap grog to comfort us on our way. Then on to RAF El Adem for a night stop – dry and warm thank goodness.

17th Dec – Departed for Cairo, all ready changed into civvies for refuelling there as RAF uniforms weren't popular. An uneventful trip until inside Egyptian airspace, then bedlam. Excited Arab voices on the RT instructed us to hold our position, so we did a racetrack. We heard a Hastings, overflying to Aden, being told to land immediately. Eventually we were given clearance to land at Cairo and park in a remote area of the airfield and not to leave the aircraft until told. We gathered that an Israeli plane had been shot down whilst approaching Cairo. (Later found out that it was an American Oil Company light aircraft with four civilians on board.) We taxied past the Hastings which had been en route to Aden. Pongo's in civilian clothes were lined up under armed guard. What a welcome! I went to Air Traffic to file a flight plan on my own. The lift boy spoke good English and showed me both the Met Office and Flight Planning, and then took me down again. Having a few minutes to spare, I decided to go into the Terminal building where I could see some shops. I always bought stamps when landing in a new country for my children's stamp collections, so I tried the nearest door, but it was locked. A nearby Arab grabbed my arms and held me tight while shouting hysterically to others nearby. I said in 'Haltonese' – "Unhand me you Oriental gentleman, I don't want your dirty postcards" or something like that!! The shouting got worse and a sizeable crowd gathered, all shouting and waving their arms. The only recognisable word which I could understand was "Israeli, Israeli". As I was pulled around, I saw the lift door open and out leapt the lift boy, this time waving a large pistol. He used the pistol to make a path towards me. The first man who had grabbed me was still holding on to me tightly. He had his ears boxed by the lift boy's free hand, followed by a swift boot up the backside which sent him off cursing. The rest of the crowd were then harangued by my new friend for a couple of minutes, then they scattered. He suggested, not unreasonably, that maybe this wasn't a good time to go shopping, as feelings against foreigners were running high and there were rumours of Israeli saboteurs being active. Anyway, we shook hands and I returned thankfully to the quiet corner of the airfield. As soon as the refuelling was finished, we took off for Asmara (we didn't mention Aden in case they refused to give us clearance). Half-way down the Red Sea coast, our Aussie co-pilot spotted oil on our starboard engine cowling and the oil pressure was a bit low. Eventually that engine was shut down. Riyadh was our diversion, but that didn't seem to be a good idea after our experiences in Cairo, so we pressed on to Asmara. After landing and removing the cowling, a large crack was obvious in a metal oil pipe. Fred found a local smithy who could only braize the crack for us. Fred decided that this was on, until we could get across to Aden for some proper servicing. We dined that evening on rice and goat meat in a fairly tatty hotel.

18th Dec – Both engines behaved themselves. On landing at RAF Khormaksah and taxiing to Station Flight, who should open the door but Bob P......, ex-Engineering Officer of 49 Sqn. We had shared an old farmhouse in Marham village as a hiring. He soon had us on board a Land Rover and out to the Valetta graveyard where we had the pick of oil pipes. Bob fetched me for supper that evening and I had a bumpy pillion ride on the back of his Honda to Steamer Point to meet his family again. What a contrast to Penang! Oily gravel beach, no green anywhere, but the welcome was warm. Unfortunately Bob found plenty of problems with 814 and all the next day he ferried more bits to 814 from the graveyard. He and his lads did a sterling job to get us on our way.

20th Dec – We took off for RAF Masirah on the East coast of Oman. Feeling more confident that 814 was behaving herself, we refuelled at Masirah and left for Karachi. On landing, a different set of problems beset us. Fred's vaccination certificates were out of date! Despite vociferous protests, he was sent off in an ambulance to an isolation ward in the local hospital.

21st Dec – When we arrived at the aircraft in the morning, one engine was running and Fred was anxious to take off. I had to tell him the bad news that Air Traffic wouldn't clear us to fly to Delhi. "I must tell you that our velly good friends in India would not like you to start an epidemic" we were told with much head wagging and hand shaking. Some time later we convinced the Pakistani authorities that we were no serious danger to anybody and they cleared us to take off for Bombay. Much relieved, we took off in a much happier state of mind. At Bombay, the Military Attaché's department wanted to know our reasons for not keeping to our original diplomatic clearance schedule! I sent a signal flannelling about headwinds and fuel states. Luckily nobody wanted to see our vaccination certificates! We set off for Madras, where storm warnings were out as the tail end of a typhoon was battering the coast. The next day the winds across to Car Nicobar island were too strong, so we spent the day wandering around Madras. We saw quite extensive storm damage to buildings and dozens of rickety bamboo scaffoldings being used for repairs – dangerous to use and to pass under. All the beautifully carved fishing boats were high above the tide marks, some damaged. On the old promenade, the statues of Queen Victoria and Co had suffered from years of salt spray. That evening, Fred, a great trencherman, challenged the hotel to produce a really hot curry because on the previous evening it had been too mild! Everyone else hastily withdrew from this challenge and said a mild curry was just the ticket. Fred insisted that we all tried his curry. I swear it started my bald patch! Anyway, Fred manfully tucked into his feast, washing it down with brandy sours. I was unfortunate enough to share a room with him!!!

23rd Dec – At breakfast, with the winds moderating, we gladly accepted the Aussies offer to pilot the next leg. After take off, Fred communed with nature on the Elsan or lay on our kit until after a couple of hours he felt better. After we were committed by our fuel state to continue to Car Nicobar, the starboard engine revs started to hunt, eventually it was feathered. In clear empty skies, we made a very gradual descent and landed on the lonely airstrip of Car Nicobar. Everyone on this Indian Air Force outpost was glad to see an aircraft, as their regular visitor was once a month. Off came the cowlings – suspect a u/s constant speed unit. Eventually Vick got through to Butterworth on H/F. With three aircraft on detachment to Borneo and only one serviceable aircraft on base, the Squadron had stood down for Christmas. Now, almost resigned to spending Christmas on Car Nicobar, we nevertheless sent an appealing message for help. On the small Indian base, rations were running low and they were living on local food, but there was plenty of tea for tiffen. The CO was an Anglo Indian gentleman of the old school and he and Fred hit it off straight away. Apparently all the natives were Christians and the only real crime in their code was to lose your temper. Every year several people used to jump over the cliffs for doing just that, and we were feeling bad tempered about that engine! As we were staying the night, we were included in a general invitation to go carol singing around the island. The CO had been drilling his thirty or so men in the English words of well known carols. He had enough copies for everyone, so that evening we climbed into their one and only lorry – three Brits, three Aussies, Sikhs, Hindus, Moslems and one Christian Anglo Indian.

That night we visited the three largest villages on the island. At each one the whole village, young and old, gathered around the attap meeting house. They sang the carols and hymns most beautifully and in wonderful harmony, all in English. Then came our turn, with Fred and the CO out front as conductors. We did our best, and, much to our delight, our efforts were greeted with great enthusiasm. Then the eating started. Officially there was no alcohol, but we were suspiciously more cheerful after coconut 'wine' was passed around at each village! When we finally returned to the airfield in the early hours, we broke open the last of our Duty Free brandy. We sat on the square of coral sand outside the CO's basha, no lights but the stars, and sang amongst others "In the Stores" which the older Indians seemed to know.

24th Dec – Breakfast was of chapatti's and tea. Vick raised Butterworth again and apparently a crew of volunteers were coming out from 52 Sqn with our spares. Three hours later, Johnny B....., a sterling ex-Polish Air Force pilot, arrived. A quick hello/goodbye and he was away home. Fred insisted on doing most of the work himself – the fitter who came with the spares wasn't too pleased! Anyway, it wasn't long before we were saying our farewells to our new friends and we had an uneventful last leg. Kedah Peak had its usual bubble of cloud, otherwise it was gin clear. After we landed and unloaded our Marks & Spencer goodies, there was one final laugh. The Aussies took off the plastic cover from their Christmas tree. There was a shower of needles and a very, very, bare trunk, but Fred had kept his promise.

33. Journey North

Ginge Mushens

Tony Carlyle and I hitchhiked north and the journey was a nightmare. We had started off quite well getting to Hatfield, then St Albans, where the Great North Road passed through, in record time, having got a lift in a smart vehicle driven by some rich plutocrat. Well, he seemed very rich to we two, as we had about 4 bob (20p in 'new' money) between us! He had picked us up in Aston Clinton and we had congratulated ourselves as we thought that it was going to be like this all the way, relaxing in plush upholstery and chatting about how we often did this kind of thing. He was quite impressed at the bravery of us young stalwarts.

The next lift, after many hours of walking, was a lorry with big cable drums on the back. There was no room in the cab, so we climb onto the back of the truck. The drums were covered in axle grease and we tried to find a spot away from the grease and out of the wind, which I might add was damn cold, even though we had our greatcoats on done up to the neck. This was turning out to be a nightmare, as the roads in those days were full of ruts and potholes, also the suspension of the wagons was far removed from today's sleek road transport.

At about 02.00 hrs we were deposited near Doncaster outside a transport café. This was the most grottiest 'greasy spoon' establishment I have ever encountered, and I've been in a few. As we had no cash to spare, we asked around till this chap said he was going north and he would give us a lift as he could do with the company. We embarked on the journey in a box like contraption, which swayed like mad due to it being overloaded. By this time both of us were dog tired, and as the cab had no heat, we were very cold. With the three of us jammed together in the cab, we derived some form of warmth and settled down to get some shuteye.

Unfortunately the driver had the same thought, and as I was next to him, he requested me to make sure we didn't run off the road! This must have been his reason for company and I was, to say the least, a bit worried, as the last time I had driven any sort of vehicle was a tractor when I was 11 years old on the farm where I was evacuated to and I had a whole field to myself, and not a narrow strip of road with vehicles on either side! I managed to stay awake, tried to keep him awake and also keeping hold of the steering wheel to stop us from hitting the side of the road, thereby ending up in the ditch, or hitting another vehicle coming at us on the other side of the road. This got really scary, so I said we had better stop for a rest, or the rest would be permanent! Carlyle was away in dreamland, so I gave him a big shove to wake him and said we had better dump this lift as it was too bloody dangerous to say the least. We ended up on a stretch of road miles from anywhere, but in the vicinity of York. Our lift driver had pulled over to the roadside to get some sleep – if he was not already out for the count.

We managed to get another lift to Durham City, and by this time we were a bit cheesed off with the whole idea of hitchhiking. We were cold, hungry and dirty, and not a pretty sight. Chiefy Thomas would certainly have given us a few days jankers for our general presentation! Any rate, we decided to get the bus to Sunderland, which was only 10 miles away. This was now well into Saturday morning and we were due back in camp on the Monday morning, so no time for bed, as we could not waste any more leave, so after arriving home we got washed and pressed our gear, cleaning off all the dirt and grease ready for the trip into town to see our mates, then off to the pub and then the dance at the Rink Ballroom, which was similar to the Barrowlands in Glasgow or the Hammersmith

Palais in London. Needless to say we got the train back to camp, borrowing the fare off our parents.

The preface above was to give a background for the reason for my next travelling decision. I normally went to Jack Smith's home in Goffs Oak for any 72 hour passes, but I decided that this bird in Sunderland was missing my attention, so a visit was required to allay any fears of neglect on my part. The hitchhike idea was obviously not considered, as previously mentioned, so what to do? I had worked out that if one got the train to Baker Street from Wendover, then the train – after changing from steam to electric at Rickmansworth – came in on the underground line. So, to get on the Inner Circle line was a simple matter of jumping over the barrier, as the platforms were adjacent. Then, when one got off at Kings Cross, you paid 6d at the barrier, the fare for a full Inner Circle line ride which the collector put in his pocket, and here you were at stage two. I might add at this point that, as there was no corridor on the train, then you need only purchase a ticket to Great Missenden and stay on the train to Baker Street, as ticket checks were out and also it was cheaper!

At Kings Cross I banked on the trains being jam packed, which they were, and, with the excuse ready "I'm seeing my mate off", I purchased a platform ticket from the machine next to the Kiosk, got it clipped at the barrier, then made my way to my previously selected train. Just seconds before the train departed, I boarded and pushed my way through the crowded corridor to a spot near the toilets, where I could view two carriage corridors. As luck would have it, the toilets were full of Guardsmen, and as there were no seats vacant, the corridors were also packed, so I reckoned on being safe from ticket collectors till I got to Newcastle. If the collector did manage to get near, he would have to check out the Guardsmen and I should be able to slip by while he was engaged in sorting out the drunken squaddies.

The journey was uneventful, apart from me having to ask the squaddies to move so I could use the toilet. On being refused, I said it was possible that one of them could get wet, as my adrenaline was a bit high. They were quite affable after that, possibly due to the big words I used and my funny red-banded hat, which puzzled them. Newcastle was my next test and it was so simple. There were two wooden sentry type boxes at the exit, each having a uniformed ticket collector. They had the boxes so placed to form two separate queues, which normally was okay, but the rush from the train, with hundreds of passengers, completely surrounded the exit, with people pushing and shoving to get out and so on to other transport to complete their journey home. They more or less pelted the tickets at the collectors and rushed through. I just followed the crowd and slipped through. It was a simple matter then to purchase a single to Sunderland, walk to Platform 5, board legitimately and journey home, where I arrived about 11 o'clock in the evening on the same day, so all in all it beat hitchhiking.

34. Some Dreams Do Come True

Eric Mold

Before World War ll broke out, I was a young lad living in Greenford, Middlesex, and my mum and dad subscribed to two boy's weekly magazines for me – the Modern Wonder and the Hotspur. I could not wait to get my hands on the Hotspur every week. It contained a story about a chap that did all kinds of daring deeds flying around in a plane that was made of steel, had wings as sharp as razors and flew as fast as a bullet, with the flames of a rocket coming from it's tail.

Little did know that 25 years later I would be flying that same plane. The F.106 Starfighter flew faster than a bullet, and in the afterburner a sheet of flame shot out of the tail 10 to 20 ft long. Only bits of it were made of steel, but I have actually sharpened my pencil on the leading edge of one of its 7 ft wings (it was 57 ft long).

Eventually I flew 1,200 hours in that bird, it was by far the highlight of my career, right next to the three years I spent in Station Workshops, Schools and on the Henderson Parade Ground at RAF Halton during my apprenticeship.

35. I Learnt About Flying from That…

Fred Hoskins

At one time there was, and possibly still is, an RAF flight safety publication or journal called *Air Clues*, and in it was a column entitled 'I Learnt About Flying From That!' in which pilots would confess various errors from which they claimed to have learnt and which were intended to help others from avoiding the same. I often wondered how many confessions had still to be told, and lately I have been thinking of a few of my own.

In 1950 I started my pilot training on a Percival Prentice Mk.T1, which had replaced the Tiger Moth. The Prentice had a fixed undercarriage and was fairly spacious, with side-by-side seats for instructor and pupil, under a large canopy with a sliding hatch or window on each side. There was a third seat in the back for, it was alleged, a second pupil to sit and learn from what was going on in front. The adverse effect on the pupil struggling in the front, of having an audience in the back, had presumably not been considered. However, the only time the back seat was used, so far as I am aware, was when an instructor took two pupils to a satellite airfield for a spell of circuits and landings. Perhaps the Prentice might reasonably be described as being like a taxi with wings, a good aircraft for going away for the weekend – not that we Flight Cadets were permitted such liberties.

Not long after my first solo I was sent up to do a session of solo spinning, and when spinning or doing aerobatics solo the rule was to recover by 5,000 ft, so this meant starting the manoeuvres at about 7,000 ft. With the low power of the Prentice, it took quite a long time to climb to that great height. Naturally, the weather had to be good for inexperienced pupils like me to carry out the exercise, so I enjoyed climbing out over Lincolnshire looking for a space to do my spins. I had actually enjoyed the spinning I had done dual, but as it was my first time solo I was a bit apprehensive. Remembering the drills and checks, on reaching 7,000 ft I had a good look round to see that all was clear (there could be a lot of activity around RAF Cranwell at that time), tightened and locked my harness, checked there were no loose articles in the cockpit, that the flaps were up, that there was enough fuel and that the engine temperatures and pressures were within limits. At last, the spin! Straight and level, reducing power, nose above the horizon, speed falling off, throttle closed, stick further back and as the judder of the stall started, stick right back into the stomach and full left rudder. A flick and, success, a veritable spin to the left as per the book! As I said, I quite enjoyed spinning so I let it continue for a while and then I thought about recovering, the procedure for which is to apply full opposite rudder, pause and then ease the stick forward, and when the spin stops, ease out of the dive and put on power to climb up again. So, I started the recovery action. At least, I thought that was what I was doing, but, read on.......... I applied full opposite rudder and waited. The spin to the left continued unabated and I sat there with the stick still hard back in my stomach. Becoming aware that the altimeter needle was turning rather rapidly, I decided not to wait any longer but to put the stick forward. A few more turns and to my delight the spin actually stopped! I eased back on the stick, opened the throttle and as I levelled out and began to climb away, I noticed that the altimeter needle was just coming up to the 2,000 ft mark – from the lower side! For some reason this made me feel a little peculiar, as evidenced by a little shaking all over and sweating of the palms and forehead, so I opened my side hatch to get a little bit of cool air. At that moment, I made a thank-offering to the 'gods of the air' by sharing my breakfast with them, scattering it in the slipstream. The cynical might say that this was merely "Yawning in Technicolor", but I prefer the more reverent interpretation. I did not venture another spin that morning!

Did you spot the mistake? Yes, of course! I said the recovery action was "Opposite rudder, pause, stick forward", but I put on opposite rudder and then, instead of just pausing briefly, I waited for the rotation to stop before putting the stick forward. Thinking about it afterwards, I realised that in my dual spinning we had recovered almost as soon as we entered the spin and I had come to believe that rudder alone would stop the spin and only then was it necessary to put the stick forward. My putting the stick forward was done in desperation and in the belief that I was not doing the right thing! So, I can safely say that I learnt from that little fright and I can also say that when I became an instructor, none of my pupils were left in any doubt as to the correct way of recovering from a spin, even though they were not permitted to spin solo in the Vampire, with all the complications of 'B over A ratio' and the effects of applying in-spin aileron.

It was not long after the spinning incident that I was sent off to do circuits and landings to include some flapless landings. Unusually, the grass runway in use was the short one running south to north at the village end of the south airfield. As I said, it was short and there was little or no wind. I recall that it was rather a hazy morning. After a few uneventful circuits, I turned on finals for a flapless landing. By definition, this would entail a longish flat approach and it was made longer and flatter by the absence of wind. I did not do it very well, came over the hedge a bit too fast and just floated on and on instead of putting on power and going round again. So, when I finally touched down, there was very little runway left, and having run out of grass I had perforce to use the field full of cabbages at the end of the runway! I found that it is not easy to taxy a Prentice in a field of cabbages, so I had to shut down the engine and sit there waiting for help. I called the tower, which was then situated near the old swimming pool and gymnasium, and told them what must have been obvious if they had been looking. Quite probably they had not been looking, as it seemed that they had not been listening either. I came to that conclusion because, although our callsigns indicated our Flights, they asked me my Flight so that they could telephone the Flight Commander to arrange to get me out. Not understanding what I had been asked, I repeated that I was in the cabbage field, whereupon a laconic voice, presumably an instructor, intruded with the drawling remark "They want to know your Flight, you fool, not your plight". The Prentice? There was no damage, just a bucket or so of earth and some greenery in the undercarriage fairings. What happened to me? I can't remember.

After getting my wings and commission in 1951, in January 1952, I moved all the way from Cranwell to RAF Swinderby to join No.204 Advanced Flying School and then went with the same AFS when it was transferred to RAF Bassingbourn. Having completed the course on the Mosquito Mk.T3 and Mk.FB6, I was sent to Singapore, where I converted onto the Hornet, another de Havilland design, at the Far East Training Squadron (FETS) at RAF Seletar. From there I was fortunate enough to be posted to No.33 Squadron at RAF Butterworth in the north of Malaya, right opposite the island of Penang. Butterworth was a small station in those days and was commanded by a Wing Commander. Effectively, it comprised just 33 Sqn, an Armament Practice Camp and the support for those units. This was my first squadron and in due course it turned out to be my last, as I had the added good fortune to command it at RAF Odiham from 1971 to 1973, when it was equipped with Puma helicopters. Butterworth, in 1952, had the reputation of being somewhat 'wild'. This reputation had something to do with its remoteness – far from the delights of Singapore – and something to do with drinking Tiger beer, I seem to recall. Indeed, the instructors on FETS advised us that we would have to be prepared to play liar dice and drink Tiger beer when we went to Butterworth for the armament training phase of our course. Without those attributes it seemed that we would lack what is now known as 'street cred'. In fact, the favoured tipple was Anchor beer, and those who drank Tiger were thought to be a bit on the rough side, even by Butterworth standards. Anchor was so popular that there was a hush of disbelief and horror when the Padre referred one day to St Paul, when caught out in a storm, "Casting out three anchors". Anchor was even consumed at the table on dining-in nights without the knowledge of the top table. All that was necessary was for those preferring it to wine was to ask the bar boy to bring 'Chateau Anchor', whereupon a bottle would be produced wrapped in a napkin and poured very carefully to minimise the head. But I digress. Butterworth's reputation was also related to the fact that everyone had been living in attap huts until just before I arrived, and to the fact that all the aircrew and officers carried pistols at all times (this was during the Emergency). At lunchtime, all weapons were deposited (i.e. left lying about) on a table in the entrance to the Mess. All in all, there was a certain element of the Wild West – particularly as it was known that a few of the more unconventional souls would think little of firing at, e.g. a snake, if such was to be seen in the

Mess. By the time I arrived, brick buildings had been erected, but the squadron offices were still in tents and the crewroom was an attap shelter with no sides – much more romantic than the brick edifice that took its place, and a sight cooler. It was in one of those tents that I had my arrival interview with the Squadron Commander, Sqn Ldr C.C.F. Cooper. After the usual exchanges, he said "Tell me, Hoskins, have you ever had an accident?". "Oh, no sir!" I replied (forgetting about the cabbage patch), to which he responded "Good. Keep it up" – or words to that effect.

Our aircraft were parked in line along the disused north/south runway, which was not very wide, and it was necessary to taxi into the line from the front and then execute a tight 180 degree turn to end up facing forward. This entailed using a lot of brake on the inside wheel and a lot of power on the outside engine. Not long after my interview, I returned from a flight to find that I was being marshalled into a rather narrow gap in the line. I started my 180 degree left turn and could see that it was going to be tight, but had the reassurance of an airman at the starboard wingtip giving me the thumbs up. By this means I managed to slide my starboard wingtip over the port wingtip of the next aircraft. Looking back, I wonder if the National Serviceman thought he would get his revenge for being called up, was bored and thought it would be funny, or whether he put his thumb up in mistake for down. Nevertheless it was my fault, but I do not recall receiving any punishment for this offence. In fact, I am not sure whether the situation became known beyond the Flight Commander, because good old Chiefy Sinfield (an ex-Halton brat) just took off the wingtip fairings, knocked out the dents and screwed them back on again.

As I have indicated, 33 Sqn was equipped with the Hornet Mk.F3 (the trainer version), and we also had a few Mk.F4's which could carry a vertical camera for photographic reconnaissance, but the role of the squadron was fighter/ground attack. The Hornet was, to put it simply, a smaller and single seat derivative of the Mosquito, with a wingspan of 45 ft instead of 54 ft, and entry to the cockpit through a sliding canopy instead of squeezing up through a small hatch in the bottom corner of the cabin. In my eyes the Hornet was one of the best looking aircraft ever built, its sleek lines enhanced by the de Havilland trademark, the elliptical tail fin and rudder, and, in the case of the Hornet, made even sleeker by a dorsal fairing into the fin. The Hornet was designed for long range bomber escort in the war with Japan, but the war ended before it could be used in that role. In Malaya it was employed on strikes against the Communist Terrorists, and for that purpose was armed with two 500 lb bombs, four 60 lb rockets and four 20 mm cannon. It was fast (420 knots) and as the propellers were 'handed' it had no tendency to swing on take-off, unlike the Mosquito where it was necessary to lead with the port throttle and then bring up the starboard, repeating this process several times, because if you opened both throttles together you would find yourself going at right angles across the grass instead of along the runway. The squadron had two Mosquito Mk.T3's for dual checks and for instrument flying training. They were not very serviceable aircraft and so one did not get the chance to fly them very often, and when the day came it all seemed a bit difficult after the sweet little Hornet. Shortly after joining 33 Sqn, I was detailed for some solo instrument flying in a Mosquito, which entailed flying out to sea north of Penang to find a cloud to fly about in. However, that was not the problem. The only useable runway at that time ran east-west. There was a taxi track running to the east end of the runway and it was here that trouble started. I thought to myself that it would save a lot of time if I were to do my checks before take-off while taxying, instead of at the halt just before moving onto the runway. I got to the bit where you check that the flaps are up and reached for the flap lever..... you've guessed!

The undercarriage, flaps and bomb doors were controlled by three levers, grouped together in the centre of the bottom of the Mosquito's instrument panel. To avoid confusion, each lever had a different shaped knob and the undercarriage lever also had a safety catch on it which had to be depressed in order to unlock the lever and lift it. Taxying along, I reached out my right hand and grasped the undercarriage lever instead of the flap lever, released the catch and raised the lever. Immediately there was an amazingly loud noise in my earphones coming from the undercarriage warning horn. Fortunately, this caused me to jam the lever down again, but when I looked at the undercarriage indicator lights I saw that one was Red and it would not return to Green. My thought processes were dominated by this noise in my ears and my reaction was to think that everyone at Butterworth could hear it and must know what an idiot I was. That ought to have caused me to do the sensible thing, namely, to stop the engines, tell the tower and wait for someone to come out and put in the undercarriage locking pins. Remember, the Mosquito had a tail wheel, so the backwards tilt of the fuselage and the undercarriage legs created a geometric lock and there was really no likelihood of the undercarriage collapsing if I shut down. However, this did not occur to me and my one thought was to get into the air as soon as I could! Therefore I continued to taxi, cautiously, using the brakes as little as possible and pushing down on the undercarriage lever every few seconds. I simply cannot remember whether I ran up the engines and checked the magnetos before going onto the runway, but I suppose I must have done. The Red light was for the port wheel and the turn was to starboard, so at least the brakes were not acting against the unlocked leg. However, it might be argued that the extra power on the port engine for the turn would have the same effect. Nevertheless, I lined up for take-off and began to open the throttles. As I have explained, the Mosquito had a marked tendency to swing and to prevent this it was necessary to lead with the port throttle and then bring up the starboard. In itself, this could be a little challenging if one was relatively new and did not have much continuity on the Mosquito, but I was also intent on changing hands from throttles to stick so as to free my right hand to push on the undercarriage lever as often as possible. Also, the wretched horn was still blasting away at me! Suffice it to say that there was a decidedly dodgy feeling about the take-off run. In the event, the port leg held until I attained flying speed – just. I felt the leg go and the wing drop just at that moment and put on opposite aileron to lift the wing at the same time as I eased back the stick to get off the ground. After climbing away and settling down, I found a cloud and did some IF as if nothing had happened – well, almost. I then returned to base and was glad to find that the undercarriage came down satisfactorily and locked with both warning lights Green. It had not occurred to me that the undercarriage system might perhaps have been damaged by the lurching take-off, but luckily there was no harm done. The landing was not too good, and after signing the Form 700 my Flight Commander told me so. I acknowledged this with due humility and forebore to say what I was thinking – "You should have seen the take-off!".

The only other confession I am prepared to make at the moment also relates to my days at Butterworth. It was an interesting and exciting place to be, with Penang for off-duty pursuits and most of us belonging to the Penang Sports Club for the rugby, and to the Penang Swimming Club for the swimming. With rugby on Wednesday and Saturday afternoons, and probably two games of water polo on a Sunday morning, I can see now why I was a just a bit slimmer in those days. As to work, we had plenty of opportunity for dive-bombing, rocketing and firing on our own ranges and, of course, plenty of the real thing on anti-CT strikes. This was perhaps the most active time of the long Emergency, but strangely enough we did not have to do much at weekends even though the Army could hardly pull out of the jungle every Friday afternoon. However, we always had four pilots on standby at the weekends in case of need.

As well as sport, there were some opportunities for other social activities, and one Saturday evening a crowd of us, including all the duty pilots, were over in Penang for a dance at the Eastern & Oriental (E & O) Hotel. So far as I can recall, it was the St Andrew's Society's celebration of the Saint's day; it matters not, but it was a formal affair and we were all in our white sharkskin dinner jackets as in the days of the Raj. It was in the early hours of the Sunday morning that we made our way from the E & O in Georgetown to catch the last ferry, crossed to the mainland and then journeyed the last few miles from Butterworth town to the airfield. We had imbibed reasonably freely, so it is possible that we might have chosen to travel the 4 or 5 miles by trishaw instead of by taxi, and in that case we would probably have raced the trishaws for part of the way, with the trishaw men in the seats and doing the pedalling ourselves. Whatever the situation, we arrived back at the Mess at about 02.00 hrs in a state of merriment and thought it highly amusing to be greeted by the Station Duty Officer with the news that we were to have a call at 05.00 hrs for briefing at 06.00 hrs for a strike. "Ha ha!" we said, "Pull the other one! It's got bells on". Although all this was hilariously funny at 02.00 hrs, somehow we could not see the humour of it three hours later when the early call materialised, followed by the briefing, with a breakfast in between for which we could find no enthusiasm. I suppose the reason for this must have been something we had eaten at the E & O. Briefing was a fairly quiet affair and the met forecast did not lead to joy unbounded – low cloud over base, with drizzle, cloud at various heights on our route and, in short, not the sort of day for which you would spend money on going to Malaysia today. Not much was said while we were getting changed and drawing lines on our maps. These lines were long because the target area was near Chukai, in Trengganu, on the other side of Malaya. After picking up our parachutes and signing the authorisation book and the F.700, we mooched out to our Hornets, still very quiet in that gloomy grey morning with a covering of low cloud. Our state is illustrated by the fact that one of our number walked right past his aircraft and seemed intent on going to the other end of the airfield until he was called back, and another one of us had great difficulty in climbing the ladder onto the wing of his Hornet. However, we started up and taxied out to the west, the sea end of the runway, where the armourers plugged in the pigtails of the rockets. Take-off was in two pairs at an interval of 30 seconds. I was flying as Number Two, on the starboard wing of the formation leader. The take-off in close formation went off satisfactorily, strange to relate, and I found afterwards that although we did not usually use oxygen because we rarely flew high enough, that morning we all decided to plug in the oxygen from ground level. By this time the layer of cloud was not very thick so it was not necessary to keep close formation for more than a few minutes, and as we turned to allow the second pair to catch up we opened out and settled down in battle formation in 'finger four'. We found our way to the target and identified the area of jungle to our satisfaction.

The aim of air action was to annoy the CT's (Communist Terrorists) and keep them on the move. Usually our target would be a pin-point or a few map squares of jungle and mountain. Occasionally there would be a clearing and perhaps one might see a hut, but there were never any people to be seen on the ground. Our routine was to try to upset the CT's for as long as possible by staying over the target for as long as we could, making the strikes last rather than dropping all our bombs and firing off all our rockets and cannon in one or two attacks. With two bombs and four rockets, this meant six attacks before starting with the 20 mm cannon. My logbook shows the sortie as lasting 2 hours and 25 minutes. A 'run in and break' was the accepted method of getting a formation back on the ground, and in the squadron it was quite common for those in the crewroom to saunter outside to watch, criticise and use their expensive aircrew watches to time the event from break to last aircraft to put wheels on the runway. So, naturally, we had to close up in echelon for that run in. It would have made much more sense to slide into a very long line astern and creep in from a long straight approach. But no; the Mess was on the beach, only a few hundred yards from the sea end of the runway, and on a Sunday morning just about everyone would be watching, so there was really no alternative but to get into close echelon, bore in from over the sea at 250 knots or so and then, on arriving at about 50 ft over the end of the runway, to break formation at two second intervals. This manoeuvre entailed simultaneously hauling back on the stick, whanging on lots of aileron and closing the throttles. Then, continue the climbing turn, losing about 100 knots in the process, radiator flaps open, down with the undercarriage, flaps half-down, keep turning, start descending and aiming for the end of the runway, check the undercarriage lights Green, call finals, full flap, straighten up for a second or two and grease it onto the runway. With a mixture of skill and luck, a formation leader could make a virtually continuous turn from the break to the touchdown without touching the throttles, but the rest of the formation would have to straighten up on the downwind leg. Though tired, we made it successfully.

It was of course, Sunday, and the event of the day in the Mess at Butterworth on Sundays was, inevitably, a huge curry lunch after a few beers. As it was not all that often that we were called out at weekends, we concluded that we could relax; we all thought that we had done our share for the day. But the idea of beer was unappealing, and, funnily, that Sunday, the curry did not seem as attractive as usual, so three of us slunk off to our rooms after a glass of orange squash! The other, being of a stronger constitution, and having decided that the chances of more flying were simply non-existent, indulged in a beer or two, though I doubt whether he ate much curry! Imagine our horror and disbelief when, after only an hour or so on our beds, we were called out again in the afternoon! Luckily, the second target was not all that far from home and the sortie lasted only an hour and 20 minutes, but the close formation was not at all steady on our return and I recall quite vividly some very jerky antics as we closed up for the final run in.

Today, one hopes, this could not happen. One wonders why it did not seem to occur to any one of us to question our fitness to fly on that day, and, moreover, to fly for almost four hours, and for over half the time with a full load of armament. It is impossible to guess whether any of us would have passed or failed a breathalyzer test at the time of take-off! Whatever the alcohol situation might or might not have been, the plain fact is that we were all very tired and unfit for that reason alone. Clearly, if we had any doubts ourselves we were not going to say so – but I don't think it even occurred to us. Who would wish to be seen as either unable to hold one's drink or trying to duck out of an arduous sortie? I dread to think of the repercussions that would have attended an apology from all four of us that the operational sortie would have to be cancelled! In the case of my spinning incident in the Prentice, it never occurred to me that my instructor might perhaps have been responsible, at least in part, for the fact that I was less than completely clear about the correct recovery procedure. But I did not confide in him afterwards, as I ought to have done, because I did not want anyone to know that, as it seemed to me, I had been stupid. The difficulty I had with the Mosquito undercarriage incident was completely down to me and I could blame no one – but, hang on a moment, surely it was bad design to put three levers so close together? After all, the Hornet had a much better layout.

I think I can safely say that I did learn some lessons from those experiences. The fear of appearing foolish in the eyes of others has a very strong influence. In retrospect, I can now see that in those earlier days I did not learn perhaps the most important lesson of all, which is to overcome pride and the fear of looking foolish, and to speak out at the time so that others may learn then, and not later, or never at all.

36. Go (Middle) East Young Man

Robbie Roberts

There was I (in August 1959) in a nice cushy number in the Training School at Smith's Aircraft Instruments at Cheltenham, teaching anyone RAF Brampton cared to send me about auto-pilots and flight systems, when this PWR bombshell descended – "Posted to 114 MU, Steamer Point, for AIS duties". Remembering the brief visit I had made to Aden in 1950 en route (by boat) to the Far East, the first thing I asked was "Can I get out of it and go to Bomber Command instead?". The answer was a resounding "No"! The second question was "What is AIS?". Answer – "You'll soon find out, you're going to do a 6 week course on it at RAF Melksham".

Well, I found out! What was then AIS is now called QA. "Me a Quality Inspector? Come on, I'm an Instrument Basher". "Not for the next 2 years you're not". So I got on with it and finished the course as a fully fledged (!) AIS Inspector. But that wasn't all! I was immediately sent to the Standards Room at RAF St Athan for a fortnight to learn how to check all sorts of things used to measure other things – if you follow me! Precision Measuring Equipment (PME) they called it.

By now it was well into October, and, bursting with all this new found knowledge, I was transferred from Training Command to RAF Innsworth to be prepared for the boat. That wasn't too bad, because I was occupying a Quarter at Innsworth whilst working at Smith's, so I only had to walk up the road. I was doubly fortunate because I became 'time qualified' for Chief Tech while I was being 'processed'. The promotion was published in local POR's and yours truly put up the crown. This immediately qualified me for a berth in a 2nd Class cabin on the troopship, the Empire Orwell, instead of having to travel on the troopdeck. You've no idea how much this meant unless you are prone to sea sickness as I am. By the time I got my sea legs, the voyage is usually over! The cabin made all the difference going through the Bay of Biscay, when the sea was very rough – I was able to stay in bed and be miserable in some comfort! Rough! You had better believe it! I mean, at one stage the mattress (with me on it) was thrown across the cabin on to the floor. Our steward (?) had to tie everything down after that to stop having a repeat performance! After we 'turned the corner', we made an unscheduled stop in Gibraltar for the injured to be disembarked (OC Troops with a broken arm, children's nurse with a fractured skull etc) and the rest of us were given a day's shore leave in Gib to recover! At least it was calm going through the Suez Canal and the Red Sea, and I was back to normal by the time we disembarked in Aden.

So there we were, myself and two other guys with whom I had shared the cabin, on the beach waiting for the transport to take us to the Sgts Mess at Steamer Point and looking at the barren rocks all around us with no enthusiasm whatsoever! I remember thinking "A 2 year tour here is going to feel like a lifetime". When we finally got to the Mess, which was halfway up a hill overlooking some of the barrack blocks, sports field (sand) and sea, we were told by the Mess Manager that accommodation was at a premium and most of the new arrivals had to be billeted on the verandahs until a bunk became available. It just so happened that there was one bed free in the only air-conditioned billet in the Mess. Guess who got it? The Mess Manager had been at Innsworth during my time there and our past association now paid off without any effort on my part! Finally, there I was, installed in an air-conditioned bunk, sharing with the Flt Sgt in charge of the MT Section, who decided that, being older than I, would take me under his wing. It pays to look green sometimes!!

As for work, well 114 MU was an Equipment Holding Unit, which means that all the bits and pieces for everything belonging to the RAF in the Colony were stored within its walls. The AIS Section, to which I was posted, had a SNCO inspector in each aircraft trade, plus a SNCO Chippie, with a WO and Flt Lt in charge, to carry out regular inspections of everything in order to make sure it wasn't deteriorating in storage. I had been sent out to assume charge of the Standards Room, and the guy whom I was supposed to relieve had already gone home to the UK! So much for the handover/takeover! Anyway, when I went to look at my new domain, it turned out to be a concrete building, about the size of a garden shed, with no windows and a door which led into a kind of 'air lock', with another door leading into the working area. When I opened that, I stepped into a room with benches all round the walls (like a fitted kitchen) loaded to the gunwales with PME of all sorts, and, because of their sensitivity, it had to be maintained at a temperature of 65°F. When you remember that the shade temperature outside varied between 80° in the 'winter' and 95° in the 'summer' (April to October), coupled to high humidity, this amounted to a considerable bonus and automatically made me President of the Unit's Prickly Heat Club!! Everybody at 114 MU came in to see me on one pretext or other when it got really hot, because it was the only air-conditioned building on the MU.

There was one disadvantage however, the MU had a Police Dog Section. Not many people know that once a police dog is sent overseas it never goes back to the UK, consequently, in a place like Aden, the dogs are likely to suffer from heat exhaustion when they get older. The treatment was to put them into a cooler atmosphere for anything up to a week. Yes, you've guessed it, I was the only person who had such a place! During the hot season I was always being asked to provide some relief for whichever dog was suffering. The poor old things used to lie near the air-conditioning unit absolutely flat out, not interested in anything. Unfortunately, because of the general reduction in the cleanliness which resulted from their stay, I couldn't do any work in the Standards Room while they were there. Still, the handlers cleaned up when the dogs were well enough to leave and I was able to take over again.

Mind you, there was plenty of other work to be done. I was on call for any aircraft instrument work which required AIS inspection at RAF Khormaksah, and we had to attend the docks regularly to inspect incoming cargo, particularly those items 'damaged in transit'. It could be very interesting. One day you could be inspecting aircraft parts, the next it could be paint, clothing, furniture. You name it, we inspected it. Of course we had to negotiate (argue) with the local Arab agent about who was responsible for paying for missing/damaged items. It was just co-incidental that all the Arab stevedores seemed to have better KD shorts and shirts than we did!

Another job which I had never done before, or since, was to attend the ritual burning of Married Quarter furniture at a special site dedicated to that purpose. It appears that in the Colony there was a particularly hungry and prolific insect, popularly known as the 'woolly bug'. This would eat any sort of fabric and was very partial to an appetising dish of Married Quarter, Issue 3-piece suite, or anything similar. Once infestation had been identified, there was only one solution – burning. The reason why AIS had to attend was because the destruction certificate had to be stamped by an unimpeachable authority (!) to verify that burning had actually taken place. This was to ensure that the said furniture did not appear either on the second-hand furniture market in Crater (the capital of the Colony) or in the homes (!) of any of the Arab workforce. When you consider that the Services as a whole employed about 20,000 Arabs, the effects of spreading woolly bug throughout that lot could have been quite serious – but not for the local furniture manufacturers of course. It is difficult to describe the pleasure of standing next to a pile of blazing furniture, the size of the Guy Fawkes bonfire which we used to have at Halton, in an ambient temperature of 95°F!

Life did have a social side of course. We were supposed to finish at 13.00 hrs each day, so that if you didn't mind the heat you could go swimming (in the sea), play football (on sand), or cricket (on sand), or golf (on sand), or go fishing in the harbour, or just participate in horizontal PT. Sailing was also very popular and there always seemed to be racing of one sort or the other at the Yacht Club. Steamer Point was itself a town which had grown up to service the passing commercial and tourist trade. At that time, about 400 ships a month called at Aden for bunkering services and the cruise ships called in because it was a duty free port. The main street was parallel to the shore line, with the shops all lined up on one side as if they were waiting for the tourists. Since there was no deep water quay at which boats could tie up, all loading and unloading had to be carried out by lighters. The passengers were ferried from the ship to a sort of covered landing stage and thence to the shops. The streets had no names, but were numbered. The main street being No.1 Street, with No.2 Street behind and parallel to it. The numbers continued to rise the further you went back and the streets got more and more grotty. Anywhere behind No.4 Street was 'Out of Bounds'! When a cruise ship was in, there was no point in going shopping because there was a special price for cruise ships. I have been asked to leave a shop full of tourists so that I couldn't tell them how much they were being overcharged. (Same applied in Change Alley in Singapore!) There were also passable cafes, restaurants and an open air cinema or two. Being a free port, most things were much cheaper than in the UK and one of the first things many people bought was a pair of binoculars; they could then sit at some vantage point overlooking the harbour and identify the various ships going in and out. I was assured that it could be very interesting if you really got to know the finer points. The only ship which I was able to identify was the 'Canberra' when she called in on her maiden voyage.

    I took up full bore shooting (again) and soon found myself in the squad training to represent the Middle East in the 1960 Bisley competition. We used to go to the range at Khormaksah to practice, but running down from 600 yds and diving full length into the sand wasn't much fun, even in the early morning when it was relatively cool. I was actually selected to go to the UK as part of the team (they must have been pushed!), but my (then) wife would have arrived while the team was away, so I declined the offer. I didn't want to think about what would have happened if she had arrived to find that I wasn't there to meet her but was at Bisley!

    Life in the Mess was frequently enlivened by visitors from the other Services who stopped over when going to or coming from the Far East. On one occasion, we had some US Navy bods in the Mess from a visiting destroyer; they had such a good time that they invited us back to the ship the following night, on the proviso that we could 'smuggle some booze aboard'. The excuse for the visit was that they had a cinema projector in their Mess capable of showing Cinemascope films and they were putting on a show that evening. We duly turned up at the appointed hour and were ferried out to the 'Samuel P. Roberts'. As we walked past the Master at Arms at the head of the gangplank, the bags which we were carrying made muffled clanking noises, but although I am sure they knew what was going on, we were not stopped. Once on the Mess deck, the bags were unloaded and the bottles hidden. In order to fool the powers-that-be, the liquor had to be added to two jugs of fruit juice on the table around which we sat, with no alcohol in sight. I can assure you that both jugs were heavily laced! I don't remember what the film was, but we all returned to shore without incident. The destroyer had weighed anchor by the time I was able to look for it the next day.

One thing Aden did not lack was water, and you could grow anything provided that it was watered constantly. We even had a flourishing 'camel's foot creeper' outside our bit of the Mess. My roommate had the access to the contents of fire extinguishers (ox blood) which made a very good fertiliser. You could almost see the creeper growing in front of your eyes. All this water came from artesian wells which were about 10,000 ft deep. There was so much available that one of the local Arab towns, Sheikh Othman, about 15 miles away, even had its own version of a Botanical garden. This contained all sorts of flowers, shrubs and trees, and was well worth a visit even if only to take advantage of some welcome shade once in a while. In another part of the Colony there was a series of seven brick-built reservoirs (known as Sheba's tanks) attributed to the Queen of Sheba, which must have been an early attempt at water conservation long before such things as artesian wells were known about. It did serve to remind us just how long a settlement had existed in that part of the world.

Once I was living out and drawing the appropriate allowances, I managed to buy a car which qualified me for membership of the Forces Motoring Club. There may have only been 86 miles of road in the whole Colony, but we had some sort of competition most weekends – rallies, sporting driving tests (the sort where you rush backwards and forwards round lots of bollards, arranged in patterns, trying not to knock any over), sprints (for which I borrowed a DKW coupe from the local agent) and even motorcycle trials. We also had competitions with the Motoring Club in the Shell refinery in Little Aden. I remember in one trial, I shared an ex-WD 500 cc side-valve Triumph with two other guys; we didn't do too well but it was enjoyable. At least it provided something else to do in a place where diversions were very necessary to take one's mind off the local surroundings. Oh yes, just as an aside, my daughter was born about 6 months before I was 'tour-ex'. She took part in her first car rally when she was 6 weeks old, which must be some sort of record. In later years she used to take great delight in telling her school chums that she was actually an Arab, because "I was born in Aden". She is now a married lady who has given Margot and I four of our eight wonderful grandchildren.

Funnily enough, the 2 years penance doesn't seem too bad in retrospect. At least, when I had finished my tour I did come back to Instrument Bashing in Bomber Command (RAF Scampton), but that didn't last too long and within 12 months I had volunteered for CSDE (the Central Servicing Establishment at RAF Swanton Morley) to join the VC.10 Project Team – but that's another story. I often wonder what Aden is like now. I did hear that the RAF hospital at Steamer Point had been taken over by goats after we withdrew, and the place must have had a rough time when the Suez Canal was closed. I shall just have to wonder – I'm certainly not going back to find out!!

37. Flight Commander at Halton

Dave Williams

From 1945 to '48, I was 582604 A/A D.J.T. Williams, stationed at No.1 Radio School, RAF Cranwell. From June 1956 to November 1957, I was still 582604 D.J.T. Williams, but now stationed at No.1 School of Technical Training, RAF Halton as a No.3 Wing Flight Commander. I was 28, married, and due to leave the Service on completion of an 8 year Short Service Commission, which had commenced in 1950, only 2 years after graduating as an AC.2 (Aircraftman 2nd Class) from Cranwell. You will conclude correctly, from the 'AC.2', that I was not among the leading technical lights of the 51st Entry!

Before this posting to Halton, I had flown the interim night fighters, Meteors and Vampires – the Javelin programme having slipped badly by about 7 years. Almost immediately before being posted to Halton, I had declined an offer made by the Air Ministry to extend my Service contract to December 1983, in which year I would be celebrating my 55th birthday. This meant that I was no longer eligible for another operational posting, and so to Halton.

When I first learned the nature of my final job in the RAF, I had a minor panic, recalling my life as an Apprentice and all the tricks we used to pull to avoid any activity not pleasing to us – such as hiding on top of a wooden tabletop slung across the heating pipes in the drying room, and many more plots and stratagems, all designed to 'get out of something'. I could remember them all of course, as it was not all that long since I had finished at Cranwell. Where best to smoke to avoid a F.252 (Apprentices were granted a Smoking Pass at the age of 18 years. If you were caught under that age, then you were charged on a Form 252 and punished), how not to be bored to tears by the Sunday Church Parade, how best to scrounge a '48' (weekend pass) from a not too switched-on Officer, etc etc. Would I be too 'street wise' for them, thus making their lives dull and uneventful? Or they for me? I remembered asking my Flight Commander at Cranwell for a 'compassionate' 48 hr pass to visit my sister in Nottingham. Her husband, I related, was an Officer based at RAF Newton, and he had been ordered away for a few days, and that my sister was most unhappy about being left alone in their isolated cottage in Sherwood Forest. Bad move. "What's your brother-in law's name and rank?" he asked. "Morgan, Sir. Flt Lt Edmund Morgan" and the so-and-so picked up his phone and said "Put me through to Newton please" and invited me to leave the room. Two minutes later he came out of his office, eyed me up and down a few times and said, "Don't ever try anything like that again Williams, or you'll be in real trouble". That's all. I was very lucky. But back to 1956.

My immediate boss was a Sqn Ldr Newman and we always had lunch together – sandwiches in his office. My fellow Flight Commander was Plt Off Robertson, who could hardly wait to complete his National Service and become a student at Wye Agricultural College. I wonder if his plans came to fruition? After a week or two, I found my feet. The rogues soon discovered me to be not only their equal in their craftiness and various ploys, but just that little bit more sophisticated. My 11 years of Service experience, and especially the 3 years apprenticeship, were paying off, and in no more than a few weeks I was confident and very happy at my new job. My relationship with the boys generally was good and the Boss told me that I was 'very able' at getting the mix of 'Flt Lt' and an 'older brother' just about right. Praise indeed. But that approach didn't pay-off with all the lads, as some of them were not sufficiently mentally mature to accept my two faces and had to be sorted out. A few were just naturally bloody-minded and would respond positively to nothing! The majority were great. It came as no surprise to me when I was 'invited' to take over both the pipe band and shooting team, as I had been in both at Cranwell, and I was happy with that. As a sometime side drummer, I couldn't resist having a go occasionally, and my efforts, which I thought were pretty damn good of course, always reduced those currently in practice to gales of laughter and remarks such as a smiling "Yes Sir, er, very good indeed". I was also very pleased to learn that there was a Chipmunk Flight at Halton, which meant that I needn't travel to another Station to keep my flying pay warm! It also meant, of course, that I could still horse around the sky now and again doing what I loved doing most.

After I had been at Halton for a couple of months, I let it be known that Thursday evenings were my 'Open Door' times, which meant that any of my lads could just knock on my office door, walk in and discuss anything with me that might be bugging them. I wore 'civvies' for these sessions and they, the sessions, proved to be quite successful. I wasn't all that mentally mature myself – not from where I see those days now, nearly 50 years on! – but sufficiently so to be able to address, in a positive way, most problems and personal concerns presented to me. Of course, there were 'The Usual Suspects' who would spin some remarkably inventive tales in an attempt to gain privilege of some sort, but they soon ran out of steam and gave up. I made one mistake for sure, something that I realised I had omitted to consider, and fortunately the Padre helped me out of the hole I had dug for myself. One of the boys, a Pakistani, was desperately unhappy and I saw him several times. With a mixture of the philosophical capacity of a young man (!) and 11 years in the Service, I was able to turn his life around, and, after a month or so, he was enjoying living once more. His Dad, who had headed writing paper which proclaimed him to be a 'Retired Station Master', actually travelled to England soon after that time to talk things over with me (I assumed the Railway pension funds were in good shape!). He was a most pleasant man who cared deeply for his son and eventually insisted on taking my wife and me to dinner in Aylesbury. Was it 'The Bull' or 'The Black Bull'? Too long ago, but I think it was in 'The Square'. There was no suggestion of anything untoward in his demeanour – he wasn't looking for privilege for Junior in other words. We enjoyed both the meal and his company, and his boy settled comfortably into Halton life. A 'chancer' I must mention was the lad who wanted a '48' in order to be able personally to comfort his girlfriend whom, he said, was pregnant with his child and currently experiencing a very bad time with her parents. A few questions elicited from him the 'facts' that she was 2 months 'gone' and that he hadn't been with her for 3½ months! Not at all like today's 'know it all' youngsters. After a short chat, he had the sense to admit he was 'trying it on' and I sent him away with a flea in his ear and a recommendation to read a certain book.

The Chipmunks contributed significantly to my delight with my final posting. I think things hadn't changed much since my days at Cranwell, inasmuch as Wednesday afternoons were still 'sports' afternoons, a euphemism for 'scrounge' for many. But for me, they were Apprentices

'Flying Experience' times, and I was able, most Wednesdays, to fly at least 5 boys in the time available. I always asked my passengers what they would like me to do, and the replies were nearly always the same.... "Aerobatics?" or "Can I have a go?' One or two wanted to see something specific from the air, while one or two others would leave it up to me. With the 'have a go' lads, I would climb to about 3,000 ft and just hand over. There was no danger in this of course, plenty of height to put things right if needs be. One or two showed real promise, and I told them so, much to their delight of course.

A/A David Finn was either Australian or a Kiwi – I can't remember which – and there are several details of our relationship (a bad word, nowadays) which I either can't recall or they don't make sense when I think I can. Certainly, he was not 'one of my lot'. The other Flight perhaps? He first came to my attention because of his frequent absences from the shooting get-togethers, and I learned that Finn and jankers were anything but strangers, and eventually I decided to discover why he was being so frequently punished. I also obtained reports from schools and workshops reference his application and general performance, both academic and practical. None was good! In summary, he was idle and anti, and seemed almost to set out deliberately to attract trouble. And yet....! And yet there was a maturity about this lad, and he always maintained eye contact when in conversation – with me, anyway – and that was not too frequent a happening in my experience with any age group. After a few one-to-ones, David Finn began to reveal the real 'him'. He was humorous, articulate and unselfconscious, but my cautious probing about his work and jankers drew from him only evasion. To cut this short, I eventually got to know him fairly well, despite the fact that I had to be always cautious not to be judged overly concerned with his welfare or to be too concerned about him personally, especially as he was not 'one of mine'. I am neither going to claim here that I was a major influence in his life nor that I was some Svengali-like figure. Perhaps what I did, or helped to do to David Finn, was a bad thing, and that I would have been well advised not to interfere in his life in any way. What I brought about in that young man's life was nothing more than to introduce him to a different way of looking at things, a new angle on his life particularly. I got him to see a bigger picture of the future and his position in that. He responded very positively to all this, and over a period of 3 months he changed completely. I had no more significant contact with him until not long before his Passing Out Parade, when I sought him out to congratulate him on winning a place at the College 'up the road'. There was no emotional occasion that day between us; all that was said, other than my congratulations, was his "Thank you Sir" to me. Was that more than a formality I wonder? Did he intend to convey more, hoping that I would understand? Who knows? Five years later David Finn was dead. His Government, sponsors of his Apprenticeship, refused to allow him to remain in England for a further period and offered instead a Cadetship at their college, their equivalent of Cranwell, which he accepted. In 1964 – I think it was – I read in Flight magazine that a Fg Off David Finn had been killed by enemy gunfire whilst flying a Canberra over the Malayan jungle. I didn't feel too good about that for quite some time. Tales like this I could relate at some length of course, and that causes me to remember one A/A Diffey. I promoted him to L/A/A (Leading Aircraft Apprentice) and a few months later, on knocking the door of the room at the bottom of the barrack room and walking in, I found him and a chosen few having a puff. Place thick with smoke. Diffey was not pleased at all to be caught like this. I just looked at him for a few seconds, turned and left the room. I didn't know what to do and, cruelly, did nothing. Poor lad, he must have been very worried by my silence which really was a demonstration of *my* immaturity.

At the time of leaving Halton and the RAF, I was a happy bloke. I had had several 'Above Average' assessments as a Night Fighter pilot pasted into my log books and, latterly, a rewarding association with the boys. Rightly or wrongly, I felt that I had done a good job. I had been recommended for a General List Permanent Commission, but had performed pitifully before the Board, so 'Civvy Street' it was. On my final day, a group of the boys presented me with an engraved cigarette case/lighter. It said, "To Dave.. Good luck Sir". I liked that.

38. The Christmas Mail Pick-Up From Aldabra

John Oakes

An article in the Beverley Association's magazine called Mag Drop prompted this story. One of the members was asking if any of the readers knew anything about a Christmas mail pick-up in 1962 from an island in the Indian Ocean called Aldabra, where an airfield was being built. It was pretty much a 'One Off' operation and although I know airborne pick-ups were done during the war, it wasn't something we practiced.

I know little about the conception or the planning stage, but on the 7th November 1962, with Sqn Ldr Evans in the Captain's seat, we were airborne out of RAF Eastleigh in Kenya at 15.05 hrs in Beverley XB263. Our total load was a 2 ft wooden cable drum wound with nylon cord, with a rusty three pronged hook about 3 ft long, on the end of a 2 inch steel tube about 6 ft long, and two standard passenger seats, fixed-to-face forward in the last positions in the boom.

Once airborne, the AQM and myself threaded the drum onto the steel tube and pushed the tube through the folding parts at the back of the seats. The boom parachute doors were opened and the hook was hung outside in the airstream. As you can imagine, the hook flew away and the drum spun round out of control. We were within the airfield boundary and high enough for no real damage to be done. I imagined that if we had been lower and over the local village, we could have retrieved some of those pink parachutes (now made up into pink underwear!) that we had dropped to them a few weeks before. Anyway, with enormous effort, we were able to control the flight of the hook (erratic though it was) with myself sitting on the floor behind the drum, gripping it between my hands and knees, and the Q giving "Up-a-bit and Down-a-bit" instructions to the Captain. We did about ten or so runs across the airfield and to all intents and purposes it all went well. A small modification to the hook was all that was needed before another try the following day at 12.05 hrs, with crew and rig as before.

This time the hook was to be 'flown' at about 10 ft above the ground and all went well until the "Up-a-bit" communication did not translate to the lazy old Bev and the hook tore up a sizeable chunk of Eastleigh. We were only aloft for 15 minutes on that day, but with repairs needed to the hook and the last posting date for Christmas being brought forward, it was decided we had enough experience for the operational sortie to go ahead the next day. It was all very rushed, but the last posting date was crucial if the letters were to get to the UK in time for Christmas. Flt Lt Holloway, who had been acting as Co-pilot, was given the job of making up a parcel containing enough cord and instructions to be dropped with the main load. That was all very rushed too, for he was due to catch a flight home to the UK that evening.

The take-off time in my logbook says '9.11.62, 02.55 hrs', and that is all I can remember until sighting the island of Aldabra (or was it Paradise?). A DZ had been marked out on the beach and the main load was dropped. I seem to remember doing several circuits round the island, while the party on the beach were reading the instructions and preparing two long bamboo poles. A loop of cord was stretched between the poles and secured lightly to them. The rest of the loop was drawn back to a point where a small bag was attached. It had been intended that a bag of up to 60 lbs was to be lifted, but discretion had divided this by ten and we almost heard the groans when the ground party read this in Dick Holloway's instructions. The Q and I positioned ourselves in the boom, and a run-in was begun. Great consternation ensued, for, in spite of the danger of a bloody great metal hook flying out of control at great speed (well Beverley speed) at zero ft, the beach party had all gathered around the rig to see it work (or not!).

I am sure that a countdown was given, but suddenly the drum spun away between my knees and hands. Luckily I thought to put on a pair of the standard issue asbestos gloves for this run. The cape leather aircrew gloves would not have stood a chance! Grip as I might, there was no way I was going to be able to slow things down. Then as suddenly as it had started, the drum stopped as the end of the cord secured to the drum was reached (Who was the clever lad who tied the knot!) Perhaps a second or two elapsed before the cord appeared to leap back into the boom, ably assisted by the Q in a frantic hand-over-hand. Then the hook appeared, with one leg almost straight and precariously caught on it was the double cord of the loop. OK so far, then the light ties from the poles arrived and finally the bag of mail. Success!!! This all happened within a lot less time than it takes to read this, including the dash to the cockpit with our prize. From out of the blue, the Navigator produced a rubber stamp saying '1st uplift of mail from Aldabra' and each letter was cancelled. The remainder of the flight was uneventful; though I paid a bit more attention to the Engineers log, for the round trip would be 12 hrs 35 mins. Probably not the longest of flights, but for me one of the most rewarding. In retrospect, there was no way this exercise was going to be a success, and, given more time to plan, I am sure it would never have been attempted, but in its simplicity it worked. Had any of the parameters been slightly different, that Christmas mail would still be floating in the Indian Ocean.

P.S. If anyone knows the whereabouts of any of the envelopes (covers) from that pick-up, then as a bit of a collector I would very much like to hear from you.

P.P.S. Or was it all a dream?

39. CB or Not CB? That is the Question

Tom McHarry

In my second year at Halton, I had been transferred in disgrace from 'C' Squadron back to 'A' Squadron, having been demoted from C/A/A back to the ranks. My offence? I had been caught red-handed (with a Royal flush in Diamonds!), gambling with the Junior Entry who were in my charge, by no less a stickler for discipline than Chiefy Thomas. He, as was expected by King and Country, did his duty and I was duly charged, found guilty and got my marching orders.

However, my buddies were all in 'C' Squadron and I tended to join them whenever the occasion arose. I cannot recall as to how it came about, but some eight or so of us managed to dodge the 'column' and were walking down to the New Workshops – all being FIIA's. Once again, I, along with all the others, were caught red-handed (or should it be 'flat footed') by WO Pearce, who, as all the Riggers will remember, was a nasty piece of work. Unfortunately he did not accept our various excuses (surprise, surprise) and we all had our names taken and were promised swift and just retribution.

Several days later, the strangest thing occurred. The 'C' Squadron Flight Commander arrived down at workshops to hear the charges, and all the bods who had been caught walking instead of marching down to work were paraded outside the New Workshops Admin office. I had never heard of anyone ever being 'tried' at workshops before and took it to be 'just one of those things'. Number, rank and names, were read out and we all in turn acknowledged our own names. It was then a case of "Hats off. March them in". Once we were all assembled in the office, the names were again read out, but this time from the charge sheet and the 'crime' was detailed. "Wait a minute" I thought, "my name wasn't read out this time".

"Seven days CB (Confined to Barracks). Do you accept my punishment?"

"Yes Sir" came the mumbled responses from the assembled troops.

"March them out".

"Left, right, left, right. Halt. Right turn. Dismiss".

That night I prepared my kit and waited until it was almost time for the first jankers call. I hid round the corner of 11 Block, ready to sprint onto the parade when my name was called from the roll – but it never was – not on that parade nor the next. Narcy Burford (bless him) and quite a few others of the 51st may have clocked up more 'days' than I did, but as far as I know, none of them spent seven of them lying on their pits! I was never hauled before the 'A' Squadron Flight Commander, so I can only assume that my transfer back to 'A' Squadron had not at that time been notified to the workshops administration office.

"Theirs not to make reply,
Theirs not to reason why,
Someone had blundered."
(With apologies to Alfred Lord Tennyson!)

40. Rags to Riches or A Chequered Career

John McLaren

Having wasted 3 years at Tech School and a further 3 years of Halton training, I marched up the hill for the last time, having amassed 34% on my final exams. Added to my failure at 'Schools', I managed 4th out of the four failures! Retribution was swift. A Flight Mechanic examination board and I became a Flt Mech AC.2! You don't get much lower than that! In no time at all I was posted to the ATDU (Torpedo's) at Gosport, whilst the rest of the Entry headed for RAF St Athan. Maybe I got the best of that one. No sympathy was forthcoming either from my own Entry or the other ex-brats at Gosport, nor did I deserve any.

Two years on, in 1950, I found myself on a short fitters course at Athan. This was intended to eliminate 'SAC's below-the-line' and promote them to J/T (Junior Technician) under the new trade structure. I got through the course with little trouble, was posted to RAF Leuchars and thence to A&AEE Boscombe Down, where I volunteered for Aircrew. My subsequent interviews at Biggin Hill seemed only to consist of in-depth discussions on my criminal past. That's that, I thought. Not so. Four months later I was on the OCTU course at RAF Jurby, as a u/t Navigator. I must have built my imaginary bridges correctly, because I then found myself at RAF Thorney Island doing flying training as an acting Pilot Officer (on probation). During the next few weeks, I returned to Boscombe Down to renew old acquaintances. To a man they were speechless! It couldn't last! I was much too near my gorgeous new wife, and this, plus a Tiger 100 motorbike with no rear springing, saw me in Halton Hospital with a slipped disc. I took the opportunity to look up Flem Carlton, the Sgt in charge of the Apprentices Pipe and Drum Band, and at the same time bummed a few cheap salutes from any passing airmen and rooks (junior apprentices). I eventually opted for discharge, left the Service in November 1953, and got a job with Fields at Croydon Airport.

I was immediately advised by all of my ex-brat workmates to get back in the Service. Nine months later I did just that. With the rank of Cpl, I was posted to RAF Tangmere, where I became an 'experienced' Meteor man – after 5 years on them I should think so too! Whilst beginning to have dreams of the Sgt's Mess, I was posted to Aden in 1958. Skimming over two very hot and uncomfortable years on the 'hot rock', I did manage a one hour trip in a Meteor Mk.7 with Flt Lt Beaky Leach. I came back to RAF Manston in 1961 as a Snr Tech, soon to be reversed to Command Sgt. With time on my hands my thoughts turned to

'Branch Commissioning'. "Why not" I thought. One day I was bribed by the promise of a Rate I to ferry three aspiring 'O' level candidates to Hawkinge for Maths and English exams by the Education Officer. I happily chugged over there in my Morris Minor, but I was not so happy to find that I too was entered for the exams as part of the deal. Only one out of the four passed both exams. ME!! Both of these subjects were required for commissioning, so I was on my way. Some hopes! Station Orderly Sgt came round every 10 days at Manston. My married quarter was at Sandwich, 8 miles away, so I usually asked one of the station NCO's to do the night part of this duty. This worked well until one weekend the 'stand-in' got pie-eyed in the Mess and forgot to lock the NAAFI. There followed a Police report, a very serious looking charge and a 'severe dig' for me. Good-bye commission. I then decided on an NCO career and accordingly began to prepare for my Ch Tech examination boards. I spent several days at Stations operating current aircraft, and spent time in propeller and engine bays talking to people who had recently been on the boards at RAF Weeton, garnering current trends on questions etc. I came up with a short list of about twelve and worked on them. I took a week's leave immediately before my boards, went up to Weeton, made contact with several examiners, modifying my short list accordingly. I suppose these days this would be called 'examination technique'. I don't know what Weeton would have called it! I passed the Pt.1 by one mark. Failure in this (it was 'Safety Precautions') disqualified you immediately. I passed the other parts quite easily and then came to the four long questions. One ex-brat examiner had been particularly unhelpful to me, in spite of being stationed with me previously. He was my examiner. Two of the questions were OK, the other two I'd never heard of. The WO i/c interviewed me last. "Questions have difficulty factors" he explained. "You scored over 90% on the two Ch Tech difficulty factor questions, and less than 30% on the other two". These were questions usually set for J/T and Cpl Tech boards. Could I explain this? There was a long silence and he suspected what I suspected. My examiner had tried to be helpful; some help! It was late on Friday afternoon by now and he wanted to get away for the weekend. After a short conference, it was decided to give me two further questions under his eagle eye, and if I obtained over 80% I would be given a nominal pass. They reverted to form and I passed them easily, thus becoming a Chief Tech.

All this trauma severely disrupted my carefully laid plans for the train journey back to Manston. Avoiding changing at Crewe had been carefully worked out, but the unexpected delay had changed all that. I had a 10 hour wait at Crewe and decided that a celebration was in order.

My kit was in the buffet, together with a large holdall containing about 30 AP's (Air Publications) which I had brought with me to study. One of my duties at Manston was custodian of the small Tech Library. I thus had access to every AP which I required. Three sheets to the wind, I boarded the train 2 hours later, had a few more bevvies at Victoria and fell asleep on the train. I awoke at 04.00 in a railway siding in Ramsgate! I managed to phone Manston and a friendly duty driver ran me home. Sometime on Sunday, with my head threatening to fall off, I unpacked. No holdall!! I eventually concluded it must be at Crewe and I rang the station on the Monday, not a sign. During the next year I replaced all of the AP's by demanding a new one and 'scrapped' the old one. What worried me was if somebody found the holdall and its contents, but I never saw or heard of them again. Phew!

My 6 years at Manston brought me in contact with a few 'names'. Two come to mind. Hughie Green was in a Summer Revue at Margate and he flew a posh twin-engined aircraft in every Monday morning and out again Friday night. The euphoria of meeting such a star soon evaporated; he proved to be more obnoxious off the stage than on it. He insisted on showing his wisdom of all things mechanical and insisted on carrying out his own A/F and B/F inspections. One of the fitters advised him one Friday night that neither oil/water traps under each engine had been emptied for some time. We all gathered round for the fun. As he unlocked the last securing clip, about 2 pints of filthy oil/water mix sprayed down his £300 suit. His agent and the rest of his entourage had hysterics. They seemed to dislike him as much as we did. We didn't get any complimentary tickets to his show after that!

Douglas Bader arrived, also in a twin-engined aircraft, for a weekend stop. He and I immediately struck up a rapport and he seemed to prefer my company to either the Station Commander or the Search and Rescue helicopter crews. I finished up ferrying him and his wife to their weekend destination in my trusty Morris Minor when their taxi failed to appear. I had been on PWR (Preliminary Warning Roster for Overseas) for 2 years for Singapore, a very difficult place to get to at that time. This matter came out in conversation with the great man and he considered a man of my experience and talent shouldn't be rotting at Manston. When he reappeared on Monday morning he drew me to one side and said, "I stayed with your C-in-C this weekend Flight (Ch Tech's were completely unknown to him). I've fixed your Singapore posting". A month later, with 2 days notice, I left for Changi in December 1964!

At RAF Changi I entered the commissioning stakes a bit more seriously. OC Eng, OC Mech Eng and my Flt Cdr were all ex-brats. I passed the additional education GCE's required, read the Flight and

Aeroplane magazines, and during the next 18 months was passed up the interview ladder. Biggin Hill awaited.

We came home to RAF Valley in 1967. I needed very little motivation to pursue a commission after 2 weeks there! My Biggin Hill interview came up in spite of the efforts of my particularly miserable Sqn Cdr to stop it. He said as a new boy he would want 12 months to look at my suitability. As I had already been accepted I could see no logic in this. I collected the paperwork from the office and drove down to Biggin Hill. As we all do, I thought I had done poorly and returned to complete 5 or 6 years at Valley.

A few weeks later I went to the Cup Final at Wembley with a bunch of the Station footballers. Coming back on the train to Holyhead, we took over the restaurant car and all got very drunk. The train to Holyhead runs right through the Valley Camp and at this point a lot of cutlery, china and beer cans were thrown from the train. We docked at Holyhead, escaped by taxi and laid low waiting for retribution. Sunday morning the hangar WO knocked on my door. "Boss wants you first thing tomorrow, his office 08.30, best blue". My heart sank; that was quick I thought. At 08.25 the next morning I was there. The miserable ****** kept me there till 12.30. He called me in and he was laid back in his chair toying with a piece of paper. I tried desperately to see if it had a British Rail motive on it, or any Police connection – no luck. He finally threw it across the desk but his aim, like everything else about him, was poor and it skidded to the floor. "Read that", he spat. Trembling fingers picked it up, turned it over and read. "You have been selected – Branch Officer terms – RAF Henlow 4 July 1967 etc etc". I collapsed into his armchair, chalk white and totally incoherent. "I'll give you a week on that course", he hissed. Then he looked a bit worried. "You had better get a drink" he said, "You look as if you've seen a ghost". Little did he know. I never heard another word about the train affair, but his nibs got a bit of revenge by making me spend the remainder of my time, prior to reporting to Henlow, in charge of a 'recruiting safari' to Halifax, Huddersfield and Rotherham. Places I never want to go to again. He finally signed my blue clearance chit at 16.55 on 3 July and I was on my way.

OCTU proved to be hard physical labour. The dreaded 'Officer Qualities' being the key to success. I found these easier to cope with than the academics. There were three of us SNCO's and the other two quit after 2 days. The powers that be didn't like this at all, and I was interviewed at length as to the reasons and whether I intended to go the same way. I said that they would have to drag me out by the heels and this went down very well. Having got off to a good, if lucky, start, I did quite well, kept my head down and my mouth shut, and finished up in the top six on OQ's and obtained a 'nominal' pass on the rest.

During our final project (OCTU loved projects), my team had chosen 'The Qualities of a Leader' as our subject. As we approached presentation time it became clear that we were in for a roasting for our total lack of effort. We chose Douglas Bader as our 'leader' and just prior to the presentation I phoned his London flat, and explained our dilemma. Could he possibly help? He agreed to appear personally and give a 10 minute talk on the subject and then take questions from the floor. He did just that. At the end of our abysmal Pt.1, I arose and introduced the great man to speak for himself. He proved to be an admirable speaker and he brought the house down. It also earned me a very one-sided interview with the Air Commodore CO the following morning. There was also a hurried review of Officer Cadet's SSO's regarding V.I.P. visitors! Flying Officer McLaren and family left the Valley hell-hole to become the new OC Mechanical Transport Flight at RAF Leuchars. It was a tough baptism and I shudder at the hours I spent on the runway in the middle of the night, clearing the snow and ice with the infamous MRD. Fortunately I knew the Derwent engine, which was fitted to this 'runway de-icer', and I managed to keep them serviceable enough to burn a few holes in the runway. I was also blessed with an ex-brat OC Eng who certainly helped me control the rougher element. I also ran the Station Pipe Band, during which time we won the first ever RAF Pipe Band Championships at RAF Waddington. Another plus.

Two years later, in 1969, I was posted South. RAF Hullavington certainly knew something I didn't, because they dis-established me 6 months later. Fortunately Spider Webb was about to come out of the MT slot at RAF Lyneham, so in I went. I sat in 3 MT chairs during the next 14 years, apart from 2 years in Cyprus and 6 months at RAF Brize Norton. Promotion to Flt Lt followed in 1972 after the requisite 5 years.

During the next few years, due more to good attendance than skill, I became, in the eyes of the powers that be at least, an experienced MT man. I preferred it to the alternatives, and sharp end aircraft jobs invariably went to Cranwell-bred youngsters, so I never struggled to leave the MT world. Promotion to the coveted 'Scraper' (Squadron Leader) brigade came surprisingly predictably in August 1979. A call to OC Eng's office (another rollicking I thought) resulted in the cracking of a bottle of the good stuff and long gratters. No misery or tears this time, but I did spend a moment pondering July 1948, but it is certainly better to be born lucky than clever!!!!

My Service days finished at Lyneham in July 1984.

41. My Last Operational Sortie in the RAF

Sandy Sanders

Ring … Ring … Ring … I switch off my alarm clock, check the time, 02.30 hrs on a cold and frosty January morning in 1967, 'Somewhere in England' as the wartime saying went. In fact it was RAF Marham – El Adem with grass to you ex-Air Force types! The sortie of the day was to ferry four Lightnings to RAF Akrotiri in Cyprus. To achieve this, it required six Victor tankers of 55 Squadron – three Victors for each pair of Lightnings. Victor No.1 refuels the fighters five times between the UK and Malta, then lands there; No.2 refuels twice after Malta and lands at Cyprus, the Lightnings having sped off at a great rate of knots after their last refuel. Victor No.3 acts as a standby for the other two. I was detailed as the Crew Chief for the standby Victor, so I was not expecting to be going anywhere – famous last words!

Anyway, back to the story. I grab a couple of shredded wheats (no, not three – I'm no longer a growing lad!) – pick up my over-night kit, and rather than scrape the ice off my car windscreen, I jump onto my pushbike and head for the Squadron, calling into the Operations Block to pick up my flying kit on the way. I meet my crew there, checking their helmets, oxygen masks, etc. They offer me a cooked breakfast, which I turn down saying "I will have one when the others have gone". I give a hand to the Crew Chief who is preparing the aircraft for the sortie, doing pre-flight checks, storing the spares and luggage, de-icing the aircraft etc, until the crew arrive one hour before take-off.

The crew and I get on board and carry out the necessary checks and prepare for engine start-up. At this point in time it comes over the RT that one of No.1's engines fails to start, so we have to fill the slot. Still, I didn't mind having a night in Malta! The take-off was uneventful and we climb to our operational height of 37,000 ft where I carry out my first duty of inspecting the upper surface of the aircraft for any damage or loose panels, using the rearward viewing periscope. All satisfactory. We arrive at our first refuelling point and attempt to extend the refuelling hoses from the two Mk.20 wing refuelling pods – no such luck! One comes out, but the other decides otherwise. After a quick chat to the Captain of the other tanker, it was decided he would take over the refuelling for the first leg to Malta and we would use the one serviceable pod to refuel the Lightnings, one at a time, for their last two refuels to Akrotiri. I have not had an over-night stop in Cyprus before, so it would be a new experience for me and I'll be able to have a night out in Limassol. Once again – famous last words!

The sortie is carried out successfully, with the Lightnings arriving safe and sound at Akrotiri. It is quite an impressive sight watching the refuelling through the periscope. The two Lightnings position themselves at the rear of the Victor tanker ready to couple up to the refuelling hoses. The length of the hoses is only 51 ft and they have to be pushed 10 ft into the pod by the receiving aircraft before fuel will flow, so it does not leave much room for error.

We arrive over the airfield at Akrotiri, select the undercarriage 'down' in preparation for landing. A few swear words from the Captain came over the intercom, followed by "Chief, I've only got '2' greens, check the circuit breakers are made correctly". I carried out the check – everything was satisfactory. Air Traffic Control was informed of our problem and we were asked to fly low past the Tower for a visual check. To them everything appeared normal with the undercarriage, so the next move was to do a 'roller' down the runway to check if the undercarriage would bear the weight of the aircraft without collapsing. I should mention at this point that the Victor's tail number was XH648. This aircraft had a history of undercarriage trouble, in fact it was known on the Squadron as 'Tugboat Annie' because of the number of times it had been towed by tug to the hangar for retraction tests and always without the fault being reproduced. I informed the Captain of this and he decided to make the next circuit the final landing. All loose items were stored securely and I made sure that I was firmly strapped into my seat, with everything crossed! As it turned out, it was one of the smoothest landings I had experienced.

Although I was greatly relieved, it meant that I would not be seeing Limassol that night, instead I would be endeavouring to rectify the snag. It also meant that I would need a space in a hangar to do a retraction test. This space was not available until early evening, so arrangements were made for the crew and a tug to meet at the aircraft at 19.00 hrs. During the 2 miles tow to the hangar, the skies opened and we all got drenched. It was just not my day – and there was more to come!

The Victor was jacked up – not the easiest of tasks when using aircrew rather than tradesmen, considering the weight is roughly 135,000 lb and balanced on three points the size of 1p each – but it was achieved without further mishap. The undercarriage was retracted several times and just as I thought, no problems whatsoever. '3' greens – locked down, '3' reds – travelling, '3' lights out – locked up. By this time it was getting late and the Mess bar was due to shut, so it was decided to leave it on jacks and give it more checks in the morning before lowering it to the ground again. Wrong!!! I got my pint in, plus a sandwich, in the Sgts Mess, before retiring absolutely shattered after a 22 hour day. I was asleep by the time my head hit the pillow, but not for long, as just after 02.00 hrs there was a banging on the bunk door. My presence was required at the hangar to get the Victor off jacks and towed out to allow the aircraft at the back of the hangar to be towed out for use in an exercise that had been called for the Island. The task was carried out and as it was about 05.00 hrs, the crew decided that we would have breakfast and then set off for home without any further investigation into our undercarriage fault. I must say that I was not sorry to see the back of Cyprus. The flight home was uneventful, in fact I cannot recall anything of the flight – perhaps I slept all the way! The runway at Marham came into view and all the crew had their fingers crossed when the undercarriage was selected 'down', but it was not necessary as it locked down with '3' greens. Perhaps it was the crossing of the fingers which did the trick – we will never know. As it turned out, this was my last trip as a Victor Crew Chief, having completed my 7 year tour of duty, so I still have not been to Limassol. Instead I was posted to RAF Ballykelly in the Emerald Isle to look after some Shackletons (10,000 rivets flying in close formation!!) – what a come down! From one of the most advanced aircraft to the oldest.

Footnote:- If you ever visit the Imperial War Museum at Duxford, you will come across a Mk.K1A Victor standing there with a smug look. By a coincidence, it just happens to be XH648, so give the nose wheel a kick from me to let it know that I haven't forgotten my last flight in it!

P.S. On July 12th last year (1995), I met up with John Greenslade at Duxford. I had previously arranged with the Museum to have access to the cockpit of XH648, so we were able to spend some time looking round, but not for long as it was too b y hot inside.

P.P.S. It could do with a paint job!

42. Girl Katie

Eric Mold

Life aboard our little ship, the *Girl Katie*, named after our first grandchild, is not all ladies in silk dresses and fancy hats, or gentlemen in white flannels and reefer coats, sipping pink gins and lowering the ensign as the sun goes down. We do manage to do a bit of that, but not too much. Mostly it is a labour of love – a continuous 'work in progress'. Vera and I do most of the maintenance work ourselves because it is almost impossible to find knowledgeable and competent workers. Here they charge $50 per hour for (very) unskilled labour just to scrape the barnacles off the bottom when we are in dry dock. A ritual we go through once a year.

Girl Katie is about 39 ft overall length and 13 ft in the beam, built of fibreglass in Taiwan in 1984; in the days before they knew how to build things down to a price as they do today. She is what is called a Sundeck Trawler and, as expected, she has a nice sundeck and the sea keeping qualities of a small fishing trawler. Not fast, but her twin turbo charged diesels propel her at a maximum speed of about 10 knots. Before leaving the engine room, I should mention that we have a three cylinder 8 Kw diesel genset down there, which provides all of the 110 volt AC power we need when we are not tied up to a dock drawing shorepower. In addition to AC power, we also have a 12 volt DC system, the basis of which is two massive D8 batteries which are charged by alternators on each engine and a 'smart' charger that runs off the genset. We carry 350 gallons of diesel fuel and 200 gallons of fresh water. The plumbing system delivers hot and cold running water to a shower on the swim platform aft, wash basin and shower in our cabin, the galley and a shower and basin in the guest cabin (now my office) forward. Hot water comes from either a heat exchanger on the starboard engine or a 110 volt water heater. There are two toilets, together with their related plumbing, holding tank, flush pumps and transfer pumps etc. Work on these is not a job for the squeamish, but I got all that knocked out of me when my room job ar Halton was 'stand-ups and pans!'. Climate control consists of two reverse cycle air conditioning units, which normally cool, but can work in reverse to provide warmth on chilly nights. The system is controlled by another 'smart' unit which senses the temperature and monitors the operation of the units themselves. Occasionally the cooling water intake gets plugged with debris and a unit will begin to overheat, so a sensor shuts it down. When that happens, I've got to get out of bed (it usually happens at night), lift up a panel in the floor, close a seacock and clean out a filter. Sometimes it gets so plugged that it is necessary to use the pressure hose to blow it through. Once it got plugged up with jellyfish.

The accommodation consists of the guest cabin forward with a ¾ berth, which will extend to a double, a toilet and shower en-suite, seat, wardrobe and sundry cupboards and drawers. Amidships is the saloon, with dinette to port and galley to starboard. The forward part of the saloon is taken up by the lower control station, helmsman's seat, wheel, throttle, gears, autopilot control and engine gauges to starboard; the navigation and chart table are to port. Above are instruments such as radios, speed and depth gauges, radar and stereo entertainment centre. For navigation we have both LORAN and GPS (Global Positioning

System) which can be hooked up to my laptop which is loaded with 'glass charts' on a CD-ROM. This equipment constantly displays the boat's position to within a few feet as it moves across the charts on the laptop's screen. We also carry paper charts in case the system crashes (as it sometimes does). In the galley, Vera has the usual electrical appliances and a four burner stove with oven, microwave, electric oven and two stainless steel sinks. The refrigerator/freezer runs on 100 volts AC, but automatically switches over to 12 volts DC if it senses an AC power failure. On the after bulkhead of the saloon we have a 20 inch TV set and VCR, plus a Grundig 7000 short wave radio. Three steps lead down to our stateroom aft. It is quite large – the full width of the boat. We have a comfortable Queen sized bed, vanity table, drawers, wardrobes, hanging lockers and a good sized toilet, wash basin and shower en-suite. Mounted high up on one of the wardrobes we have a 13 inch TV set. The furniture is all teak and the boat is carpeted throughout.

Outside on the foredeck, there is an electrical windlass to handle our 60 lb anchors and chains. Side decks run aft on either side of the boat to four steps, which lead up to the sundeck. Since we are no longer interested in sunbathing, we have had a special enclosure made for the sundeck. We designed it ourselves, but had a hard job in finding someone to make it for us. Eventually we found a young Russian who took it on and he made a brilliant job of the stainless steel, vinyl and Plexiglas structure. We call it the Florida Top and it has been featured in Southern Boating, a popular US boating magazine. It gives complete protection from the scorching sun and allows us to dine on the sundeck, even in a tropical downpour. It can rain quite heavily in the Tropics, as many of you will have experienced.

The sundeck is carpeted with indoor/outdoor carpeting. Up there we have another refrigerator, mainly for keeping the beer cool and making ice cubes for our martinis. On top of this fridge we have another 13 inch TV set. There is also an L-shaped settee and a table with chairs to seat four for meals. A dumb waiter window connects the galley with the sundeck. Up four more steps from the sundeck we come to the flying bridge where we have a duplicate set of controls, seating for six people and a gas grill. Our 'Follow Me TV' antenna, which keeps the satellite dish pointing at the satellite when the boat is underway or gilling about at anchor, is also mounted on the flying bridge. This neat but expensive device is our latest toy. First trip out it went U/S. Apparently its internal compass went on the fritz and we had to dismantle the whole thing and return it to the makers to be fixed. More agro, more expense. What's even worse, we had no Coronation Street for the two weeks it was away! To wind up our little outfit, hanging on the stern we have a 10 ft inflatable boat with a 5 hp outboard to take us ashore when we are anchored off and for our granddaughters to play with when they visit.

Vera and I, with practically no outside help, keep this expensive, highly complex box of tricks looking nice and running reasonably well on a relative 'shoe string". Sir Thomas Lipton once said "You can get the sensation of boating by standing fully dressed under a cold shower, tearing up £100 notes". One would need to be well into the six-figure bracket to own and operate a boat like ours if you had to leave all the maintenance and repairs to the stick handlers and rip-off artists found around here. It is only the training that I picked up at the bottom of Chestnut Avenue at Halton that enables me to do all of the things I have done on this little ship over the past eleven years.

"Why do we do it?" you may ask. We do it because we love it. We don't do many long distance cruises these days, and it gets more and more difficult for me to climb down into the engine room, but we are not ready to give it up just yet. When I do have to work on the outer side of either engine, it takes about 20 minutes for me to crawl inside there. It is like working on your belly at the bottom of a coal mine. Fortunately I have a lovely little gopher, always ready to go for this and go for that. I don't know how I would cope without her. Vera has picked up a lot of technical know-how over the years and she would have made a great 'Bratess' given the chance – and a hell of a lot prettier than you lot! We enjoy the constant exercise of mind and spirit, planning, scheming and figuring out how, when and what we are going to do next. There is a fair amount of physical activity involved, especially as we don't own a car – just two folding bikes. (We rent a car for 24 hours every two weeks or so to do all of the jobs and the major provisioning which we cannot do by bike.) We walk a lot and travel by bus, but we don't exercise, mow lawns nor shovel snow. It is wonderful to have your morning coffee on the shaded sundeck with palm trees swaying in the breeze, the odd dolphin poking his snout out of the water to say "Good Morning" to, or a flock of pelicans diving like Stukas into the sea trying to catch their breakfast. There is something really special about owning and living aboard your own little boat – your own little world.

That's all for now folks. Vera, who has been busy all day making a new cover for one of our seat cushions, has just called me to the sundeck – it's martini time!

43. Schoolboy Impressions

JMR

How can we explain how it was sixty years ago?
The war had only been over for a few months, as you know;
and the whole country was a bit run down and tired.
Not us; we were starting on a post-war adventure -inspired.

We got on the train at Marylebone.
At Wendover there were trucks;
"Well, at least we'll get a ride".
Not ?????? likely,
"Put your luggage inside"!

Could anyone forget that P38?
I thought it was great
and was waiting for it to come back.
Pity it didn't.

What about the march up to Camp?
I hadn't a clue how far it might be,
I can't even recall if we marched in sixes or threes.
Still, we eventually got there -
Some nearly on their knees.

Luggage was united with owners.
Medical – breathe, cough, sample,
food, bed in shared temporary room,
rise, breakfast, get uniform, post 'civvies' home.

"Please step inside this room gentlemen".
"I swear that I ………."
"GET OUTSIDE ON PARADE YOU 'ORRIBLE AIRMEN"!!!
Ambition realised.

44. The Shepherd

Geof Bradshaw

When, early in 1961, it was announced that No.46 Night/All Weather Squadron (Javelins) would disband in six months, an unusual chain of circumstances found me in the post of Flight Commander. As a supplementary list Flight Lieutenant, this was not a position I ever anticipated since it was a general list Squadron Leader post, but there I was. I mention this so you will appreciate the unbridled happiness with which I reported to RAF Hospital Wroughton less than a month later, victim of a passing Mobile X-Ray Unit.

My protestations fell on deaf ears. They were determined to treat me and proceeded to do so to the extent that when I left there, 3½ months later, I really needed my 28 days sick leave. It hadn't been *all* bad, but 90 shots of streptomycin (odds on the left, evens on the right) had left me unable to walk a straight line. Corridor walls had a magnetic attraction for me. A visit to Central Medical Establishment (CME) then confirmed that I would be grounded for two years while I completed the course of some revolting medicine that I was having to take. I mentioned to the Doc that, with my recent background, it would probably mean I would go 'down the hole' as a fighter controller which was not my scene at all – could get typecast. "No sweat" says he, "I'll just say that you should be employed out of doors".

Back at RAF Waterbeach, 46 Sqn was no more, so I lurked in Flying Wing HQ for a month or so until I was told to report to 229 OCU at RAF Chivenor; something about a convoy and a range in Wales. At Chivenor, the OC Flying Wing told me that their air-to-ground range at RAF Castlemartin in Pembrokeshire had hitherto been operated as and when by one of the Unit's Pilot Attack Instructors (PAI) and I was to take a crew there to set it up on a more permanent basis pending the arrival of "Some chap who had to have an outdoor job"....... "Who dat?" I wondered....... With a ground attack tour behind me, and a PAI qualification, I had talked myself into it.

I drove into Pembroke on a grey November day, quite unimpressed by the rows of equally grey houses I passed, and checked into the Sundial Guest House where I was made welcome by Mr & Mrs Thomas and was joined by one of the staff PAI's who had come to show me the ropes. Three days later he left and I was Detachment Commander/Range Safety Officer, RAF Castlemartin. The whole range covered about 6,000 acres, most of which was used by the Army for tank training and I had one end of it next to the village of Bosherston. It is totally exposed to the south west winds and averages 32 gales a year. After a while my uniform became stiff with salt from the spray breaking over the 100 ft cliffs and the 'gold' in my cap badge turned green. I had a control tower, crew shed and a deep hole in the ground with a little hut built over it. We generated our own electricity, via a monstrous Petrol/Electric set, and brought water in from a tap in Bosherston. The range equipment belonged to the Navy, so I dealt with RNAS Brawdy for targets, etc; Merrion Camp (Army range HQ) for fuel; REME in Pembroke Dock for vehicle servicing; and Chivenor for admin.

There were 16 of us – me, an ex-air gunner Flight Sergeant, two Corporals and a mixed bag of airmen. We were later joined by a Warrant Officer armourer who was probably the only one of us who wasn't there because he could best be spared by his previous Station. We were all billeted in boarding houses in Pembroke, but after a couple of weeks I was able to move into the Army Officers Mess at Merrion, bringing the membership up to about six. Then I discovered that there were some empty married quarters up for grabs and was able to arrange allocations for the family men among us.

I went home at Christmas, made all the removal arrangements, and then it snowed. I had to get back to the job, so it had to be by rail. I had managed to contact my Senior NCO, Paddy Dougal, to ask him to leave the Landrover at Pembroke station and sure enough it was there when my train arrived 4 hours late, but also there was a note with the Station Master to the effect that the roads were bad and my old room was available at the Sundial, and the door would be unlocked. It was nearly midnight and snowing, but I thought I'd have a go at getting to Merrion and tackled the first hill. I got to the top, in 4 wheel drive, just, but with another 6 miles of narrow, winding hills ahead, common sense dictated a turn around. When I crept into the Sundial, there was a note by my bed that the kettle was on the stove and to make myself a cup of tea. Next morning after breakfast, the Thomas' refused to take any money because they had invited me to stay.

By the following weekend the snow had cleared enough for me to risk getting the train back to Waterbeach to collect the car, as my wife, Jill, was a little unhappy at the thought of driving a long way in winter conditions with a three year old prone to travel sickness. There was now flooding outside our 'quarter', part of an old cookhouse on a hutted site hidden from the Main Camp, but I had to leave Jill to deal with the move and drive back to Castlemartin. Some friends gave Jill a tremendous amount of help, lent her a car when she needed to go into Cambridge, put her and Sarah up for the night and took her to the train when she left. The removal men had loaded the van, then found a puncture and had to get another van and transfer everything so the whole episode had been a lot for her to cope with. After all that and about 10 hours of travelling with a travel sick Sarah, Jill was very pleased to see me when I met her at Pembroke. I'd arranged for them to stay at the Sundial until our things arrived and then finally, after 8 months of uncertainty, we were settled together again in a house on top of the hill between Pembroke and Pembroke Dock, overlooking the town and castle.

The original plan had been to spend three weeks at Castlemartin and one week back at Chivenor, but I suggested to OC Flying Wing that we were wasting our time at base and could more profitably be employed permanently at the range. He was happy with the idea of a more flexible firing programme and my crew and I enjoyed the freedom of detachment from the main base. I also protested at the rubbish on wheels I'd been given with which to keep the range active (one Landrover took 18 hours to make the journey from Chivenor because of breakdowns) and was given some more reliable vehicles. This was of course before the days of the Severn Bridge and motorways, and the road distance to Chivenor was 260 miles via Gloucester.

I told my motley crew that as long as the range was ready for use whenever required and, apart from travelling to and from work in the truck, they were properly dressed when in town, then we'd get on OK. They knew they were on to a good thing and it worked well. I dealt with the odd petty 'criminal' on the spot and only invoked the ultimate punishment (banishment to Chivenor) three times. One chap for hopping into bed with another's wife while the husband was away attending court on a paternity charge, one for wetting his bed in his boarding house for the second time (drunk) and being insubordinate about it, and the third for being totally incompetent. I'll draw a veil over the Corporal's wife who formed a friendship with the local prostitute and allowed her to make use of her quarter!

Around about March 1962, I went to CME for my six monthly check and was told I was still grounded. I reminded the Doc that after one year medically grounded I would lose my flying pay and that my year would be up before my next check. "We can't have that" he said, and gave me a flying category; 'Dual only and not above 10,000 ft'. I made use of it later during one of my brief visits to Chivenor and cadged a ride in the Hunter 7. We stayed below my ceiling and did a few dummy attacks on the range and a barrel roll or two, but by the time we landed I was totally exhausted. I felt scarcely able to pull myself from the cockpit, and when I did get back to the Operations Room I just sat on the edge of the dais drinking a cup of coffee. I was surprised at how out of condition three months in hospital and a year off flying had left me.

During the winter months the hill farmers were allowed to graze their sheep on the range, so the first job every morning was to drive them away from the target area. At first we were meticulous about this, stopping firing when they wandered back, but the sheep became so used to the aircraft and gunfire, that after the morning roundup I only bothered when they got close to the real danger area. During the summer, German Panzers used the tank range and we had to drive them off too when they inadvertently crossed into our area. One Landrover versus two tanks! The rocket target was an old tank and we didn't want an international incident.

If the range was not needed and maintenance was up to date, we'd sometimes go beachcombing in Bullslaughter Bay, which was inaccessible to the public and not easy to climb down to. You'd think it was a school outing seeing a tough Scottish airman running around with half a lobster pot float on his head and clutching a dustbin lid and a stick. Paddy and I bought a 5 ft cross-cut saw and set up a 'sawmill' to convert the timber we found to firewood. The blokes were quite enthusiastic, but I had to draw the line when the Adjutant from Merrion rang me to say he'd just seen three of them cutting down a tree in a council owned wood.

I learned from their landlady one morning that a policeman had called about some airmen who'd been kicking over dustbins the night before. I contacted the Police who were happy to leave it to me, then went back and walked all over my bunch; not for the dustbins but for not telling me that the police were interested. Another time, when a certain Army officer had complained to a publican about them drinking in the same bar as he and his wife, they did tell me, and afterwards were heard by Paddy to say, "Old Brad'll fix it". I did nothing of course and heard nothing. Mind you, this particular lady once sent her batwoman round to complain to Jill that our labrador pup had stolen her dog's bone. A careful search behind the settee revealed what had once been a lamb chop, which was dutifully returned.

Two of my airmen missed the transport one morning, which, in accordance with my strict instructions, left their billet at 07:30 hrs. They were then in a hostel in Pembroke Dock 10 miles away and when they rang in for transport were told by Ted Usher, the Warrant Officer armourer, that they'd better start walking and it would be one day jankers for every half hour they were late. They turned up remarkably quickly having had a lift. They never told me and it wasn't till several weeks later that Jill told me she'd picked them up on her way to Merrion. She had realised they had to be two of my bods and when they told her their problem, she agreed to keep quiet. They received their 'reward' via one of my 'Petty Sessions' and no one ever missed the truck again.

The Navy crew turned up one day on one of their occasional visits with a German incendiary bomb, which had been found in the roof of an old cottage. They weren't sure what it was (having spent the war in Birmingham, I had no doubts) and had carried it, admittedly in a bucket of sand, 40 miles in a Landrover. They threw it off the cliffs into an inaccessible cove……and it went off! Armourers!!?

I spoke about the wind earlier. There was one occasion when we had to try three different routes to get to the range because of fallen trees, but the winter of 1962-63 really got to our vitals. It snowed, then, for something like six weeks, the temperature stayed around freezing while a bitter east wind sliced across the range. There were four access points, which had to be guarded when firing was taking place, and normally the sentries would spend up to four hours on a shift depending on conditions. Now I rotated them every hour. I obtained four calf length storm coats and coke braziers, but that was all the protection they had. One chap came off his stint and in great trepidation presented me with a sort of bolero jacket, all that was left of his coat after it caught fire while he was huddled over his brazier. It was difficult to look serious as he told us how he had tried to put it out when everything around was frozen solid. Another of them stood the brazier on the step of the stile he was guarding and burnt a neat round hole through it.

Came the great day when the specialist at CME gave me a clean bill of health and a full flying category. I'd spent two years at the job, during which time I'd spent a total of 16 days at my Chivenor base and received one visit from the three Wing Commanders there. They flew into Brawdy, where I collected them in my car, had a quick look round and departed muttering things such as, "Blurry 'eck".

True, conditions were primitive and we had to be prepared to help ourselves, such as building a ramp out of driftwood so we could load the generator into the truck when it had to go to Chivenor (it also served for servicing our cars), but the weather wasn't always bad and in summer could be idyllic……barring the horse flies. On the plus side, we were living in a holiday area yet to be developed and had access to empty beaches and little coves, some of which were out of reach of the general public, and were left alone to get on with the job. Our daughter Sarah had her introduction to school at the excellent village school at Bosherston. The head commented on the noise of the aircraft the first time Jill went there and she didn't dare tell him who Sarah's father was. I went there with misgivings, some of which were borne out, but I could have had a much worse ground tour.

On the principle that 'them as don't ask don't get', I put in an application for posting to helicopters and was delighted to receive it in about six weeks, which is practically by return, so I must have done *something* right. I was dined out of the Mess at Merrion in spite of the various blacks I'd put up caused by different Service customs, they just regarded me with tolerant amusement as that funny 'blue' chap. My crew gave me a party in town, a bottle of Black Label Scotch and presents for both Jill and Sarah, and we left. I didn't know it then, but I was on my way to Borneo and the 'Confrontation' with Indonesia.

45. It Was Only a Golf Prize

Stan Downton

I came all the way from California to play in the 2004 HAAA Golf Society 3-day Away Day meeting in the Swindon area, where they played three different courses. The other 51st golfers, who are members of the HAAA GS, consider they are too old to be able to manage to play 18 holes on three consecutive days, so they don't know how I manage it. Perhaps the Californian climate has something to do with it, which enables me to play most days of the week and the course is only at the end of our garden. As it happened, I was fortunate enough to win the 'Nearest the Pin' prize at Ogbourn Downs GC, which was a letter opener in a presentation case.

On the day of my return to the States, Dave Bidgood (75th), the HAAA Golf Society Captain, drove me to Swindon station and I took the 06.45 train to Paddington, caught the Heathrow train and arrived at Terminal 1 at 08.45 and found the Staff Travel office round about 08.55. On previous visits to Heathrow, we always travelled out from Terminal 4, but British Airways, in their wisdom, decided that the flights to Los Angeles, San Francisco and Moscow would now operate out of Terminal 1 instead of Terminal 4. Most of we ex-BA employees are very familiar with Terminal 4. Staff Travel is directly opposite the check-in gates and we just dump our bags and golf equipment at position 25, then go through security and head for the Gate. All very simple. But at Terminal 1, Staff Travel is located in the Queen's building, which is situated between Terminal 1 and 2. Incidentally, I qualify for Staff Travel, having joined BA at JFK in New York in 1977. I then moved around Canada and the

US, working in Montreal, Seattle, San Diego and retiring when based at Los Angeles airport. Anyway, back to the Staff Travel office at Heathrow.

I checked in and was informed that I should not have been issued with a 'positive space' ticket as the flights were overbooked. Due to the miracles of modern science, the ticket had been issued in Jacksonville, Florida. They were duly chastised via the computer, but they processed me anyway. The check-in bags were weighed and the attendant informed me that the golf bag had to be taken to the area that dealt with oversized bags. To do that she would have to issue me with a temporary boarding pass that I was to take to Zone K to get rid of the golf bag. I trotted off to Terminal 1 with all my baggage and found Zone K, where I was told, "You want the oversized baggage position, which is in back of us". Lo and behold, I found a place that just looked like Aladdin's Cave, complete with Turbaned attendant, who put my golf bag down a massive chute. I then went back to Staff Travel with one case and a holdall, and surrendered the temporary boarding pass. The young lady then said, "Come back here at 10.55 and we will see how the flight breaks". Incidentally, the flight was scheduled to leave at 11.50. I went to W.H. Smith's, picked up a Daily Mail, and also had good look around Terminal 1, which was a Zoo! Got back to Staff Travel at the allotted time and at 11.15 I was given a Business Class seat, a standby release tag for the golf bag and directions to get to Zone R. So off I trotted with case and holdall to Zone R, where I was greeted by 2 ladies, one of whom was under instruction. I presented my boarding pass and the standby golf bag release tag. The boarding pass was OK, but the release tag gave them trouble. Eventually, after a couple of phone calls, they ascertained that I should present the tag at the departure gate, where the golf bag would be released for the flight. They then informed me very sweetly that they could not take my case down their chute, as it would be too late to make the flight. "Take it to the departure gate. They will take care of it". BIG MISTAKE. I go over to security, put my holdall on the security belt and told them that the other case goes in the hold. I go through the arch, pick up my holdall and look across and to see a girl looking through my case tagged for the hold. I asked her "What is the problem?" and she said, "There appears to be a dagger in the bag, but I cannot find it". The penny then dropped. I said, "If you look in the lid of the case, you will find a letter opener in a presentation case which was I won as a prize in a golf competition". Now the game is on. "Sir, you cannot take this on the aircraft, we will make out some paperwork in the office and the letter opener will eventually be returned to you". It is now about 11.40 and I have to get to Gate 56, which I estimated was about ½ mile from my present location. At this point in time, I didn't exactly lose it and tell her where to put it, but I did make her a present of it, and she did say she was very sorry. I replied, "Not half as sorry as I am!" and took off running with case and holdall. Eventually I got to the Gate, only to find what appeared to be complete chaos. I got rid of the case, surrendered the standby golf bag tag and boarded. The bad news was that we left 40 minutes late. The good news is – the case and golf bag made it, and I had a bed to sleep in. When you go through that performance often enough, then three straight days of golf is dead easy.... end of saga!!!

46. For Whom the Bell Tolls

Ginge Mushens

After a lot of searching in pockets, kitbags and kit lockers, and cajoling several residents of Room 16-3, we managed to rake together the grand total of 3d (1p in 'new' money), this being the price of a seat in the 'Dog End' of our local Camp cinema or 'Dream House'. This Emporium was the nearest we could get to 'Zanandu', the land where dreams came true, for about 2 hours twice a week and so offset the grind of life as an A/A (Aircraft Apprentice). Of course 3d only purchased one seat, so we had a small dilemma as to how to get the rest of the crowd in to see the object of our desire – one 'Ingrid Bergman'. Even now my heart leaps at the thought of even being refused a liaison with such a delectable female. Back to the task.

<u>Scheme 1</u> – confuse the girl in the ticket office and block her view whilst the mob got in. The grill on the front of the ticket booth was very small so it might be feasible, apart from the gorilla stationed at the inner door employed to tear the tickets, who might prove to be a problem.

<u>Scheme 2</u> – someone do a 'pretend' collapse very near the front of the queue and ask the gorilla for help, at which time, in the confusion, entry by the mob was affected. This had one serious drawback, as the fight to get into the cinema by rival Entry's to occupy the few seats available was nothing short of GBH, in other words injuries were commonplace, so our appeals for help would have been ignored.

<u>Scheme 3</u> – (my idea, and not without cunning if one thinks – self first!). I go to the cinema with our roll of cash and purchase a ticket, then legitimately take my seat until the lights go out for the start of the show. Upon which time I find myself caught short, i.e. I need to go to the toilet. Now, opposite the toilet door is the emergency exit which cannot be seen by our gorilla friend, so yours truly opens the door and they are 'in' – problem solved.

This last scheme, on the night, worked a treat, apart from the fact that some loudmouth had told his mate, who told his mate etc etc. When I opened the door expecting to see Jock Wardlaw, Tommy McCallum, Paddy Waddell, the Colemans and a few more – half the camp was there!! I rushed back to my seat, making sure I still had my unsurrendered half ticket proving I was a legitimate customer, and, assuming an air of total innocence, watched the invasion of the 'Dog End' with some incredulity. The cinema had been fairly empty at our end, but after the trailers, when the lights came on for a short interval, it was literally heaving with A/A's. Gorilla dashed around with a look of abject horror on his face as he looked at the mob then at the half dozen surrendered tickets on his string. Of course the clever ones soon found some discarded tickets on the floor and proffered these as a sign of their innocence. Gorilla knew he was beat, so he then went to the emergency exit and, with about 200 yds of chain, proceeded to baulk any further attempts at this ruse.

The Main Feature: Without boring any of my readers as to the attributes of our Ingrid, suffice to say I never liked Gregory Peck after that because of what he did to her under that blanket when he should have been fighting the Spanish Civil War! It was during that campaign that the subject of this article came about. As total shock horror, Franco's troops were using 'Dum Dum' bullets! After the film show, on enquiring about this with my Plumber (Armourers to you) mates, I was informed that this method of warfare was not allowed as it made a great big nasty hole in the victim, which didn't give him much chance of recovery. "How's that?" queried yours truly. "Well" spoke Roach with some authority, "They file the point off the sharp end of the bullet and it punches out whatever it hits". All the Plumbers nodded their heads, the noise of rattling brains was tremendous. "And to demonstrate this I will show you" spake he.

We retired to the barrack room and from out of nowhere a number of .303 bullets appeared. "Seeing you want a demo Ginge, we'll use your rifle so you can clean it after" spake our demonstrator. (A note here about the rifles. In those days we all had a rifle, which was kept in a rifle rack in each barrack room.) With rifle and bullets, we went to the end window of the room, lifted the sash then loaded the rifle with three bullets, with the ends having been filed off prior to loading. The first shot was dispatched into what was supposed to be a lawn just outside 16-1's window. A .303 makes a bit of a crack and of course, heads popped out of the windows below. These were quickly withdrawn when on looking up they saw the rifle! The demonstration was not satisfactory to our mates, as the hole in the lawn, although quite large, did not show a comparison between the entry and exit holes. "What we need" one participant said, "Is something to simulate a body". A quick survey did not elicit any volunteers. "I know," said someone, "We'll use that new lead bumper weight, as that has give and some thickness". All were in agreement and the weight was tossed onto the lawn. Again heads popped out below complaining about noise and muttering about danger, and being irresponsible, and all that stuff. Of course they didn't realise they were in the presence of skilled men who were conducting an experiment to educate an ignorant Instrument Basher. Of course one could sympathise with them, they being only sprogs of the 53rd Entry! Whilst the complaining went on, the rifle was fired and a quick retreat was observed below. The bumper weight was retrieved by the usual method of descending and ascending, to and from ground level, via the drainpipe. Inspection of the weight proved beyond any doubt that dum dum bullets made a small hole in the front and a damn great hole on exit, proving friend Roach's point without doubt. We then retired to the NAAFI to further discuss this subject, passing groups of agitated Snoops looking for something or other, which was their task in life I believe.

47. Full Circle

Jack Wetherell

The distance from Huntingdon railway station to the bus terminus is not long, but in full webbing plus a kit bag slung over the shoulder, it becomes a marathon, especially on a hot summer's day. I did that little hike in 1949, for, after 3 years at Halton plus a year at 32 MU (RAF St Athan), RAF Wyton was to be my first posting.

Life had been hard at 32 MU, but it had also been very interesting. Most of the Fitter IIA's were engaged on re-building Meteors, while the Engine lads were turning out re-built Merlin engines for the Berlin Airlift. After a short time on Meteors, I was attached to the Special Installation Squadron. This was to be quite an experience, for the job entailed flitting around the country installing TBA sets (Tuneable Beam Approach for the uninitiated!) into such aircraft as Lancasters, Mosquitos and Harvards. Then there were Gee sets into Ansons and many, many, one-off jobs. The boffins would come down from RAe Farnborough and tell us what they wanted. That done, you would probably get an instrument thrust into your hands, told where it had to fit, and then set off to design and make an attachment bracket. Offering the finished product to the boffins, they would either say "Fine" or "No, that's not quite what we want". It was all very interesting, even if, when going on detachment, the changing of trains did take hours due to you having to hump the Mod kits, plus tool boxes, from platform to platform.

In those days, people on detachment seemed to be fair game for the snoops (RAF Policemen) and many the battle we had. RAF Manby was one place where they definitely did not like us, but you could say the feeling was mutual! There was a shortage of most things during the winter of 1949 and one result of this was that the barrack room lights had to be switched off at 08.00 hrs. One morning I neglected to do this as, being Room Orderly, I had the morning newspaper to read! So this 'moth', dressed as a policeman, appeared and proceeded to inform me the error of my ways and to report to the guardroom forthwith. On reporting to the guardroom, the snoop there had bad news to relate; he could not find the S.O.R. pertaining to the 08.00 hrs lights-out order. Naturally I was very sorry for him, but felt that it would be wiser to say nothing. Did I get away with it? Well, almost! He said he would put my name in the book so that if I boobed again he could have me. I pointed out that I would be leaving in a few days, but with great wisdom, he countered my remark by saying that I may well come to Manby again. Sure enough, one evening later, we were on our way to the cinema, when out of the darkness loomed this snoop who promptly had us for having our hands in our pockets. You had to give it to them, they never gave up, but at the same time they would never have been accepted into the Mounties! It was beginning to get nasty when one of our number, (not me Chiefy!), gives this snoop a swift kick on the shins and tells us to run. We, of course, departed hastily. They must have had a fair idea of who we were, because a few nights later I got done for not wearing a hat. Mind you, it was after midnight and I had just left the Camp dance, but that did not seem to matter to our Fabian. Next afternoon, without a hat, I told the CTO that I did not go much on it and he seemed to agree with me. He must have done so, because he dismissed the charge but told me to get a haircut. You couldn't win!

In the summer of 1949 we went to RAF Little Rissington, where we were accommodated in the Sgts Mess. It was a wooden affair and was used for many things, including a store for married quarters' furniture. One Saturday we decided to go to Cheltenham and that decision turned out to be the smartest we had ever made, for on returning we found the whole lot on fire. We managed to save our belongings before they became fuel for the flames, but it was early morning before we got new accommodation. As you can imagine, we really got the third degree over that lot, but if you will excuse the pun, we were fireproof. Actually the cause was put down to a smouldering love affair bursting into flame!

Returning to 32 MU again, I was done for wearing gym shoes to the Camp stack. Apparently it was on Station Routine Orders, and as ignorance of orders was no excuse, I was awarded 3 days. As was usual in those days, I was charged on the last call of the night for dirty webbing. Well, if they give you jankers, they should expect your webbing to get dirty! My Flight Commander evidently thought I was going through a bad patch, so decided to help me. The first I knew of this was when the Flight Sergeant came up to me and told me to say that I had no blanco. Well, I thought about this and came to the conclusion that he was trying to get me put away for a stretch. Hats off for the Flight Commander who asks "Why the dirty webbing?" I told a wonderful story, but he seemed a little put out by it and suggested that what I really meant was that I had no blanco. Being quick on the uptake, I hastened to agree but was unprepared for the next bit. He asked me if I was interested in cricket and I was so flabbergasted, I said "Yes". It was the wrong answer because I found myself as wicket-keeper for the Section team! As it was only for one performance, I will draw a veil over the result. On coming out of the Flight Commander's office, the Flight Sergeant threatened to punch my ear, but you couldn't really blame him, could you?

In those days, you had a 48 hour weekend pass every month and always you were threatened with dire punishment if you were late back. I had decided to go to Halton to see a girl friend of mine and yes – I was late back – collecting 5 days as result. Actually I reckoned that I deserved a Duke of Edinburgh's award, for, having missed the last train from Wendover to London, and with the 'don't-be-late' warning fresh in my mind, I had to do something positive. A friendly engine driver stopped at Wendover station and offered me a lift on the footplate of his engine as far as Wembley. This was great, but even that, plus some inspired hitch-hiking, failed to get me to Paddington in time to catch the Cardiff train.

At 32 MU you did guard duty at night; usual thing, two hours on and four off. You were given a rifle and bayonet, but of course, no ammunition. As was normal, the Orderly Officer used to come round on a bicycle, but always without lights. My companion on guard one night reckoned that this was too much and decided to do something about it. As the night wore on we trudged round the hangars, ears alert for the sound of tyres on tarmac. Eventually we heard it, stood still and waited. When the rider was only yards away, my companion leapt into action shouting the age-old challenge. Well, the poor Orderly Officer fell off his bike and I'm sure he must have thought that his last moment had arrived. He never, as far as I know, came that trick again, but I could never quite make up my mind if my companion had only meant to scare him.

So here I was at Wyton again, the home of four squadrons of Lincolns – Nos.15, 44, 90 and 138. It promised to be, and eventually proved to be, a great Station. None of the hangars were heated in those days and it was as cold as charity working on the aircraft during the winter months. Somehow though it all seemed worthwhile, especially during exercises when you could see as many as thirty Lincolns taking off one after another. It was a much different Station to what it is now; everything was spread out, with none of the new buildings squeezed into the empty spaces and no long runway. Funny in a way that my first 'real' Station should also be my last. The 'wheel' has really turned – the Full Circle.

48. An Unofficial Modification

Fred Hoskins

Just before Christmas 1952 there was a discussion in the crew room of No.33 Squadron at Butterworth, Malaya, as to the desirability of delivering some toilet rolls by air to RAF Tengah in Singapore, where our sister Hornet squadron, No.45, was based, together with 60 Squadron (Vampires) and visiting Lincoln squadrons. The usual method of delivering toilet rolls by air, and I do not mean in the normal course of supply, was to lower the flaps, put in the rolls, and then close the flaps again. Over the target the flaps were lowered and out would fall the rolls of paper. Obviously, speed had to be reduced to below the maximum for lowering the flaps so as not to damage the aircraft. This method, we thought, was somewhat basic and, indeed, pedestrian. How much better it would be to devise a way of delivering at speed, preferably in a dive attack! Bombs would be out of the question of course, whether dummy or live, but we also had rockets which were fired in a dive attack so, after some consideration, we came up with a way of using the rockets without actually firing a live projectile.

The rockets comprised iron tubes with a bore of three inches into which the cordite propellant was inserted. The 60 lb warhead was attached to the front end of the tube and in the rear was a venturi restriction to speed up the flow of gases when the cordite was ignited. On pressing the firing button on the control column, ignition was achieved electrically through cables culminating in a 'pigtail' connection to the rocket itself. For our peaceful employment of the rocket, we took the empty tubes and mounted them, reversed, on the rocket rails under the wings. Thus the venturi was at the front end, leaving what had become the rear end open for the toilet rolls to be loaded and ejected. To prevent the airflow in flight from pushing the rolls out, we taped fabric over the front ends of the tubes and also taped paper over the rear ends to keep the rolls in place. On the cloth at the front we taped detonators which we connected to the rocket circuits. Our calculation was that on pressing the firing button the detonators would blow away the fabric, the airflow would enter the tubes with sufficient force to break the paper at the tail ends and the rolls would be ejected. So it proved to be.

Two Hornets were 'armed' with four tubes loaded with toilet rolls and on Christmas morning they flew to Tengah and back, a distance of 320 nautical miles each way. By the time they reached Tengah, the traditional Christmas programme was in full swing and it was apparent from the crowd outside the Sergeants Mess that the officers had arrived there to gather refreshment before going on to the Airmens Mess to serve the turkey and pudding. The crowd looked up with surprise as two Hornets dived on them with some élan and streams of toilet paper floated down. Witty inscriptions had been added to some of the paper, including "Hang this on your Christmas tree, Champion de Crespigny" – that being the name of the Tengah Station Commander. I cannot imagine anything like that happening today!

49. The Ring

Eric Mold

It would be true to say that my Air Force career worked out exactly as I always dreamed it would. Although I joined as a boy, all of my dreams while I filed away in basic fitting, or bashed away on the parade square, or blew into the trumpet, were to fly. I was lucky enough to realize my dreams soon after I left Halton's hallowed halls. Good luck was to follow me all through my Air Force career. I was lucky enough to get all of the flying jobs I really wanted. But there was one time when I didn't know exactly what I wanted to do. I was just coming to the end of a 6½ year tour flying Starfighters in Germany and wondering what would happen next. One day I got a phone call from a friend in Ottawa, (Canadian Air Force Headquarters), saying that they had a job opening up which they thought I would be just right for.

Two months later I found myself on the staff of the Aerospace Engineering Test Establishment, (the Canadian equivalent of RAe Farnborough or A&AEE Boscombe Down), with a small office overlooking the tarmac at Ottawa's Uplands Airport. My job was to co-ordinate the flight test and acceptance programme of all Canadian military aircraft that were being repaired, overhauled or modified by civilian contractors. Nice work if you can get it – and I had got it. I had small detachments of quality control people and aircrew at several contractors' plants in Canada and the US. Where 'production' didn't warrant establishing a detachment, I organized crews from operational squadrons to do the job. I went along to monitor completion of the test card. Most of the time I dashed around the continent in my own T-33. Sometimes I'd do a bit test flying myself, if one of the resident guys was on leave or they had a particularly heavy workload. Getting checked out on most of the aircraft types involved went with the territory – as they say. A real fun job. I can tell some good stories about it like the time the lid blew off a large thermos urn of soup when we de-pressurized the cabin of a Saberliner we were testing for the USAF. It had just been fitted with a beautiful VIP interior by CAE in Winnipeg. We really dropped in the soup over that one! But that is not what I want to tell you about today, this is all about 'The Ring'.

We had a small detachment of people at Scottish Aviation in Prestwick, where they were doing work on the Starfighters which we had based in Germany. Eventually the time rolled around for me to do my annual Flight Safety Survey of this detachment. I was to be there for a couple of weeks, while the resident test pilot took a few days leave. I intended to take one of the twice weekly Yukon sked flights that the RCAF operated between Ottawa, Gatwick and Europe. However, when the time came for my departure, I found I had been 'bumped' by someone with a higher priority than me. I suppose I could have rescheduled my visit, but I was thinking of the resident test pilot's leave plans. I had authority to travel by commercial air, but even in those days it would have cut nearly $3000 into my meagre travel budget. I had all but given up on going when I heard that a C.130 Hercules was leaving from Trenton, a base about 150 miles away and it was going directly to Scotland. A phone call to Transport Command Ops got me a ride in the jump seat, as supernumerary crew. Someone flew me down to Trenton in the beautiful old Dakota we kept for such duties. Before long I was sipping coffee and munching away on sarnies, learning how the other half lived, as the Herc climbed up and set course for the Atlantic.

The C.130 was going to RAF Machrihanish. I didn't have a clue where that was but compared with Canada, Scotland is not a very big place, so I did not think it would take me long to get from there to Prestwick. Later I wandered back to the navigator's station and took a look at one of his topographical maps. Machrihanish was on one of the outer Scottish Isles. Wow! – miles from anywhere! But there must be transportation to the mainland – mustn't there? Apparently our Maritime

Command Argus's had been operating from there on NATO exercises. The Herc was going over to pick up ground handling equipment that was left behind when the Argus detachment returned. They would only be on the ground for a few minutes while the gear was loaded and then they were going on to Germany before returning to Canada.

When we landed at Machrihanish, it was pitch dark and the place appeared deserted. Apparently it was only manned by detachments during exercises. I remember walking away from the Herc, carrying all of my flying gear and other bits and pieces, and wondering how was I going to get 'down town'. Luckily I found a phone box which had a taxi firm's business card stuck to the wall, so I was able to call a taxi. About 30 minutes later a small car arrived and the driver inquired if I was the one that called the cab. On the way into Campbeltown, I asked the driver if he knew of anywhere I might get a room for the night. "Auch, sure I do" he replied, "Tha hey a few rooms at tha pub". That sounded fine to me. A couple of pints right now would just hit the right spot. Eventually we drew up outside a small pub. I forget the name now, it was such a long time ago. I paid the driver and staggered out of the cab, carrying all of my gear.

As I pushed open the door of the saloon bar, the 20 or so punters inside suddenly went silent. They just stood and stared at me. I suppose I must have been a rather curious sight. Wearing my orange flying suit with maps and whistles and knives and things sticking out of it or hanging from it, a yellow Mae West, carrying a biliously painted crash helmet and various other bits and pieces of military gear. I grinned, rather sheepishly and said "Hi", whereupon the hum of conversation gradually resumed. I asked the barmaid about the possibility of a room for the night and she quickly summoned the publican's wife. After a few sceptical glances and a couple of questions, she took me upstairs to see the room. It was not easy struggling up the narrow stairs will all of my kit, but eventually we reached the third floor and I was shown – with great pride – into a small, cold, room. If Robbie Burns himself had been standing there, I would not have been surprised. All of the furniture was well over a hundred years old. The enormously high double bed, massive pillows and eiderdown, large marble washstand, complete with a matching water jug and washbowl. Even a 'you know what' under the bed. The landlady was obviously very proud of the room she was offering me. I was very tired, grateful – and thirsty. I dumped my gear on the bed, put on a pair of jeans and sweater and 'retired' to the bar and made friends with most of the lads and lassies therein. After a few drams and a pint or two I could not keep my eyes open any longer. By the time the landlord called "Time", I was ready for bed. I slept like a log.

When I awoke, the sun was streaming in through the windows – unusual for Scotland. When I looked out, it was just like a scene from Gulliver's Travels, or perhaps a set from the movie Whisky Galore would be more apt. The beautiful little harbour, fishing boats, lobster pots, all bathed in glorious sunshine – it looked like paradise to me. A tap on the door and a young lady asked if I was ready for my tea, and a few minutes later she produced a tray containing a teapot, milk and sugar and a plate of shortcake cookies. Then she asked if I was ready for some hot water to wash with and she said, "There's a shower on the floor below". Half an hour later I walked into the Saloon Bar where a small table had been set for one; apparently I was the only guest. This was one of the finer moments of my Air Force career. Sitting in that quaint Scottish pub, sun streaming through the windows, enjoying a delicious 'Full Monty' (in the original sense) and the Queen was paying the bill. "Thanks Ma'm". The landlord told me that there was a Viscount plane service to Prestwick once daily, or I could take a series of buses and little ferries, and island hop over to the mainland. That sounded much more fun than a 20 minute flight. I decided to try that way the next morning. I checked in on the phone with my people at Scottish Aviation. They wanted to send a Flying Club plane over to get me, but after reassuring them that I was doing fine they left me to my own devices.

I spent the rest of the day exploring the quaint little town, walked around the harbour, examined the fleet of brightly painted fishing boats and chatted with some of the fishermen. I had a ploughman's lunch and a pint in a quayside pub, and tea and 'pigs ears' in a little tea shop later on. Eventually I went back to the inn for a traditional Scottish evening meal. Another enjoyable night in the saloon bar gave me the opportunity to repay some of the generous hospitality that was lavished on me the night before – after they realized that I was not a Russian pilot or had not just got off a flying saucer.

The next morning, after another FM breakfast, I made my way to the harbour and the bus stop, where I boarded an ancient Bedford bus for the run up to Claunaig. What beautiful run it was, the deep blue of the sound on the starboard side and the purple heather and majestic countryside to port. On sunny days Scottish scenery is hard to beat. I was fascinated by the way the bus driver extricated himself from his seat to open the door for passengers, or to deliver the occasional newspaper. He sort of threaded himself between the centrally mounted engine and over the hand brake lever and gearshift in a most peculiarly contorted manoeuvre. I wondered what the result of this peculiar form of exercise, a hundred of so times a day, would have on him over a 20 to 25 year career? But he was a jolly fellow, he knew everyone and had plenty of chit chat with each passenger that got on the bus. When we arrived at Claunaig, I had just sufficient time to grab a sandwich and a pint, as there were no dining facilities on the ferry. When the boat drew in, a couple of cars drove off of it and a few that were waiting on the quay drove on. Then a shepherd with a flock of about 30 sheep boarded. There were several foot passengers like me and a few boxes and packages, including two crates full of chickens. The ferry captain and his helper knew everyone. Everyone was greeted with a joke or other light hearted banter and before long we were off across the sound to Lochranza. There was a canteen on board where it looked as if they could rustle up a cup of tea, but since it was nearly the end of the season, and the traffic being on the light side, it was not in operation. When I asked, they said they were sorry it was closed – but if I wanted a dram – they could arrange that. When we arrived at Lochranza, another ancient bus was waiting to take me down the spectacular east coast of the Isle of Arran to Brodick, where I took another little ferry to Ardrossan on the Scottish mainland. I was met by my colleague from Scottish Aviation, who soon had me ensconced in a modern, rather boxy, hotel in Ayr.

After a couple of days on the job, the weather changed. And my, how it changed. It rained like it only can rain on the west coast of Scotland, it comes at you horizontally – not from above, like it does at most other places. There was nothing for me to do except lay on my hotel bed and wait for it to improve. Then I got to thinking – I had an old aunt that used to live in Stranraer, which was only about 85 miles away. I wondered whether, if I rented a car and drove over there, I might be able to find out what had become of her. I decided to try.

My mother died in 1942 and I can remember my aunt from Scotland coming down to London for her funeral. After the funeral, my father and I took her to Euston Station to see her off back to Stranraer. Just as she got on to the train, my dad pressed a small box into her hand and said, "Here, I know Lil would want you to have these". The box contained two rings. One of which has an interesting history. Apparently, one of the great aviatrix pioneers, Amy Johnson, Jean Batten or Emila Erheart, I don't know which one it was, sold off some of her jewellery to help finance her flights. One item, an earring in the form of a fleur-de-lis of diamonds mounted in platinum, was among the items purchased by a jeweller friend of my dad's. Apparently the other earring had been lost. The jeweller suggested that mounted on a gold band it would make a beautiful ring. So my dad commissioned him to make it for my mother. My aunt always admired the ring and my mother often jokingly said, "I'll leave it to you in my will when I die".

I had not seen my aunt since the train drew out of Euston Station that night. Now, near Stranraer, with time on my hands, it would be nice to find out what had become of her. I picked up my rented car and set off, in the pouring rain, to find Stranraer. A couple of hours later I rolled into the small town, the layout quickly came back to me – we often spent our summer holidays there before the war. I soon found The Swan Inn, which was owned by my uncle and aunt long before WW2. In those days it was a favourite with the crews of the Stranraer flying boats that were frequently moored on nearby Loch Ryan. The present landlord told me that my aunt was still alive and he directed me to her little cottage, nearby. I rang the bell and the door opened a few moments later. I said to the old lady standing there, "Hello Auntie Vi, I'm Eric, Lil's boy". She smiled but seemed confused, she thought that I was my dad. She was expecting the chimney sweep that day, so all of the furniture was covered with newspapers. Well into her eighties, she obviously had difficulty hearing and cataracts greatly limited her vision. But we had a pleasant couple of hours together – she soon produced a half bottle of *Dimple* and we had a dram or two, all the time I'm trying to convince her that I am me – not my dad.

Eventually, when the time came for me to leave, I asked her, as tactfully as I could, if she would leave my mother's rings to me in her will when she died – I wanted to keep them in the family. "Auch bairn, ya can hay the rings – ya can hay the rings" she replied. With that she disappeared and returned a couple of seconds later with a grubby little black box tightly secured with elastic bands. It contained one of the rings – the important one – she did not know what had happened to the other. I offered her some money, but she would not think of it. I hugged her and kissed her good bye and drove away.

The weather eventually improved and I was able to finish my work at Scottish Aviation. Then I had to find my way back to Canada. I made my way to London, where we had a headquarters, and asked the movements people if there was any chance of a service flight back. The sked flight was full, but a couple of day later, His Excellency Roland Mitchener, the Governor General of Canada, would be returning and he always allowed ordinary guys, like me, to travel with him if there was room. During the two day layover in London, I took the ring to Bravington's where, after it was ultrasonically cleaned and put it into a nice little ring box, it looked just like new. I had a great flight back to Ottawa – no one eats box lunches on that plane! His Excellency circulated throughout the cabin and had long chats with most of us, and he listened with great interest when I told him this story. He was a very popular guy.

Vera was waiting to meet me when I arrived at Ottawa Airport. When she asked if I had bought her anything, I nonchalantly replied, "Yes – I've got you a diamond ring".

50. Trials and Tribulations

Robbie Roberts

Trying to recall events of nearly 40 years ago is some challenge. Unfortunately I didn't make any notes at the time or keep a logbook, so the following account relies only on my (increasingly) fallible memory.

As part of the preliminaries to coming home 'tour-ex' from Aden in 1961, I was asked to nominate three areas of preference for my next UK posting. Nothing unusual in that you may say, except that I got my first choice – Bomber Command – in the shape of a posting to RAF Scampton. Now, I had nothing against the place or the 'V' Force for that matter, suffice to say that after 12 months in the Electronics Bay, I was reasonably happy with my lot until a signal came through asking for volunteers for a job at CSDE (the Central Servicing Development Establishment at RAF Swanton Morley in the wilds of Norfolk), which involved participating in the BOAC intensive flying trials of the VC10, which would consist of 1,000 hours of route proving over a period of 6 months.

Shortly after putting my name down, I was called to RAF Upavon for an interview, along with about 60 other worthies. It emerged that what *'they'* were looking for was a team of three, consisting of a fitter, a rigger and one representative of the 'important trade', to wit, an Instrument Basher. Those of us who survived to the short list were subsequently called to Swanton Morley for an individual grilling by the OC Projects Wing. As far as the Instrument Bashers were concerned, the choice rested between myself and another 'Chief' from Scampton, and since he (or his wife?) decided he didn't want the hassle that the job would undoubtedly involve, Joe Soap got it – and was eventually posted to Swanton Morley, together with two V-bomber Crew Chiefs who had also been selected.

At Swanton Morley, we found out how we would be expected to cover the trials. The aircraft was to be under our surveillance 24 hours a day for the duration of the trials. One of us would fly each day from Heathrow to record flying time; the time and flight conditions when any fault occurred; the 'turn-round time' at our destination; all ground equipment used; together with all replenishments (kick the tyres and refuel) required. When the aircraft returned to Heathrow, a second member of the team would be on hand for the night shift, to take over and record any defects which were found over and above those which had occurred in flight; the time; manpower and spares required to fix them; as well as to prepare the aircraft for its trip the following day. The third member of the team was to arrive at least one hour before take-off to take over and be ready to cover the aircraft on its next flight, while the other two team members had to get ready to continue the sequence in turn until the trials finished. All this information was to be recorded on standardized forms and returned to CSDE for analysis for later use in spares provisioning, manpower allocation, etc.

Now, before we could be considered competent to take part in this exercise, we were to be attached to the VC10 Project Team at the Vickers (as it was then) Weybridge factory, prior to going on a BOAC VC10 Flight Engineers course. We were duly enrolled on the next one, together with BOAC pilots, Flight Engineers and two Flight Engineers from the 'mob' who were to be attached to Vickers at Wisley for familiarization with the BOAC aircraft, and subsequently the RAF variant. The aim was to give us a pretty detailed knowledge of the aircraft and its systems – no trade barriers, everybody did everything – from the operation and servicing of the toilets (recirculating of course) to the functioning of the flying controls. All in all, it took about 12 weeks, 6 of them in the Aircraft Servicing School at Weybridge and I do recall that 'our' Flight Engineers were not best pleased when they were required to take a written examination at the end of that phase. The only part of the course that I missed out on was the 2 week engine phase at Rolls Royce, because I was moving into a hiring at Farnborough. It turned out to be a flat in a large house almost directly in line with the centre line of the RAe runway, which could be a bit noisy (but very exciting) during the Farnborough Air Show. I could actually take photos of any aircraft on finals from the kitchen window, which was on the second floor.

It was now April 1963 and the three of us moved up to Heathrow into the office accommodation set aside for ourselves and the manufacturers reps etc who would also be on the trials. The VC10 (G-ARVF) was to be flown by a mixture of Vickers Test pilots, BOAC pilots converting to type and two RAF pilots. Servicing was the responsibility of the BOAC engineers, with specialist help from manufacturers reps. For the life of me I can't remember the exact date on which the trials started, but I do know that the first month consisted of a flight – Heathrow-Beirut-Heathrow – every day, and each of us flew once every three days. When I was due to fly, I got up at about 05.00 hrs and drove from Farnborough to Heathrow ready to take over from the night shift and prepare for take-off

– usually about 08.00 hrs. Since there were only about 12 engineers on each flight, (BOAC ground crew and reps), we had no cabin crew until the later flights, and only tea and coffee were available in the air – about 4½ hours – but we usually got a cooked meal at the airport when we landed. We had to eat on a rota basis however, because some of us had to 'kick the tyres' etc and get the aircraft ready for the return flight. As unlicensed engineers (in the civil sense), we RAF guys were not allowed to carry out any actual servicing, but we could poke our noses in and help if required. After the novelty had worn off, most of the in-flight time was thoroughly boring, but the aircraft was fully furnished so there was plenty of room to stretch out in. Of course, if anything went wrong, there was something to do, but most of the time the aircraft was remarkably reliable. On one occasion when we were 'Somewhere over the Mediterranean', I asked one of the BOAC aircrew "Where are we?". "Twenty five miles north of Rhodes, sir" came the instant answer (without reference to anybody or anything you notice). "How do you know that?" I asked. "I don't" he said, "But you can't tell nervous passengers that you haven't a clue where you are". So much for honesty and integrity!

Once the first month was over, Beirut became a bit old hat and we started introducing flights to Khartoum and back. This trip was normally staged through Rome, and bottles of Chianti etc started to come back as well! I think I omitted to say that as far as Customs were concerned, we qualified as aircrew and therefore had a daily duty free allowance. One of the fascinating things about these trips was that we came back after dark and coming in from Rome, we started to let down over Paris. On a clear night it was quite a spectacle. There was also a lot to be seen on the final approach to Heathrow and the flight deck sometimes became quite crowded. It got so bad on one flight which I was on, that at the post flight aircrew/groundcrew debriefing, Brian Trubshaw (later to be the Concorde Test Pilot) gave us all a stern talking to and said that in future he would appreciate having less than 12 people standing on the flight deck during finals because it made it difficult to concentrate on the job in hand!

Of course there were some problems. On one occasion we were coming back from Khartoum and Heathrow was fog bound. Would you believe the diversion airfield was Rome? So we had to turn round and go back to Rome. Having landed there, we finally got into a coach to go into Rome itself. Before we left, the BOAC purser was calling out each name in turn to tell us how much we were due as an overnight allowance. While this exercise was going on, the coach was in darkness and when he got to my name, he said something like "One thousand, six hundred and fifty five lira" and in response to my gasp of amazement, some wag said " Don't worry, it's only about fourpence halfpenny" – total collapse of assembled company! The hotel turned out to be probably the worst one that I have ever stayed in. The waitress didn't refuse to sell us any beer after the first round, she just said that they had run out. All the windows of the lower floors were completely covered with steel shutters, and the breakfast table had to be experienced to be believed – barely cooked eggs and bacon served cold. Fortunately, having gone straight back to Khartoum from Rome, we managed to get back to Heathrow the following night. Gradually during the trial, the daily flights became longer to Accra, Lagos and finally weekend trips to Nairobi and Salisbury (now Harare), which were very enjoyable. I always remember coming back from Nairobi to London non-stop with Peter Kane, the senior BOAC VC10 Captain, who was walking up and down the cabin repeatably calculating whether we had enough fuel on board to make Heathrow. Not exactly designed to inspire confidence, but we obviously made it. The trials finished with an overnight to Montreal and when I walked down the steps, I was welcomed by Stan Downton (!) who was in charge of the civilian servicing party. Stan would not hear of me spending the evening in a hotel and insisted that I should join him and his family for dinner at his home. It was an extremely generous gesture by Stan and one which was much appreciated. These 51st ex-brats get everywhere!!

I suppose it sounds as though it was a doddle from start to finish. They say you only remember the best bits of any experience. It was hard work, but there were plenty of good bits. I still feel very privileged to have been chosen to take part in what was a unique event, which, when it was over, resulted in the three of us being absorbed into the VC10 Project Team to continue working on the aircraft until we were all posted to RAF Brize Norton in 1966 to take part in the RAF Flight Trials and then to introduce the aircraft into service – but that's another story!!

51. 16 Block Drain Clearance: A Confession

Nobby Clarke

No doubt someone out there will put me right, but I think it was early 1948, just after we 'Plumbers' (Armourers) had completed our Demolition Phase, that the situation arose. It was Bull night, and, as you can all remember, things could get a little fraught, even at that late stage in our Halton saga.

Someone, I know not whom, came into the room (16-3 I believe) to say that the landing was flooded. It was, as always, all hands to the pump and of course, the inevitable result was that nothing was achieved! We tried prodding, banging, mopping up, and anything else that one could think of, but all to no avail. It may well have dawned on somebody, at some point, that it might have been worthwhile going down to the floor below and removing the plug from the U-bend, but it did not dawn on us!

Yours truly then remembered that he had some detonators and safety fuse stached away, 'won' from the Demolition Phase, and suggested that a detonator might just have enough punch to remove the blockage, and so it was agreed by one and all that this would be done. I proceeded to take a No.27 detonator and about 3 ft of No.11 safety fuse, squeezed the fuse into said detonator and placed it in the offending drain. We then cleared the landing, warning anyone standing around to stay clear until the "small" bang. I lit the fuse and we all retired to positions of safety, in order to countdown the 33 seconds burning time. Right on the dot, there was the most enormous explosion, which reverberated throughout the whole Block. This was followed immediately by yells of anguish from the ground floor, where it transpired that poor Henry Ford had been standing. A large piece of the U-band had narrowly missed his head and he had been given quite a drenching by the dirty water expelled by the blast. Whilst I had achieved the desired effect of clearing the blocked drain, I was also responsible for showering the mucky water all over the landing walls. Ah well! You win some, you lose some!

The net result of all this, as you will no doubt have already guessed, was that I was up before 'Sir' the following morning. Before being marched in, Chiefy Thomas informed me that "You are going to bounce so high, that I doubt if we shall ever see you again!"

Having tried to persuade 'Sir' that I had used various implements in an attempt to clear the drain, including the leg from a McDonald bed, I had to confess to the truth. 'Sir' said that he admired my initiative, but felt that the use of explosives to clear barrack block drains was not the best way of doing it, and moreover, I was very lucky not to be facing charges such as murder, manslaughter or grievous bodily harm. I was given 48 hours to persuade other members of the Plumbers fraternity and other trades, to hand in any items of an explosive nature which they may have secreted away – the level of such 'hand-ins' would help to determine my subsequent sentence.

As Beefy Creasey has said on a number of occasions since, "There seemed to be more 9 mm ammo outside the Squadron office than there was in the SAA Lock-up". (SAA – Small Arms Ammunition, for the benefit of the gash trades!) There were also a goodly number of other things which go 'BANG' (and not just in the night!) included in the pile, and so when I next stood in front of 'Sir', he was inclined to be a little lenient. He awarded me 14 days jankers, or the option of having a Court Martial. "No thank you Sir" says I, "I'll take what you have given me".

I think 'Sir' was a little disappointed in that he could not fine me for the cost to repair the drain!

52. By The Stroke of a Pen (What's in a Name?)

Taff Denham

On Saturday 28th February 1992, I attended the 14th South African Air Forces Association Dinner at the 'Wanderers' cricket ground in Johannesburg, which you may or may not know is the South African equivalent to 'Lords' in the UK. The day was great, this being my 8th consecutive reunion dinner with the SAAF, friends of mine being ex-SAAF. The day and evening was very hot, but only two iced beers passed my lips from 19.15 hrs till the dinner at 20.00 hrs – very conservative. During dinner I consumed 1½ glasses of white wine and finished off with a glass of port at about 23.00 hrs. Dinner finished at 23.30 hrs and I was home by midnight in order to watch the Rugby World Cup game on TV between New Zealand and South Africa. South Africa had beaten Australia in their first game, but would New Zealand win this one? Unfortunately I was destined not to see the end of the match.

At the time, little did I know that I would be confined to bed for the next 20 weeks with a chest and head harness to support my head, for, in the early hours of the morning at approximately 02.30 hrs, during half time in the match, whilst paying a flying visit to the toilet, I did a 90° wheely in my stocking feet, skidded across the tiled floor and ended up backwards across the bath, with my head and back giving out a resounding whack against the wall and it was a case of 'lights out'. My wife Pat was asleep at the time, but fortunately woke up to investigate the 'bang'. She immediately realised that I was in a bad way and managed to tuck a bone shaped pillow between my chest and chin, which was resting on my chest, and then somehow she got me out of the bath and into my bed – how I'll never know. Pat phoned our local doctor early in the morning and he came and fitted a neck brace and gave me some injections. He asked Pat if she could manage, with his help, until Monday morning, as going to the hospital over the weekend was hopeless. I felt I would be better off at home under their care and the doctor was in and out every 2 hours day and night.

On Monday, he arranged an ambulance and for a Spine Specialist to be ready to see me as soon as I arrived at the hospital. Moving me from my bed in the prone position was tricky, but somehow they managed to get me into the ambulance. The driver assured me that they had scouted the route to the hospital for a road clear of bumps, holes, road works or any rough surfaces, and that they would be going very slowly. I set off in the ambulance for the Mill Park Hospital, approximately 5 km away, wearing just pyjamas, a neck brace and being supported in the sitting position by two ambulance attendants. While I was on my way, Pat and my local doctor set off in their own cars for the hospital and Pat had my ID Book, papers and money. The next thing I knew was that I was being booked in, X-rayed and put in to bed at the General Hospital – not the Mill Park Hospital. Normally, at that time, one couldn't book into the General Hospital, but here I was. A Scots Nursing Sister took down my particulars, showed me the card to check, then handed it to an African Administration person. Meanwhile, Pat and the doctor had discovered that I had not arrived at the Mill Park Hospital and they were checking with the police and other hospitals to see if an ambulance had been involved in an accident, but they were informed that no accidents had been reported. Pat eventually located me at the General Hospital, waiting in bed to see the Specialist. I had been booked in under the name of 'Mrs Molly Drenann', but I hadn't been put into the Women's Ward! Not yet anyway – the beard must have been a give-away! On arrival, Pat was beside herself and shouted at the Nursing Sister "Don't put him in the Gynaecology Ward and don't cut off any parts which may be sticking out". The Scots Sister burst out laughing, but the Africans didn't think it was funny! By this time Pat was demented and my local doctor wasn't amused as he couldn't get me released, having been signed in and there wasn't an ambulance available anyway. After much shouting and waving of arms, I was finally released to go to the Mill Park Hospital, it now being 17.30/18.00 hrs. The Specialist had gone home and was called back. I was X-rayed again and was finally seen at 20.00/20.30 hrs and was diagnosed as having fractured my neck in such a way that my head was locked forward with my chin virtually touching my chest. A brace and head set (not the radio type!) was ordered to be delivered the next day from Pretoria. It was eventually fitted at 18.30 hrs the following evening and I spent a week in the hospital, followed by a further 20 weeks in bed at home. The brace and head set were periodically adjusted, but they only managed to raise my head off my chest by 2°.

It took a further 18 months trying to convince the General Hospital that I was a Mr Denham and not Mrs Molly Drenann. After many phone calls and letters, it became Mrs Molly Benham and they continued to send me accounts addressed to Mrs's Drenann and/or Benham which I naturally refused to pay. So you can see, that by just a slip of the pen, a Mr M.G. Denham (582548) becomes Mrs Molly Drenann / Mrs Molly Benham. Unfortunately I'm not fully back to my old self. The head is still not far away from my chest and I can usually recognise people by their shoes, and have to sit down to be able to see their faces. But, most importantly, I'm back to being called Mr Denham!

53. There Was I ... With My Neptune's Cold War Diversion

Don Ellis

In May 1955 I was a comparatively experienced Navigator on 217 Squadron, operating Lockheed Neptunes and based at RAF Kinloss in Northern Scotland. The Neptune, a bit bigger than the Lancaster, had only two engines, each of 3,500 hp, and unlike the Lancaster, Shackleton and almost any British aircraft one could think of, was remarkably quiet to fly in. It performed well, but was said to be not too happy on one engine when heavy. It had originally been intended as an Airborne Early Warning aircraft, and was equipped with a massive, powerful radar ideal for that purpose, but had been lent to the RAF by the Americans to form four maritime squadrons. This would bolster up the existing Coastal Command force of Shackletons and Sunderlands now that the Cold War was developing.

The Cold War affected us in that occasionally Russian naval forces would put to sea, and NATO wanted to know what they were, where they were going and what they were up to. The Command had a brief, on such occasions, to mount Operation Reason, and crews would be detailed to 'Locate, report and shadow'. Perversely, the Russians invariably embarked on these expeditions at weekends, and on our squadron we all believed that World War 3 would begin during the Easter, August or Christmas Grant. Sure enough, one Sunday, 15th May, my crew was called in to briefing, to 'locate, report and shadow' a force of two cruisers and four destroyers which had been sighted on Saturday coming out of the Baltic, and were expected to turn North after clearing the Skaggerak. At that time, a Summit Conference was in progress in Geneva, attended by Anthony Eden, the then Prime Minister. We were briefed that having found the Russian task force, we were not on any account to close nearer than 20 miles, lest we initiate an international incident. In his next breath, the Intelligence Officer said that if we were able to bring back photographs they would be much appreciated! We also learned that we would be defensively armed – at that time the Neptune had a mid-upper gun turret with 2 x 20 mm cannon, as well as nose and tail turrets, and all our Signallers were trained Air Gunners as well. We took off at 07.10 hrs and headed off to the Northeast, heavy with fuel and our 20 mm ammunition, our brief being to remain until PLE (Prudent Limit of Endurance). I was navigating (there were two navigators on the crew) and being a recent graduate of the Staff Navigation Course, I had worked out an interception course based on the last known position (on Saturday afternoon) of the Russians and their likely movement.

Flying at 2,000 ft, we reached a point where I had estimated that we would be within radar range of the force, so the set was switched from 'Standby' to 'On', and lo and behold a force of six blips was visible on the screen within 20 miles of the position I had predicted (guessed?). Radar gave me a range and bearing on the force, which I plotted from my DR (Dead Reckoning) position, and we decided to climb to 4,000 ft, so that radar could obtain a firm fix on the Southwest corner of Norway, some 80 miles away. The Captain put on climbing power, and up we went. As we levelled off at 4,000 ft, the RPM on the starboard engine ran away and the pilots carried out feathering drill. We had by now been airborne for about 1 hr 30 mins, so had not burned off a lot of fuel, and as the propeller was being feathered, the aircraft dropped about 1,000 ft so we set off for Kinloss on one engine at 3,000 ft with an estimated 1 hr 30 mins to run. Pilot's Notes told us that we should be able to maintain height at 135 knots on the live engine, but inside half-an-hour we had lost another 1,500 ft, so with full climbing power and speed down to 120 knots and still going down slowly, the decision was taken to get rid of some excess weight.

Behind the mainplane, which went right through the fuselage, was an area known as the beam, from Coastal's Flying Boat days. Above it was the mid-upper turret. In the floor of the beam was a large hatchway and adjacent to it, one of our five Signallers was asleep. He was woken by our Senior Signaller, a Flight Sergeant, who thrust a pannier full of 20 mm ammunition into his hands and indicated the wide-open hatch and the sea beneath with the instruction "Throw that through there!". The young sergeant did as he had been bid at once, then said "Why, Chief?". A splendid example of crew discipline! That pannier, and others, were simply not enough, and after some agonising, the pilots and engineer decided that the tip tanks must go. These tanks each carried 300 gallons of fuel. The port tank also carried some expensive, secret electronic equipment, while the starboard tank housed a very powerful searchlight and another radar scanner. However, the engineer jettisoned them (they were pushed away from the mainplane by very strong springs) and they peeled off gracefully into the water. Rather them than us! We now were able to begin a very gentle climb and decided to divert to Sumburgh, at the Southern tip of Shetland.

We discovered en route that Sumburgh airfield was closed on Sundays, and that its runway was a mere 3,900 ft, with a hill just off each end! However, dry land was dry land! When we arrived overhead we could see sheep on the grass below and for the only time in my flying career I fired a red Very cartridge in anger. Whether the sheep understood or not, I don't know, but the runway was clear and we landed. The Neptune was equipped with reverse pitch propellers, one of the first RAF aircraft to have them, and fortuitously both of our pilots had practised reversing pitch when landing with only one live engine. We stopped with feet to spare, and taxied in.

Sumburgh is a civil airport and in those pre oil rig days was very much smaller than it is now, so we were somewhat surprised to be marshalled in by airport firemen. We were given to understand that they had come on duty as a result of our red Very cartridge, and as they entertained us with cups of tea and biscuits we wondered whether they were just a wee bit disappointed that we hadn't made a more dramatic arrival. We also learned that they were being paid double time for all the time we were there! We discovered too that an Air Traffic Controller and a telephonist were manning the Tower, and a taxi had turned up from Lerwick in case we wanted to go somewhere! Our Captain telephoned Kinloss and was told another aircraft would come to pick us up later in the afternoon. It was now around lunchtime.

We were told that the Sumburgh Head Hotel was about 20 minutes walk across the airfield, so we left one unfortunate Signaller, who drew the short straw, in charge of the aircraft while we set off in search of nourishment. I think we all enjoyed the nicest pint of beer we had ever had before going into the dining room for Sunday lunch. The dining room was quite busy and we were rather conspicuous in our uniforms, but nevertheless it was good to eat in civilised conditions. When the manageress brought our bills she told us that Sunday lunch was normally priced at 5/-, but because it was an emergency she would only charge us 4/6d!

We were glad to get back home, and for some time afterwards people kept telling us what we should have done, one of such gems being that we should have operated the live engine at take-off power to maintain height. I need hardly add that in the aircraft we were well aware that our live engine was the only one we had! Our reply to all the experts was that we had done what we did, and were here to prove that it worked.

54. The Great Escape (Halton Version)

Ginge Mushens

These things happen, so the saying goes, but why I ask does it have to always happen to me?

It was the evening prior to our 72-hour weekend pass and spirits were high in 16 Block in anticipation of the release from the shackles of Chiefy Thomas, and his little band of helpers, to celebrate the forthcoming events of late nights, dancing, girls and hopefully conquests. We, (the previously mentioned gang of Smith, Wardlaw, McCallum, Hutchison and others whom I will not incriminate!) repaired to the nearest pub in the village of Halton, out of the ken of the Snowdrops (RAF Police) to quaff the local brew. As signing out at the Guardroom was inconvenient and not 'cool' to use the latest lingo, we went the back way out of Camp, skirting the Married Quarters (where on one occasion a bugler, much to our twisted sense of humour, played Cavalry Dismount at 05.30 hrs one morning!) and the Hospital, and then onto the road to the village.

The revelry was at it highest when time and money ran out, so it was to Camp we set off, and as it was late the local bus was our way to get back before lights out. The problem was that as we had not signed out we had to get back in by another route to miss the Henderson Guardroom. This was accomplished by alighting the bus outside the Maitland Guardroom and nonchalantly strolling past as though we had just been to the Camp shop opposite, which if I remember correctly was called Thomas's. All seemed to go well until we were cutting in through the huts of the Dental Centre, when a bull voice bellowed "Stop where you are you apprentices". Of course, this was a ridiculous request, and in true apprentice fashion we split up and ran like hell for No.1 Wing. My route through the huts was suddenly barred by a very thickset bloke, who was obviously somebody of rank but dressed in Cricket Whites. "Stop there immediately Apprentice" he shouted as he extended his arms to prevent me making my escape. "No bloody chance" said I as I barged past, knocking him out of the way and to freedom and my 72-hour pass. Unfortunately he had caught my head with his arm and knocked off my hat, and in doing so displaying my full crop of red hair – and I do mean red. As my Mother always said, if we were lost in a crowd I was easily spotted!

Back at the Block, all was present and correct and no mention was made of the incident, as it was of little importance to the nights events. Next morning we had Workshops and a rumour was going round that the Snowdrops were picking up all Redheads from 1 Wing. Ginger Fraser and Ginger Tuck had been released, but the hunt was still on. I was not unduly worried, as I knew my name was not in the hat that had been knocked off, and they must have given up by now as it was lunch time and time for the 72-hour passes. At the Block, a message came for me to go to Chiefy Thomas's office. I suddenly had a sinking feeling that all was not well, and my brain raced at a pace usually well in it's excess of its normal panicky speed. God, I've been caught, now how to get out of this, as it was more than just a scrape? I knocked at the door and on entering came face to face with my cricketing friend, only now he was dressed in the uniform of a Sergeant of the RAF Police. My knees shook a bit, but I quickly recovered and said to Chiefy "You sent for me Flight Sergeant?" Addressing the Police Sgt, Chiefy said, "Is this the apprentice you want to Charge?" "That's him" said the Sgt, "I want him charged with disobeying a command from a Senior NCO; obstructing arrest; assaulting a Senior NCO; refusing to stop after knocking over a Senior NCO; plus the usual performance of Kings Regulations about the good order etc of His Majesty's personnel."

This was not going to be 10 days Jankers if I get found guilty thought I. Chiefy told the Sgt to wait outside whilst he got a detail to march yours truly to the Guardroom. Chiefy looked at me, shook his head, and said, "If this sticks, you'll be going down for a long one, and I mean the Glasshouse" (The Military Prison at Colchester). I suddenly felt sick. "I'll arrange for the Flight Commander to see you as soon as possible" said Chiefy, "In the meantime you will be under close arrest in the Guardroom". A Police Cpl appeared and I was escorted to the Guardroom, where they took my tie and bootlaces, emptied my pockets and put me in a cell, clanging the door behind me. The cell was about 7 ft by 5 ft, and had four 6 inch planks for a bed, with a block of wood 6 inches square by 18 inches long as a head rest, with a concave depression in the middle to put ones weary head I suppose.

I must remind readers that I was just 17 yrs at the time, so you can imagine how I felt, and I must admit I was near to tears, especially when the cell door opened and my accuser stood there with a look like the Foreign Legion Sgt in Beau Gest! "I'll ensure you get at least 9 months in the Glasshouse for this you little b.....d and you'll be discharged out of the RAF" said the Foreign Legion look-alike. It dawned on me that failure to get off would mean more than a lost 72-hour weekend pass and nights of pleasure – more like the Stockade and its mentally deranged NCO's.

The door was slammed shut. They can't shut doors quietly, these people, they must be trained like that I thought, trying to lift my spirits. After what seemed an eternity, but could only have been an hour, the door was opened by the Police Cpl and he gave me my gear and said "Get dressed. We are to go to the office for a formal hearing". He wasn't a bad bloke and said the Sgt was a bit of a swine and nobody liked him. I thought fat lot of good that is going to do me, as it wasn't a popularity contest we were in but a hell of a mess. Back at the office, Chiefy was waiting with a very worried look on his face, as we all know he was really like a father to us and he did really care. He chased the Police Sgt outside of the office, and said to me "Tell me everything that happened and do not miss anything out if you want to beat this set of charges". I truthfully recounted the whole tale to him and to our Cpl PTI, who was Chiefy's 2nd in command who had come in to help. The Cpl said, "Go over the first part again, especially when you heard the command to stop by the Sergeant". I did, saying, "This chap in the cricket outfit tried to stop me running through the huts and I didn't know who he was, as he could have been anyone dressed in cricket gear". The Cpl looked at Chiefy and a sign or something like a grimace, went between them. Next I was marched into the Squadron Office, one two, one two, quick pace, halt, right turn, to face our Flt Lt whose name I forget to my eternal shame. The charges were read out and my heart sank to the ground. It didn't seem possible that I was guilty of doing all those things that I was charged with, just for dodging a man in cricket gear. The Flt Lt called the Police Sgt in and he gave his evidence of how he was proceeding to the Guardroom when he observed the apprentice running from the direction of the Guardroom and decided to apprehend me to find out what I was up to. He told me to halt and when I rushed towards him, he put out an arm to stop me and I hit him and knocked him over and ran on. In the confrontation, the apprentice lost his hat and I was later able to identify him. I was then asked to give my side of the story, which was that I was returning to 16 Block and, as it was nearly 'lights out', I was hurrying, when suddenly this chap in cricket gear appeared and tried to stop me. As I did not recognise him, I thought he was about to hit me, so I brushed him aside and made my way back to the barracks.

The Sgt was marched out and then I was marched out by the Cpl PTI. Chiefy stayed in with the Flt Lt, obviously to decide what could be the outcome of these charges, and knowing Chiefy, how he could influence the Flight Commander to go easy on yours truly, one of his little charges.

To admit to any of the charges meant the Glasshouse. I was then marched in to the Squadron office and the Police Sgt followed. Chiefy stood at one side of the officer, I was in front and the Sgt was near the window in the corner.

"Tell me Sergeant," said the Flight Commander, "What was your dress when you tried to apprehend the prisoner?"

"I was dressed in my cricket whites" said the Sgt.

"And did you identify yourself to the prisoner?"

"No Sir" said the Sgt, "But he could tell by my command that I was a NCO."

"You did not, after the command to halt, say that you were a Police Sergeant?"

"No Sir."

"Then how was the prisoner to know if you were going to assault him or not, when you raised your arms to him?" said the Flight Commander.

The Sgt started to bluster. "I was adopting a proper senior stance and anyone would know I was an NCO" said the Sgt.

The Sgt was then dismissed and the Flight Commander turned to me. "I have discussed this case with Flt Sgt Thomas, and the conclusion which I have come to is that the Police Sergeant did not behave in the proper manner. He was not in uniform and he made an attempt to restrain you unlawfully without identifying himself. You were possibly frightened he was going to hit you and you reacted as you did. The result is that the charges against you are dismissed and you are free to go on leave."

I was marched back to Chiefy's office, where the Police Sgt was standing. When he heard the verdict, he went berserk, upon which Chiefy kicked him out of the office with the words "Leave my lads alone". The Cpl PTI had a huge smile on his face, but warned me that this Sgt would be after me from then on. I was marched back to the Guardroom to get my pocket contents from the Police Cpl and to sign out, when the Sgt burst in. His face was Puce and he let forth on how he would make sure my stay in the Service would be difficult, and he would never forget this day and he would make sure I wouldn't either. This tirade was interspersed with language I cannot repeat, suffice to say that two can play that game and I was not bothered.

Jack Smith was waiting for me when I got back to the Block, and we got our passes to go on leave to his family in Goffs Oak, who I must thank for the great welcome I always got when I stayed there, even though it must have been a bit of a squeeze seeing he had a sister and two brothers at home. It is also of interest that we always hitch hiked to his house to save on money, as 10 shilling a fortnight did not go far.

There is a sting in this tail, as when Tony Carlyle and I went on Christmas leave, we were stopped by two RAF Policemen on Kings Cross Station and we were made to empty our gear onto the platform while it was searched for what I do not know. I learned later that the Sgt had been transferred to RTO in London and still hoped to catch me. Ever the Optimist!

55. The Last Man Left in the Air Force

(Author unknown – sent in by Jack Wetherell)

I'm the last man left in the Air Force
I've an office in MOD
And a copy of Queen's Regulations
Which only apply to me.
I can post myself to Leuchars
And detach me from there to Kinloss
Or send me on courses to Cosford
Then cancel the lot – I'm the boss.

I'm the last man left in the Air Force
I suppose you imagine it's great
To be master of all you survey,
But I tell you it's difficult, mate.
I inspected three Units last Thursday
As C-in-C (acting) of Strike
Then I cleaned out the bogs at Brize Norton
And repaired Saxa Vord's Station bike.

I'm the last man left in the Air Force
My wife says I'm never at home.
 When I'm not chairing meetings
 I'm at Manston
Laying gallons and gallons of foam,
Or I'm flying the 'Red Arrows' at an airshow
Then I'm Orderly Corporal at Lyneham.
It's an interesting life, but all go.

I'm the last man left in the Air Force
I'm Equerry to the Queen
I'm Duty Clerk at St Mawgan

I'm the RAF Rugby Team.
Tomorrow I'm painting the Guardroom
And air testing several planes
The day after that I'm in London
To preach at St Clement Danes.

I'm the last man left in the Air Force
And I'm due to go out before long
There's been no talk of any replacement
And I won't even let me sign on.
I hope to enjoy my retirement
I've put up a fairly good show
But I won't cut myself off entirely
There are always reunions you know.

Apprentice Barrack Blocks - No. 1 Wing left foreground.

No. 1 Apprentice Wing Cookhouse.

GROUP A

Alan Dando Fred Hoskins Geoff Harrison Paddy Harnett Arthur Becker Tom McCallum
Don Ellis Taff White Brian Sherburn Kipper Morton Sam Bugg Joe Smith Eric Buckley
Bunnie Warren Jimmy Middleton Freddie Saunders Sgt DI Jimmy Fraser Tango Addison

GROUP B
Taff George Tony Thomas Unknown Sid Vasey Geoff Souch Pete Bruce
Henry Ford Chas Rees Mike Furness Horse Mullins Frank Howard Joe Simpson John Stappard
Jock Wardlaw Don Roberts Sgt DI Twilly Wilson Mike Gill Beaky Leach

GROUP C

Johnny Attwood Robbie Roberts Ted Skinner Dave Mantrip Percy Patient Bill Clay Gus Dixon
George Dorman Pete Pegler Ray Leverage Lawrie Gillard Eric Pordham Johnny Allen Ginge Britten
Les Sprowell Maurice Allenden Sgt DI Will Ayliffe Jock Cook Ginge Mushens

GROUP D

Joe Ashworth Ray Belsham Peter Blackman Pablo Morrison Ken Gault Georgie Board
Salty Ault Cass Terry Unknown Lofty Ball Lofty Rummery Jack Smith John Shadrack
Titch Nicholas Vic Pain George Parkinson Sgt DI Skate Lee Ken Welsh

GROUP E

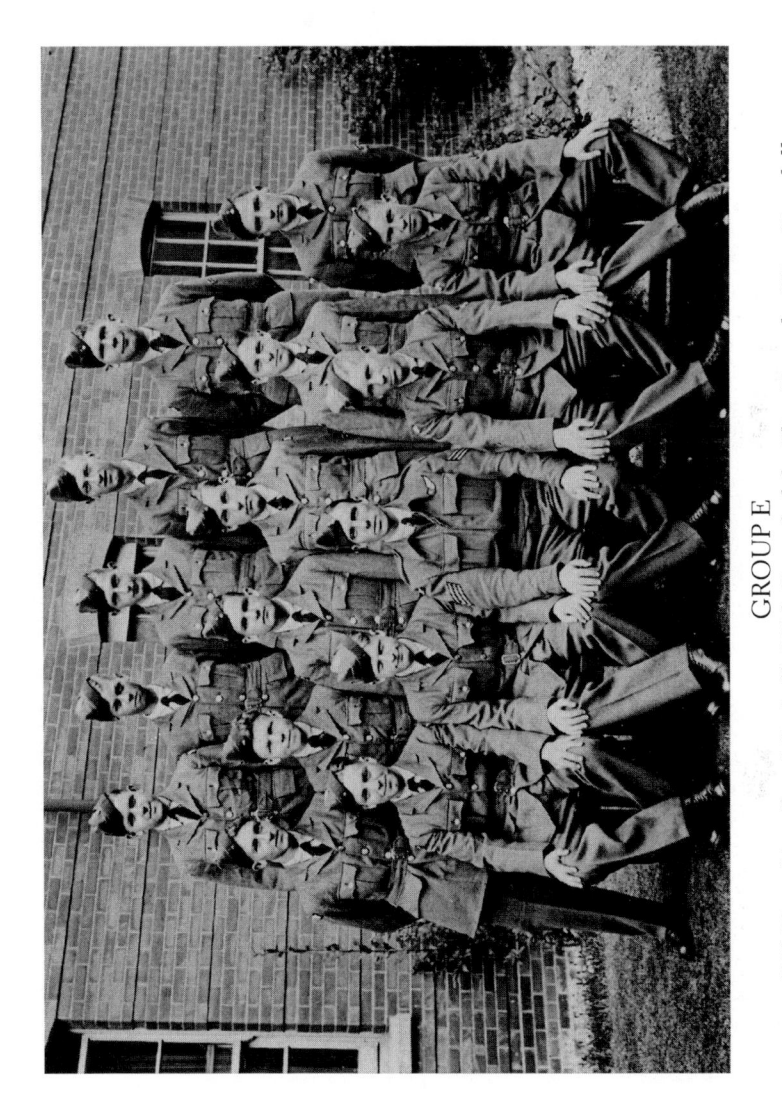

Bill Horrobin Ben Mitchell Dick Greenhalgh Slim Pocock Tiny Dowdell
Taff Denham Frank Solomon Bill Jones Gand Pinder Roy Loveluck Pete Moore
Woof Barker Bob Kelly Sgt DI Andy Magness Wag Millward

GROUP F
Joe Ranaldi   Johnny Jones   Roy Wickens   Stan Downton
Eric Wilkinson   Geoff Mason   Pete Lawrence   Sandy Sanders   Jobbie Bown   John Chapple
Brian Leak   Wilbur Wright   Vic Parker   Sgt DI   Hugh Clarke-Hunt   Len Rayne

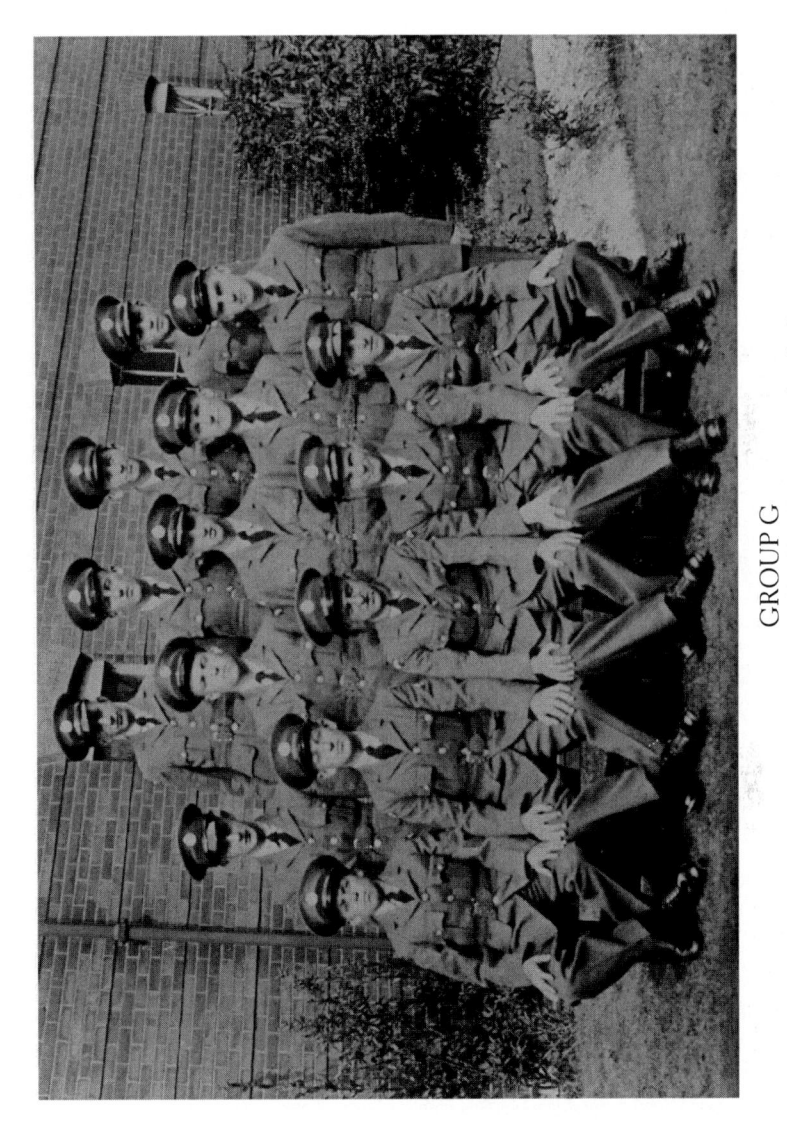

GROUP G

Ivor Lee   Don Davies   Taff Evans   Bob Clark
Taff Kavanagh   Bill Entwhistle   Alan Muxlow   Andy Andrews   Brian Ackers
Boris Pitts   Bill Northmore   Mac McPherson   Pat Graydon   Vic Lewin

GROUP H

Tom Hardie Llyn John Smudge Smith Ken Savage Snoz Cooper
Unknown Brunny Brush Stan Hyde Silas Mills Hen Brent Don Blackmore
Robert Gair Unknown Sgt DI Waaf Wynyard Geoff Glanville Dave Williams

GROUP I

John Greenslade   Roy Sherriff   Norman Black   Narcy Burford   Les Stotten
Eric Rowley   Tom McHarry   Eric Mould   Reg Chapman
Les Anderson   Roy Manington   Del Harris   Johnny Watson   Ben Coombes

GROUP J

Taff Bainton Ted Mitchell Unknown Chris Brill Blondie Dymond
Jim Coates Frenchy English Roy Hagger Spider Webb Dennis Collins
Jack Wetherell Gus Gardner Don Needham Jock Wickham Paddy Bolster

GROUP L

Colin Kinder Unknown Squeak Cottrell Timber Wood Bill Rimmer
Geordie Wallace Toddy Hood Mac McDonnell Vic Nodder Brian Perryman
Derek Ashton Paddy Waddell Unknown Sgt DI Junior Roots David Compton

GROUP M

Roy Studart Wilf Dawson Barney Barnikel Bill Williams Dizzy Cooper
Len Weston Norman Roach Brian Creasey Ted Costick Johnny Newton Ted Boobyer
Jock McClure Dinger Bell Cpl DI Art Bowker Derek Coleman

GROUP N

Barry Faulkner Gus Thorogood Don Bessant Jock Annison Pete Wilson
Dell Dellow Vic Wilson Ginge Doran Ken Claydon Jim Allen Bob Brooks Spike Malone
Taff Beesley Ken Cook George Hinchley Ginge Fraser Sgt DI Vic Fairbrother Andy Andrews

GROUP O
John Oakes Pete Ashby Les Atkinson
Roy Pollit Tommy Tucker Al Richardson Jimmy Reynolds

GROUP P

Bob Edwards   Joe Biggs   Bill Sands   Hoagy Carmichael   Eric Beale
Limey Rowan   Dennis Walker   Ginge Ward   Sgt DI   John McLaren   Ginge Cockfield   Tony Young

STANDING ORDERS - HOW MANY WERE CAUGHT?

Extracts from STANDING ORDERS:

SECTION 1

5. Private Motor Cars and Motor Cycles
Except with their parents or guardians consent and then only whilst on leave, Aircraft Apprentices are not permitted to own or drive motor vehicles.

9. Smoking
(i) An Aircraft Apprentice on reaching the age of eighteen may apply, and if his general conduct is satisfactory will be granted a smoking pass. If he is not in possession of a Smoking Pass he is not permitted to smoke or carry smoking materials.

25. Alcoholic Liquor
Aircraft Apprentices are not to be in possession of or consume alcoholic liquor.

SECTION III

5. Association with Females, including W.A.A.F.
Aircraft Apprentices are forbidden to associate with females, other than relatives, during term time. When in the company of females, Aircraft Apprentices are to conduct themselves in an orderly manner at all times, and are not to walk arm in arm.

Aircraft Apprentices are forbidden to attend dances, other than those officially arranged for apprentices.

STANDING ORDERS
FOR
AIRCRAFT APPRENTICES
ROYAL AIR FORCE STATION
HALTON
BY THE
COMMANDING OFFICER
No. 1 SCHOOL OF TECHNICAL TRAINING
(APPRENTICES).

Published under K.R. & A.C.I.
Paragraph 61.

Warrant Officer F G Marsh MBE RVM - No 1 Apprentice Wing Warrant Officer. ('Boggy' to his friends)

Flight Sergeant R Thomas - Disciplinary SNCO, C Squadron, No. 1 Apprentice Wing. ('Chiefy' to his friends)

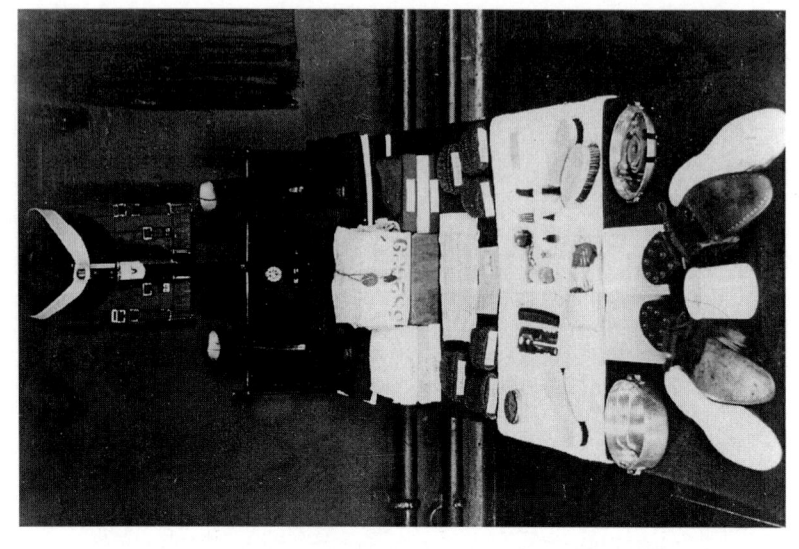

"Kit ready for inspection - Sir"

Barrack Room decorated for Christmas.

Flight Sergeant Lewis – mascot of the Pipe & Fife Band.

"Jankers" White armband indicates that the Apprentice has been caught and punished for disobeying Standing Orders.

Attentive Instrument Makers.

Radial Engine Workshop.

Final Schools night party at "The Boot and Slipper"

51st Entry Passing Out Parade - "General Salute, Present Arms"

Passing Out Parade of 51st Entry of RAF Aircraft Apprentices on 28th July 1948. Inspecting Officer Air Marshal Sir Leslie Hollinghurst KCB KBE DFC escorted by S/A/A Faulkner, No.3 Flight Commander and S/A/A Thomas, Parade Commander.

51st Entry Passing Out Parade – Air Marshal Sir Leslie Hollinghurst inspects Pipe & Fife Band, escorted by C/A/A Howard.

Members of 51st Entry on Saluting Base following Passing Out Parade of 151st Entry of RAF Aircraft Apprentices on 20th June 1991.

First Reunion at the Rose & Crown Hotel, Tring, on 20th June 1991.

Chiefy Thomas receives his LS & GC Mug from Dinger Bell at 50th Anniversary Reunion

Dinger Bell addressing 51st Entry from a bomb trolley at 1992 HAAA Triennial Reunion.

John McLaren, our piper - then and now!

Schools Building.

Old Workshops.